# ANARKALI

# ANARKALI

SUMANT BATRA

Om Books International

Reprinted in 2024 by

**Om Books International**

**Corporate & Editorial Office**
A-12, Sector 64, Noida 201 301
Uttar Pradesh, India
Phone: +91 120 477 4100
Email: editorial@ombooks.com
Website: www.ombooksinternational.com

**Sales Office**
107, Ansari Road, Darya Ganj,
New Delhi 110 002, India
Phone: +91 11 4000 9000
Email: sales@ombooks.com
Website: www.ombooks.com



ISBN: 978-93-5376-988-8

Printed in India

10 9 8 7 6 5 4 3 2

*Ta qayamat shukr goyam kard gar khwish ra*
*Aah gar man baz beenam rui yar khwish ra*

*Majnun Salim Akbar*

*Ah! Could I behold the face of my beloved once more,*
*I would give thanks unto my God until the day of resurrection.*

The profoundly enamoured Salim, son of Akbar

*For the fateful heartbreaks*

# Contents

# Preface

*Kisi se jo na khul sakay woh zindigi ka raaz hoon*
(I am that mystery of life no one can solve)

Anarkali is known to the world as a slave who fell in love with the Mughal imperial heir Salim, later, the emperor Jahangir – a love apparently passionately reciprocated by him. The name Anarkali is stated to have been bestowed on her by Emperor Akbar for her beauty and allure that compared to a blossoming pomegranate flower. The account of the love story, immortalised by Imtiaz Ali Taj's play, *Anarkali* (1922), suggests that the emperor did not approve of the debasing liaison and ordered Anarkali to be walled up alive. In his mega opera, *Mughal-e-Azam*, ostensibly inspired from *Anarkali*, K. Asif changed the end of the story dramatically. As Anarkali was being walled up, Anarkali's mother reminds Akbar of a favour he promised her years ago. The mother begs for her daughter's life in return. Akbar relents and arranges for Anarkali's escape into exile. There is an account suggesting she died of poisoning by a court official as part of the conspiracy hatched by other mistresses of Akbar's harem. Another version states she fell ill and died. There is also one that points finger at Salim for Anarkali's murder.

Some consider Anarkali a historical fact, others a quasi-mythical character. The those who believe in her existence and the love affair rely on the inscription on the magnificent mausoleum in Lahore to argue that the tomb was built by Jahangir in Anarkali's memory sixteen years after her tragic death. Some even attribute Lahore's famous Anarkali Bazaar to her. Most historians though dismiss the idea of her existence. Relying on court chronicles of the period, they emphasise that Jahangir was too deeply in love with Nur Jahan to have fallen so passionately for another woman. Citing the prince's diary, full of names of friends and family, with no mention of Anarkali, they advocate she is nothing but a figment of imagination as part of folklore. To them, instead, the only beloved who shimmers through his autobiography, *The Jahangirnama*, is Nur Jahan.

Fact or fiction, *haqeeqat* or *qissa-khwan*, or an unsubstantiated gossip glorified by Imtiaz Ali, the fascinating story of Anarkali is as famous and immortal as other legendary love stories, such as Laila-Majnu, Shirin-Farhad, Baji Rao-Mastani, and many others, and is an inseparable part of popular culture. This real or surreal character from the tragic love story from over four hundred years ago still resonates in modern times.

Surprisingly, however, none of the versions of those who believe in her existence divulge much about Anarkali or her family, beyond the legendary episode that is believed by many to have occurred in Lahore and by others in Agra or Fatehpur Sikri. What was her real name? Was she really walled up alive or allowed to escape or poisoned to death? Anarkali and her life continue to be shrouded in mystery. Neither Akbar nor Jahangir, who wrote detailed account of their rule, mention her or the episode. Amid the debate over Akbar's potential disregard for this tale, the omission of Anarkali from Jahangir's memoirs, despite his purported love, remains an enigma.

There are other perplexing aspects to the story. Salim was the prince of a vast and powerful empire, with many wives and mistresses; why would he be forbidden another love? Akbar's objection to the match is as obscure as it is feeble. These and many other questions have intrigued me and I trust others who, like me, are fascinated by the riddles surrounding Anarkali, her life and death. In some ways, the story of Anarkali was not only her own tragedy or that of Salim and hers but also of Akbar the Great.

Whoever she was or whatever she did, the legend of Anarkali is woven into history as an unresolved mystery. This novel is the tale of the enigma who came to be known as Anarkali. This fictional biographical account seeks to give her an identity, a name, a family, and a life beyond the tragic love affair she has come to be identified with. It is also an endeavour to unfold the mystery that surrounds her sudden disappearance. All of this resulting out of the flights of my imagination, my fascination with this bold and beautiful woman and, if I may add, my yearning to solve the puzzle that surrounds her life. It is an attempt to give her a long due and deserving closure.

Critics and historians may question my attempts at attributing to her a life she never had. I should, therefore, add a disclaimer for readers – this book is nothing but a work of fiction with a slight garnish of history. Many names, places and people that appear in the book are real, and that is only because it is based on documented history. However, the story itself is nothing but my fancy. It should not be read as a scholarly work. I have taken full creative liberty to offer readers a story that goes beyond the episode that follows her name.

Yet, even in this work of fiction, I could not help but reinforce the formidable message of unadulterated love and sacrifice Anarkali represents, so that she continues to inspire generations to love and to love selflessly. So that it remains one of the most fascinating and romantic tales of all times.

With this has ended my quest to find her truth. There might be as many truths to her as there are writers and their imagination.

## *London, Twenty-first Century*

# Prologue

Saima deposited the AirPods in their case as the train approached Princeton Station. She pulled the hood of her jacket over her head as she prepared to alight. It was midnight and the station was deserted. Her grandmother lived a short walk from the station. The street outside was dimly lit but there was nothing to fear in this part of town. Occasionally a drunk vagabond might step out of the shadows to ask for a cigarette smoke.

It was snowing lightly. The winter draught stabbed her like a knife as she stepped out of the station. She paused to light a cigarette and began striding towards her grandmother's house. She had been wondering why her grandmother had summoned her at this odd hour. She had not been keeping well for some time and Saima had visited her only the previous weekend to get her health check done. Although the reports indicated no cause for worry, only some age-related ailments, her grandmother's voice over the phone conveyed a deep sense of unease. It could not wait till tomorrow, she had insisted. There was a strange sense of urgency in her voice. Saima had summoned an Uber right after the call. She threw in a couple of casuals in her overnighter. The cab arrived a few minutes later. She managed to book a seat on the Virgin train on the way to the station. As she turned into the lane where her grandmother lived, she could see her house at the far end, one amongst the row of similar-looking bungalows rubbing shoulders. A few long strides and she was standing in front of the house.

The brass nameplate on the gate pillar glittered in the light of a powerful bulb. Dr Fatima Siddique, it read. Her grandmother embodied an unapologetically unconventional spirit, living life on her own terms. A rebel even decades ago, she had plunged into a dissertation that ignited a firestorm of discourse – delving into the discreet world of women shrouded behind purdahs. In a time when the mere mention of 'sex' remained an unspeakable taboo, particularly amongst conservative communities even in faraway England, her audacious choice reverberated with defiance. Unfazed by the threats that were hurled her way from conservatives, both men and women, Fatima stood resolute. For many weeks, she woke up to abusive graffiti painted on the walls of her house. Stones were pelted on the windowpanes in broad daylight. Braving the harassment, she completed her doctorate with distinction.

On the day she was awarded the degree, she planted the oversized brass plate outside her house with 'Dr' prefixed to her name. She polished it herself every day for the first few weeks to rub in the message to the neighbourhood. She received an offer to teach at London School of Social Science. Fatima served the same school for decades, rising up the ranks, eventually retiring as the dean a few years ago. Her grandmother's was a compelling tale.

Noora opened the door before Saima could reach the doorbell. She stood there wearing a monkey cap and a flowery blanket oddly wrapped around her. She hailed from her grandmother's native village and had been packed off with Fatima when she relocated to England five decades ago as a young bride. She was as old as her mother. Noora was devoted to her grandmother. So much so that she did not get married. She turned down all proposals that came her way from India and even London. Fatima tried hard to persuade her but she just wouldn't listen. Having served Fatima for that long in a foreign land, Noora was more a friend to her grandmother than an attendant.

Noora stepped aside to let Saima in. 'She made me stand at the door for one hour so that *you* don't have to wait at the door in the cold even for a minute. As if you were being carried here from the station in a heated palanquin. Your grandmother is going crazy by the day,' she said affectionately, flicking away snowflakes in Saima's hair.

Saima smiled and hugged her like she would embrace her own grandmother.

'Go, she is waiting in the attic. She has been there all day. I don't know what has gotten into her suddenly,' Noora said, pointing to the roof. 'Your black coffee is ready. I will warm it a bit. I wonder why the country which introduced India to the delightful sweetness of tea would themselves indulge in this unpleasant bitterness. I can't even add Indian masalas to it,' she added under her breath as she turned to the kitchen.

Saima hugged her again from behind and planted a kiss on Noora's shoulders. 'Ok, ok, I know you want that packet of wretched cigarettes of yours. One day I am going to let your grandmother know you smoke. You have made me lie to that old woman all these years...' she muttered.

Saima found her grandmother sitting on the attic floor, her back resting against the wall, a white box on her lap. Fatima's face lit up when Saima entered the room. Saima felt relieved to find her grandmother looking in good health. She looked so beautiful and elegant even in her early seventies.

'One's appearance wields immense power over one's self-esteem. Despite this, one must remember that true beauty is what emanates from within. Without this delicate dance of a well-nurtured mind to the tune of a compassionate heart, the veneer of the body remains bereft of beauty,' she once told Saima when she found her standing in front of the mirror to survey herself too frequently. 'With age, your good looks will wane but your inner beauty, composed of the virtues of honesty and compassion, will hold. That is the wise old secret to finding that magnetic aura that will make you truly beautiful.

Saima had adopted her grandmother's philosophy as the guiding principles of her life.

Saima bent on her knees and hugged her grandmother tightly. She planted a kiss on her forehead. 'Thank God, you are fine, *aani*. I was so worried for you.'

'My time has come, my girl. Allah appeared in my dream this morning and whispered in my ear,' Fatima said, signalling Saima to sit next to her. 'He told me to be ready to leave this awful world ... and prepare to join your grandfather and our ancestors.'

'She has been repeating this all day.' Noora walked in with a coffee mug. 'I keep telling her that the day Allah decides to summon her, he will notify me first so that I can pack your grandmother's bag. I have done it for her all these years when she travelled for conferences in distant places. Allah will also have to pack me off with her. Your grandmother won't survive a day without me by her side to assist her,' Noora said, wiping the tears that welled up in her eyes using her dupatta.

'We can't go together, you fool! Don't you realise I am heading to paradise while you are destined to go to hell with that foul mouth of yours,' Fatima retorted jokingly. 'Morning dreams are meant to come true. I am prepared to leave this world. I have lived a happy and accomplished life. I feel fulfilled,' she continued, turning serious. 'The only regret I have is I had to see your mother die so young. She was such a joyful girl and had so much life ahead of her. My *janaaza* should have left before hers,' she continued in a voice weak with sorrow.

Saima's parents had died in a road accident in Lahore when Saima was just eight years old. Fatima brought Saima up as her own child. Tears started rolling down Fatima's cheeks. Saima could also no longer hold back her tears. Looking at them, even Noor started sobbing.

Fatima was the first to get ahold of herself. She wiped her tears and shifted her gaze towards Saima. Holding her hand, she winked. 'I did ask Allah if it was possible to defer it by a month. I told him I wanted to try and persuade my gorgeous granddaughter to get married. I want to see her don the *nikaah ka joda* before my time comes to a close. I assured Him I will walk away gladly after that.

Saima hugged Fatima. 'I am not getting married for another ten years, and you, my aani, are not going anywhere till then.'

Both smiled.

'Ok, now tell me this is not a set-up plotted by the two of you,' Saima said, pretending to sound angry. 'If it is one, I am leaving right now. I have my exams coming up in a few days. I should be in my flat, studying.' Saima stood up to leave.

Fatima held Saima's hand and pulled her down. 'Sit, I need to talk to you,' she said.

Fatima sat quietly deep in thoughts. Saima waited for Fatima to speak. 'I mean it when I say my time is up,' she whispered after a while. She was talking to herself. 'It is a premonition that is surging from deep within. I will not shy away from its truth. I summoned you because I have one important duty to complete.' Fatima paused.

Noora and Saima waited for Fatima to resume. Saima looked at Fatima. She was staring intensely at the wall ahead. Saima touched her grandmother's arm gently, 'Are you all right, aani?'

Fatima turned to Noora. 'Don't you have any work to do? Get me a glass of hot milk.'

Noora took the hint and left the room, grudgingly muttering under her breath.

Fatima lifted the white box on her lap and placed it in front of them. Saima had been so engrossed in the conversation that she had failed to notice the box. 'In this lies the secret of our family, answers to several mysteries which have been closely guarded by us for many centuries. Outside our bloodline, it remains concealed. It is now your responsibility to safeguard it so that your ancestors remain in peace!'

Saima was perplexed, struggling to fathom what she had been told. What secret could a tiny box hold? Which secret had the family guarded for hundreds of years? Why must it be kept hidden? Many questions criss-crossed her mind over the next minute. She did not know what to say. A fear of the unknown filled her.

She lifted the box carefully, taking in every detail. It was a very old box and it looked like it was made of ivory. There was spectacular inlay work, studded with stones, on the lid. By their look she could make out they were no ordinary stones. In the middle of the lid was a stunning miniature painting of a woman dancing, caught taking an elegant half-turn. The box was in itself a magnificent piece of art. Some text in Persian was etched below the painting. It exuded a regal splendour, baring evidence to its aristocratic lineage – a remnant of a bygone grandeur. Saima couldn't take the mystery any further. She wanted to see what was inside and asked for Fatima's permission.

'No!' yelled Fatima, snatching the box from her. 'You can't. You must open it only after you get married so you can pass it on to your offspring. Not before that.'

'But that would be years from now?'

'That's right. I did not open it until five years ago. Promise me you will not open it until your child is old and responsible enough to be trusted with this. Your mother left us before I could tell her. I have cried every night since that fateful day when she died. She was the only generation of our family who never learnt of this box and what it hides. Promise me, Saima, you will follow my instructions and guard the secret that lies in it,' Fatima said, staring at the box peculiarly.

Saima was befuddled. She was not convinced by her grandmother's explanation but she decided not to argue and nodded reassuringly.

'No, no, nodding will not suffice. I want to hear you say it,' insisted Fatima.

'Yes, aani, I promise I will do as you say,' she replied.

Fatima embraced Saima. They clung to each other. Noora walked in at that moment holding the glass of milk. Looking at the two she thought they were weeping. She kept the glass on the table, joined them on the floor and started sobbing loudly. Fatima and Saima looked at her with surprise. Noora looked back, puzzled at their reaction. Seeing the look on her face, the two broke into a laugh. Although Noora was clueless of the joke, she chose to join in the laughter.

They laughed till tears were rolling from their eyes. Finally, Fatima stood up. She placed her hand on Saima's head to bless her. 'You go and get some sleep, my child. Noora will walk you to the station first thing tomorrow. She will pack you some *aloo paranthas*,' she said and then muttered a prayer.

## I

It was three days later that Saima received the shocking news. She was walking to her classroom when the phone rang. It was

Noora. She was crying and barely able to talk. 'Your grandmother left us. She is gone … gone without me … I served her…'

'Calm down, Noora. I can't understand a word you are saying. Tell me what happened,' she asked, stopping in her tracks.

'She passed away in her sleep last night,' said Noora, wailing inconsolably.

'Are you sure? Did you check her pulse? Have you called the ambulance? I was there only the other night. She was fine…' Saima said, refusing to believe what she had just heard.

'Yes, I did. The paramedics are here. They can't find her pulse. Come fast. They are asking a lot of questions.'

Saima went numb. Her grandmother, her only family, her idol was no more. She was now alone in this world. She felt her life turn upside down. Grief took over the shock. Saima felt her knees go weak. She collapsed in the corridor.

## II

Saima graduated with honours from King's College and received an offer from Herbert Smith, a leading law firm, to join as an associate. She was elated. She requested the firm to give her three months to join as she wanted to go backpacking in Vietnam, a trip she had planned over so many months. She did not want to give up the trip, not sure if she would be able to get away once she got busy meeting unrealistic timelines and rolling out deliverables for the partners. The firm extended the time albeit reluctantly.

She served the agreed notice on her landlady and conveyed that she would prefer to rent it back after her return if the flat was still on the market. It was situated only one tube station away from her future office. She would have retained the apartment but the rentals for three months amounted to a lot of money. She had spent all her savings on the flight tickets and hotel booking. The landlady was fond of Saima and assured her she too would like to have her back. She invited her to store her stuff in the basement while she was away. Saima accepted the offer gladly. She had been thinking of leaving it at her best friend Damini's place but felt hesitant as the boxes and suitcases would have occupied sizeable space in the modest apartment. She also suspected Damini's flatmate might protest.

It was while packing her belongings that Saima retrieved the ivory box from her wardrobe. She had tucked it away in the top shelf after it was passed on to her by Fatima. It had been two years since Fatima passed away. After a few days of curious contemplation, Saima had allowed the box to slip away from her thoughts.

Saima sat down on the bed staring at the box, deliberating how to secure it while she was away. It was too risky to leave it in the basement with her luggage, she decided. The only safe place she could think of was her bank. She decided to hire a locker and deposit the box there. Saima was still trying to figure out the next steps when the doorbell rang. Damini stood at the door with her arms crossed. Damini was her soul mate. She had just earned a law degree from the London School of Economics and received an offer from Norton Rose. They had met at INSOL International office where they were interning at the same time. They clicked instantly and became close friends in no time. Damini had also managed an extension of the joining date from her firm. Both were going to Vietnam together.

Damini walked straight to the kitchen and pulled out a soda from the refrigerator. 'It is bloody hot outside. It is warmer here in London than back home in Delhi I am told. This climate change is a real thing, I tell you. London has not been so warm before and only the other day we saw the news of countryside flooding from untimely rains. It is scary. I am really looking forward to get away from this heat.'

Saima did not respond. She was still thinking about the box.

'Is everything all right? Have you packed?' Damini asked, looking at her friend.

'Oh, yes. I am almost done. Did you have lunch?' Saima inquired.

'No. Do you want me to order something?'

'No. Let me make some rice and curry for us,' Saima said, pulling out the rice container from the shelf.

Saima had just placed the cooker on the burner when she heard Damini scream in excitement from the bedroom. 'Wow! How pretty! Where did you find this?'

Saima went cold. She realised Damini must have seen the ivory box. She had left it on the bed. How could she have been so careless? She dashed to the bedroom screaming, 'Don't open it, don't open it, Damini.'

Damini sat on the bed, admiring the box, ready to lift the lid. Saima snatched the box from her. She closed the lid and put the box back in the cupboard.

'Hey, what the fuck!' Damini was perplexed by Saima's reaction.

'I am sorry, Dan. I can't explain. Believe me, darling! Even I do not know what is inside the box. Whatever it is, must remain there, unseen. It is supposedly a secret precious to my family. I have been instructed to guard it with my life, without knowing what the box holds inside.'

Damini stared at Saima, puzzled. She did not say a word but she had relaxed a little. 'Okay. I won't push to trespass on your family secrets,' she said, waving her hands dramatically, and smiled at her. 'Come on now, we have a meal to cook.'

After they had finished eating, both sat down together. Suddenly, Saima got up and pulled the box out of the cupboard and placed it on the bed. Damini shifted back and looked at the box, mystified. Saima sighed. She gripped Damini's hand tightly and spoke in a melancholic voice, 'I have no one else other than you, Dan. You are the only family I have since aani passed away.' Noora had followed Saima soon after. 'The only reason I don't feel alone in this world is because I have you. I want to tell you what I know.'

Damini gripped back Saima's hand. In the next few minutes, Saima gave a word-by-word account of her last meeting with her grandmother, from Fatima's late-night call to the handing over of the box and her grandmother's strict instructions not to open the box.

Damini listened in awe. 'If it is as precious as your grandmother said, keeping it in the bank might be the safest option,' she suggested.

Saima did not reply. Suddenly, she nodded her head and bent to her left to open the bedside drawer. She pulled out the copy of the Quran. She touched the holy book to her forehead, opened it and began searching for a particular page. Having found it, she started reading the verses under her breath.

Damini looked at Saima, confused. She waited for her friend to finish reading. After Saima was done, she again touched the book to her forehead, kissed it this time, and returned it to the drawer. Before Damini could ask, Saima said, 'I have decided to open the box and find out what is inside.' Her tone was decisive as if she had received divine approval for her decision.

'What! Are you sure you want to do that? Your grandmother would get very upset if she finds out and ... umm ... she is bound to find out, don't you think?' Damini looked around the room and her eyes rested on the photo frame kept on the study desk at the far corner of the room with a picture of Saima, her mother and grandmother. 'But jokes apart, why would you want to do that?'

'What if I die, like my mother, before learning what is inside. I am not married; I have no child. I am not getting married anytime soon. Life is so uncertain. I don't want to die without finding out what that precious secret is. I prayed to seek forgiveness from my grandmother and my ancestors for breaking my promise. I am sure they will as I do it in good faith.' She raised her hands and muttered a prayer.

Damini got up. She picked up the photo frame with her grandmother's picture from the console and kept it upside down. She winked at Saima. 'She can't see us now.'

'You're so silly.' Saima threw a pillow at Damini, pretending to be angry at her. Damini evaded the pillow and returned to the bed.

Both stared at the box again.

Saima had thought a lot before she decided to open the box. There was no way she was going to be able to hang on to the box all her life without knowing what was inside. Her work would take her around the world. Anything could happen, an air crash, a car accident. Moreover, keeping ivory was illegal unless it was registered with the antiquities department as an ancestral property. For that she would need to produce the box for inspection which meant the contents would have to be taken out and left behind at home. And if she was going to empty out the box, she would any which way find out what was inside. She also tried to persuade herself that maybe the time had come to break the tradition and find out what the secret was while she was young, sparing her children the burden of a lifelong anxiety.

She picked up the box with her hands and placed it on her lap. She lifted the lid slowly. The box was as beautiful from inside as on the outside. There was a Belgian mirror on the inside of the lid. The surface of the box was cushioned by rich green velvet.

On it lay three leathered diaries, one on top of the other. With trembling hands, Saima carefully lifted the diary on the top which looked older than the others. Its pages had been stitched together with a silk thread. She turned the cover gently. There was some text inscribed on the first page in Persian. She turned to the next page. There too the text was in Persian. She couldn't understand a word of it. She placed the diary on the bed and picked up the second diary. That too was in Persian. The third diary appeared somewhat newer than the others. Although this too had rich leather binding with pages stitched together with a rich strand, it was certainly not the same rich silk. It wasn't as fragile as the other two. She lifted the third diary carefully and opened the cover gently. She felt a sense of relief. The text on the first page was in Urdu, a script she could read fluently. She read it aloud: *May those who carry my blood in their veins know the truth some day!* Saima felt a cold chill run up her spine. She started sweating from nervousness. She felt weak.

Damini touched her hand with concern, 'Are you ok?' she inquired.

Saima did not reply. She replaced the diaries in the box and closed the lid. Damini fetched a glass of water and handed it to her. As Saima gulped the water down, Damini spotted a piece of paper lying on the bed. 'This seems to have dropped out from one of the diaries,' she said, pointing at the piece of fragile paper.

It was very delicate and would probably fall apart if lifted. Saima bent over to read its contents without touching the paper:

> *The diaries in Persian text were written more than three hundred years ago. I have translated them in Urdu for the benefit of my future generations. I had to learn to read and write Persian at the age of fifty. It took nearly two years to translate and write the text, all of it sitting under the*

*light of a diya in the confines of my room which no one was allowed to enter. These are meant for the eyes of my lineage only.*

*Rahim Sallaludin Khan*
*Kotwal*
*Julandhar*
*1906*

Saima went cold. Rahim Sallaludin Khan was Saima's great-grandfather. By now her curiosity knew no bounds, but she felt petrified at the prospects of the secrets the diary held.

'Let us put this back,' Damini interrupted her thoughts.

Saima brought a pair of surgical gloves from the bathroom. She lifted the paper delicately and placed it back in one of the diaries.

'Beer?' Damini asked, retrieving a pint from the fridge.

'Yes, I could do with one.' Damini handed over her pint to Saima and went back to get another for herself.

Damini picked up her bag to leave. 'I am leaving, Sammy. Have my packing to finish. I will see you tomorrow.'

Saima did not notice Damini leaving. She sat still thinking about the diaries and the note she had just read. Her heart was racing. Unable to bear the suspense any longer, she picked up the box and looked at the diaries. Heaving a deep breath, she picked up the diary with the translation and settled down on the reclining chair.

# *Hindustan, Sixteenth Century*

# The Prophecy

The June heat was oppressive. Sunlight fell on the sand and lit the horizon in a hue of flames. The wind lifted tons of burning sand from the earth and tossed them at him like a swarm of locusts striking with a vengeance. The sand pierced his wounds as Mustaffa Ali struggled hard to hold on to the stirrups. The black stallion he rode was also in deep pain. Blood oozed from the deep slash in its belly. Ali was mindful that the loyal beast could collapse any time. Hopefully, it would not be before the end of their journey, he prayed.

He glanced back to check on his daughter who sat behind him strapped to his waist. Her eyes were closed and he could not tell if she was conscious. Her gentle skin had turned dry from heat and her lips were dehydrated. Her hair was dishevelled and covered with sand. Yet, she appeared unruffled. A girl of few words, his elder daughter was brave and proud beyond her age. She had refused to drink water since the previous night imploring that the little water that was left be saved for her younger sister. '*Abboojaan,* do not worry about me. Save it for Suraiya.' Tears filled Ali's eyes. She was only eight years old but had a sense of maturity about her. Despite her protest, he had poured a few drops of water in her mouth.

Ali turned to look at his wife who was riding by his side with Suraiya clinging to her breast. Jahanuma had wrapped the four-year-old in a cloak and looped it around her neck. She was also struggling to see through the sandstorm. But Jahanuma was tough, a true daughter of a Pathan father. She had seen harsher days. He was certain she would endure this crisis, but his daughters were too young to survive this. He loved his family and was pained to see them go through this situation. He muttered a prayer under his breath for their safety.

They had been riding for two days now, fighting their way forward and stopping only briefly for rest at night. The soldiers of Khwaja Hasan Naqshbandi, the exiled former prime minister of Kabul, were chasing them like mad dogs. They were still not far enough from Kabul to be able to feel safe. Ali was conscious that they would not be out of danger until they crossed into the Mughal Sultanate, the Riyasat-e-Hindustan. Their food and water were running out. His injuries were fast triumphing over his determination. He dug his heels into the horse which hastened forward despite its bleeding wounds.

Ali was not afraid of death. His only aim was to secure his family by crossing into Hindustan before he died. He was a brave man, having taken after his grandfather Muhammad Hafiz who served as the personal bodyguard of Shah Tahmasp of Persia with distinction. Ali's father Aslam Kamal was one of the five bodyguards who had been assigned to protect Humayun when he sought refuge in the court of Shah Tahmasp. Humayun was in exile after losing Delhi to Sher Shah Suri. Ali had shown no inclination to take up the family occupation. His passion was crafting weapons – swords, daggers, spears and bows.

After his marriage with Jahanuma, Ali relocated to Kabul where her father owned a flourishing trade in dry fruits. With the help of his father-in-law, Ali started a modest *karkhana* of weapons. Soon, his workmanship became popular. The admiration for his artistry spread. He started getting orders from faraway places.

He was fortunate to have Jahanuma as his wife. He loved her intensely. She was the most beautiful woman he had ever known. Tall and slender, she had sharp features. Her expressive eyes said more to him than she did with her words. He could never have enough of watching her go around the house carrying out her chores. Each evening, he waited for the day to retire so he could lay with her in the dark and forget the world in the warmth of her body. It was on these nights that they would finally find the quiet to make conversation. She was intelligent and he valued her insight. They would stay awake discussing matters of business and family, of love and their future children.

A year later, Jahanuma gave birth to Nadira. When she was born, the much-revered fortune-teller who lived a few miles away from Kabul had joined the celebrations. Using his old sigils, he had even made a prophecy. 'Your daughter is indeed an exceptional one, true to the meaning of her name. You are blessed, Ali and Jahanuma. She will grow up to be a beautiful woman, with a mind as strong willed as her heart would be pure. Nadira will live a rich life, her path defined by her fervour,' he said and everyone cheered. Then he paused and smiled gravely. 'Fate will challenge her but she will decide her destiny. She will earn a name for herself yet the forces of time will not be kind to her.' A little worried by his words, Jahanuma and Ali looked at each other. They wanted to hear more and prodded him further but the fortune-teller refused to say more. He raised his cup and before taking a sip, only declared, 'Time will tell.' By now Ali was annoyed at his vague speech and called for the festivities to commence with more food and drinks.

Ali had believed that in the entire world it was Jahanuma that he loved the most but that changed when he held Nadira for the first time. He was overwhelmed with love and promised himself to not leave any stone unturned in giving his first daughter the best life possible.

Soon after her birth, the family struck gold when the armoury of the Shah of Persia placed a giant order. Nadira was indeed a blessing, and Ali and Jahanuma kept thanking their stars for their daughter. As Ali's business expanded, Aslam Khan sought retirement and joined the business to extend a helping hand. Ali was thrilled. His work flourished with help from his father. Then arrived Suraiya. Nadira doted on her sister. Now their family was complete. They soon built a new house in an upmarket location and all seemed perfect.

But a few years later, trouble knocked on their doors. One day, Khwaja Hasan Naqshbandi visited their shop. Hasan was a loyal hand of Mirza Hakim, the former governor of Kabul who was also the half-brother of Padshah Akbar. Mirza had lost favour with the emperor and was on the run. Hasan wanted to place a bulk order for weapons. Knowing Hasan was a rebel and an adversary of Padshah Akbar, Ali's father declined citing shortage of raw material as an excuse. Hasan refused to take no for an answer and Aslam Khan was unwilling to relent. The dialogue turned into a quarrel which escalated into an ugly argument. Hasan became furious. 'Be prepared to face the consequences of your imprudent decision,' he threatened the father and son before he left.

Aslam and Ali did not take him seriously and soon forgot about the incident.

A few days later, Aslam was tipped off by a friend serving in the Shah's office that Hasan was preparing to rob the factory at the behest of Mirza. He planned to raid with his band of armed soldiers disguised as bandits and was determined to kill both Ali and Aslam before leaving with the spoils. The friend advised Aslam to leave the town with his family for some time. 'Even if the workshop is plundered, you can rebuild it after sometime.

You may even be able to recover all the loss, but lives lost cannot be reclaimed. Leave at once for Istanbul,' he asserted.

Aslam knew there was no way Ali and he could outfight Hasan. It was only prudent that they avoided a confrontation. He summoned Ali aside and described the situation to him. 'Prepare to leave for Agra at once. We will implore Akbar's protection and plead for a dignified return. I am confident that the emperor will help us when we tell him the reason for fleeing Kabul.'

Ali had retorted in anger. 'I am astonished that you – the bravest of braves – are suggesting we run away and hide. We are Turks, Father. We are not the ones to show our back to the enemy. We will fight. I prefer to die defending our honour and self-respect than be seen by our tribe as a coward running away from a fight.'

Aslam had beseeched his son to stay calm and think of his wife and his daughters, that his bravery would be foolish if it put their future and their dreams at stake. 'Remember, it is also a Turk's duty to protect the honour of the women of his family. That must take precedence over anything else under the circumstances. This is the time to think and act. We two are no match for the entire brigade of soldiers. Once your family is safe, then we think about our revenge on this rascal. Akbar detests Mirza. I am sure he will extend all the support to help us reclaim our honour.'

Eventually, Ali relented. In the dark of the night, they left for Agra along with the women of the house. Disguised by the night were also Hasan's men who were tailing them. They had only travelled a few miles when they were ambushed by a dozen armed men. Although taken by surprise, Aslam and Ali were able to slay half of them as the remaining fled to fetch reinforcement.

At night, while they were resting in a serai in a remote *kasba*, they were again attacked by Hasan's men, this time larger in number. In the fierce fight that followed, Aslam was killed and Ali's mother wounded. Ali was also injured. They managed to flee with Ali and Nadira on one horse, and Jahanuma, his mother and Suraiya on the other. Ali was devastated at having to leave without giving his father a dutiful burial. They stumbled on through the mountain passes and ravines, their horses' steaming breaths loud in the night. A few hours later, they stopped to attend to his mother who was unable to ride any more. She passed away a few minutes after. In a single night Ali had lost both his parents. But he did not have time to grieve. Teary eyed, revenge firing his rage, he had to march on and save his family.

## I

The way Ali's sturdy frame had staggered over the last few kos did not escape Jahanuma's attention. It was obvious he was struggling hard to stay in the saddle. His youthful, handsome face was covered in sand and blood. Although the wind had stopped blowing, the sand still floated in the air and flew into their eyes. The heat remained unbearable. She nudged her horse closer to her husband. 'Ali, we must stop for some time. You need to rest for a while,' she pleaded.

'No, we don't have the time. If we keep going at this pace, we might reach Lahore before sunset. It is not safe to stop. Hasan's men won't be far behind. We can't camp here at night.' To conciliate Jahanuma, who still looked unconvinced, he said reassuringly, 'Stop worrying about me, Jahanuma. Your husband has enough muscle to fight a tiger with bare hands.' However, his weak voice betrayed him. The customary roar of the Turk was missing.

Jahanuma was twice as stubborn as Ali and was determined to get him to rest. 'We shall stop,' she declared and before Ali could protest, tugged the reins to turn the horse in the direction of a large keekar tree she could see in the distance. This was the time to assert her Pathan lineage, she decided. She was the daughter of a valiant father who headed a tribe known to be the most fearless of all in Afghanistan. She could not let her husband continue to suffer just because his Turkish pride did not allow him to admit he needed rest. Ali eventually ceded to his wife, albeit reluctantly. Although in his mind, he too agreed that the cool shade of the tree would provide the much-needed relief from the scorching sun and help him recover.

Jahanuma helped Ali sit on the ground, resting his back against the tree, and poured some water in his mouth. Ali looked into her eyes. 'I love you, Jahanuma. I will fight till the last drop of blood remains in me to protect you and our daughters.'

Tears streamed down Jahanuma's cheeks. She made no effort to stop herself from crying. 'Do not lose hope, Ali. Bright days lie ahead. Whether in Lahore or Agra, we shall make a good life for ourselves. We will flourish anew, and our lives will be filled with the joyous laughter of our daughters.'

'Inshallah,' Ali whispered and took her hand in his. 'May Allah bless us and show us mercy. My little girls have not yet seen anything in life. May his kind hand protect them.'

Jahanuma muttered a prayer.

## II

Jahanuma woke up with a start. Her one hand instinctively reached out for her dagger as she adjusted her *khimar* with the other. The dagger was missing. She saw four sepahis standing around Ali. One of them, who appeared to be their captain, noticed the movement and swiftly produced the sword from his scabbard. 'Don't move or you will be dead. Who are you and where have you come from?' he asked in Pashtu, pointing the sword at her throat.

She looked at Ali who lay still despite the commotion. His eyes were closed. A horrid feeling gripped her. Ignoring the captain's warning, she stretched her hand and shook Ali. He did not move. 'Ali, Ali,' she cried to wake him up.

'He is dead. His pulse is still,' one of the soldiers said in between Jahanuma's screams. He had passed away in his sleep. Tears filled her eyes. She looked at their daughters who were still fast asleep, unmindful of another tragedy that had struck them. Suraiya was too young to realise what was happening but she knew her elder daughter would sense the loss and find it hard to come to terms with.

'Tell us who are you?' the captain barked.

Jahanuma caught hold of herself. She grasped that it was she alone who could protect her daughters. What should she tell them? Could these soldiers be trusted? They appeared to be Pashto Ahadis, the emperor's household troops, but what if they were loyalists of Hasan?

After thinking for a while, she said, 'We have come from Kabul. Ali is...' she suppressed a sob, '...was my husband and the girls are my daughters. We are fleeing from Kabul and going to Lahore to seek refuge in the shadow of Padshah Jalal-ud-din Muhammad Akbar – the benevolent and merciful emperor of Hindustan. May he live long. Our family served his father and grandfather, and we will beg him to take us under his care. Please help us reach Agra.'

'How did your husband get injured?' the captain inquired, ignoring her appeal.

Jahanuma had no intention of disclosing the details to the captain. 'I can only reveal that to the emperor,' she asserted. She had hoped her speech would yield some sympathy from the captain but he was unmoved. Irked by her defiant tone, he stated, 'I cannot help you unless you cooperate.'

Jahanuma did not want any trouble with the captain but was determined not to divulge anything till she was certain the soldiers were not part of Hasan's troop. She decided to try a different approach. 'You are a Pathan. You know very well that our women do not tell their private affairs to strangers however trying the circumstances.'

The captain looked at her sharply. She had spoken like a Pathan but he did not trust her yet. He continued to probe although his tone softened slightly. 'How do I know you speak the truth?'

Jahanuma felt a sense of relief. At least he was listening.

Realising the captain's dilemma, Jahanuma reached inside her khimar and pulled out a *kilij*. Holding its tail in her hand, she offered the kilij to the captain by its head. The captain's eyes widened with admiration as he held the dagger. He grazed his fingers across the curve of the cold blade made of the finest Damascus steel, its hilt encrusted with precious stones. It was the most exquisite kilij he had ever seen.

Jahanuma noticed the regard on the captain's face. 'My husband made this with his own hands, a labour of many months,' she said. 'This has been crafted from the finest materials. It was the wish of my husband to gift this kilij, only one of its kind in the world, to the Shahenshah-e-Hind. It was his desire to present this to the Jahanpanah personally, and convince him to take our family under his care. As he is now no more, it is my duty to make sure it reaches the emperor.'

The captain was conflicted. If the woman was lying, he would be punished for making an error in judgement. If she was indeed speaking the truth, it was expected to be his earnest duty to ensure that the emperor received the exquisite gift. If he failed the task, and the woman somehow reached the emperor and told on him, the punishment then too would be harsh. It was a complicated matter and it would be best to let his superior decide, he concluded. 'Let me take you to my commander. He will decide what to do with you. My soldiers will arrange your husband's burial.'

'Shukran.' She paused and then added, 'Can I ask for a favour?'

The captain looked at her. 'Say, but I cannot promise that it will be granted.'

'My husband was a brave Turk,' Jahanuma began as tears filled her eyes. 'He died fighting for the honour of his family. He deserves a respectful funeral. I would like to bury my husband and mark his grave so I can visit it again. He was a good man. He deserves proper rites and burial, and he deserves the honour of our memory. Allow me to give him his due and bury him with dignity.'

'We cannot do that, Bi.' This was the first time the captain addressed her with respect like a Pathan would a married woman. 'There is a protocol. The rules don't allow a formal burial unless we are satisfied that your husband was not an enemy of my emperor. I will have to get clearance from my commander.'

'I can wait here however long it takes for my husband's name to get cleared. I will not leave until I have seen his burial rites performed.'

'That will not be possible. I will, however, leave behind two soldiers. If the commander grants your request, they will be sent instructions for the funeral as per rules. You can visit the grave, too, if permitted by my superior or the emperor.'

The soldiers were not pleased with the offer made by their leader. They were in no mood to wait behind or dig a grave. Their duty roster would be over in an hour and they were desperate to get back to the comfort of their tents and indulge in their daily ration of opium.

There was no point in pursuing this further, Jahanuma realised. She had no option but to accompany the captain and hope that his superior would be an understanding man.

'How far would we need to go?' she asked.

'Our post is only fifteen kos from here. We are on patrolling duty as the emperor is camping near the post.' The soldier instantly regretted the slip of his tongue. He realised he had just disclosed the emperor's whereabouts to a stranger and broken an important rule and, probably, compromised his position in the army.

She turned to look at Ali's injured horse which lay on the floor in agony. Flies hovered over its wounds. Vultures loomed above waiting to feast on its flesh. 'May I release the beast from this misery?' she asked, stretching her hand towards the captain for her dagger. The captain handed it over to her reluctantly.

# The Travelling Capital

They reached the post at dusk. The ride took two hours with a brief stopover to offer namaz at sunset. On the way, the captain asked Jahanuma for some details about Ali's family. He needed to run some checks, he told her. Jahanuma reluctantly provided the name of her father-in-law and their village to the captain. Before they entered the post, the captain demanded the kilij back, stating that the rules did not permit anyone except the soldiers on duty to carry any weapon on them.

They passed through several security checks before reaching the post. The post was no short of a sprawling city. The horizon was covered with camps of all sizes. The makeshift city sprawled as far as she could see, covering the desert and the low-lying mountains. It was getting dark and the yellow lanterns twinkled in the night. She had learnt that Akbar's court was very mobile and he travelled frequently, often shifting the capital. But she had never imagined the provisional capital set up by him to be so grand. 'The whole official machinery – staff, records, treasury – all of it follows the emperor wherever he goes. So do the armed forces,' the captain spoke, looking at her bemused expression. 'The household and the kitchen, with countless servants also shift, as do the innumerable artists and entertainers. Even a part of his harem tags along. A city sprouts wherever he camps. And surprisingly, despite its enormity, the move happens with unbelievable precision,' he explained with a sense of pride.

They stopped in front of the commander's office. The captain instructed Jahanuma to wait and went inside. The large tent was guarded by four armed soldiers. A horse was tied to a peg nearby. An hour passed. Jahanuma was tired and the girls were famished. The captain had offered them some dry fruit and water on the way but that had not been enough. They had not eaten a decent meal since they fled Kabul. She hoped once the emperor agreed to meet, they would be offered a wholesome dinner. As she waited, her impatience grew.

The captain returned to issue some instructions to one of the guards. The guard at once climbed the horse and galloped away. He returned after a while and resumed his position at the entrance. After a few minutes, an old man with a flowing grey beard arrived on horseback and disappeared inside the tent. The guards at the entrance saluted him. He must be a person of high rank, Jahanuma guessed. The old man emerged after some time. He looked towards Jahanuma, bowed and left. The captain came out once again and released some instructions to the same guard and went back inside. The guard instantly made a move, this time on his feet. Finally, the captain came out and announced, 'The commander will meet you now. The girls can rest in the waiting room.' An *urdubegi*, a woman soldier, appeared out of the shadows and escorted the girls to the tent next door.

Aziz Koka, the commander, was a tall, well-built man. His eyes were unusually small and a long scar ran down his left ear to his upper lip. Even his dense beard failed to conceal the scar. He was in his civil dress. The captain made a brief well-rehearsed formal introduction of Aziz Koka emphasising that the commander was one of His Majesty's youngest mansabdars.

'Jahanuma Bi, your father-in-law was a brave man. He served our emperor's father with great distinction. Perhaps you may not be aware, Aslam Khan's uncle, Nazr Culi Turkistani, was a loyal of the emperor's father and was also his confidant.' He paused to say a prayer. 'And I find, not to my surprise, your husband was as brave as his father and grandfather. May they all find peace in Allah's shadow!' the commander said without exchanging any pleasantries. His face beamed with pride at the information about her husband's family he had been able to gather in a short time. Jahanuma was impressed but not surprised. Ali's father used to say that the Mughal spy network was one of the best in the world. The old man who had visited a few minutes ago must have provided the information to the commander, she surmised.

'Shukran,' she responded plainly without a hint of surprise or awe. From the corner of her eyes, she noticed the kilij lying wrapped in a green shaneel cloth and resting on a silver tray. 'When may I have the honour of meeting the emperor? I would like to present that to His Excellency personally,' she said, nodding her head in the direction of the kilij.

The commander's expression changed. He was taken aback by her indifference and lack of appreciation for the praise he had showered on her family. He made no attempt to hide his irritation. 'Shahenshah is resting. I will only be able to ask the Padshah tomorrow morning and ascertain if His Majesty is amenable to granting you an audience. As for the weapon, the same will be presented to the emperor by the protocol department as the rules command.'

Jahanuma nodded. 'In that case, can we please get a place to rest? My daughters are exhausted,' she requested wryly.

The commander's irritation increased at Jahanuma's dry tone. He had expected her to thank him or plead to arrange for an audience with the emperor. He felt like telling her off.

But her husband's family had served the emperor's late father which made her an important person and he could not risk his superiors finding out that she was mistreated.

'That has been arranged,' he responded. 'You will be provided a room in the guesthouse.' He hesitated, and then added, 'A hakim has also been arranged in case they need any care.' It was she who needed the hakim, he thought, looking at her wounds, but decided it was better not to say it.

'Shukran...' Jahanuma said, respectfully this time. It was thoughtful of the commander to have summoned the hakim.

Koka nodded and continued, pre-empting Jahanuma's question, 'Instructions have been sent to the soldiers to bury your husband along with his horse honourably. Burial will take place as soon as the sun rises. An imam has been arranged to perform the rituals. The grave will be marked and fenced. Inshallah someday the girls will visit the grave and offer respect to their father.'

The mere mention of her husband's burial made Jahanuma feel weak in the knees. The thought of him being laid to rest, devoid of the presence of his friends and family, left her feeling shattered. In a desperate attempt to steady herself and prevent herself from falling to the ground, she clutched the chair positioned beside her.

'Are you fine, Bibi?' Koka asked with concern. The captain appeared with a bowl of water. Jahanuma accepted it with gratitude. 'Yes, shukran,' she said, getting ahold of herself. 'My daughters and I will always be indebted to the Padshah and to you for the generosity you have shown us.'

Koka clapped his hand twice. Two urdubegis stepped inside. 'Escort them to the guesthouse...,' he commanded.

Jahanuma was grateful for the consideration and efficiency of the emperor's administration. In their guestroom, they were served a meal of freshly roasted meat, fruits and sharbat. The girls devoured it in no time, but she could not bring herself to eat. Alone with her daughters, the absence of Ali suddenly struck her to pieces. She did not feel brave any more. In the quiet of the room, she wept silently, letting her tears fall unrestrained. How would she take care of her little girls? Who would take care of her?

Suraiya was too young to understand anything, she could be easily pacified if she asked for her abba. But Nadira had questions. She had already asked about Ali twice. While Suraiya was in a sound sleep from the sedative that the hakim had administered on her, Nadira was lying awake in the dark, staring at the roof. Suddenly, she turned to look at Jahanuma.

'Ammi, will Abbu come back?'

Her question crushed Jahanuma. She could sense Nadira's innocence trying to convince her that her father might come back; but in her heart Nadira feared the worst. Jahanuma let the silence hang in between them. She reached out to her daughter and wrapped her arms around her and made her sit on her lap. It wasn't long before Nadira too started to cry. Her fear was real, her father was not coming back. 'How can this be, Ammi? How can I never see Abba jaan again?' she said in between her sobs. Jahanuma patted her head softly. The night moved steadily, giving the mother and daughter time to mourn Ali. Nadira soon fell asleep on her mother's shoulder. Jahanuma kept awake, her entire life flashing before her eyes – all the times she had spent with Ali, telling stories by the fireside, the girls running into their father's arms when he returned from work, memory after memory played in front of her until she too could no longer keep herself awake and passed into a dreamless state.

## I

She had just fallen asleep when the noise outside woke her up. She lifted the curtain to find out what the commotion was about. The day had still not broken out. The Uzbek guard outside smiled at her. 'The emperor announced after dinner that he will return to Agra ahead of schedule as he has an important administrative matter to deal with. We leave after breakfast. They are all packing. He will halt in Lahore for a few days on the way,' she informed. 'We are accustomed to these sudden decrees,' she added in an amused tone.

Jahanuma woke up Nadira. She splashed some water on her face. 'Freshen up. We have to leave,' she told her. No point in waking up Suraiya, she decided. She would be cranky if woken without her having slept through the usual hours. The guard shouted from outside to inform them that a coach was waiting and that they should hurry. Jahanuma settled into the waiting coach with Suraiya still fast asleep on her lap. Nadira carried their belongings and sat next to her mother. One guard found a seat at the back of the coach and the other went and sat beside the coachman.

Nadira was overwhelmed by the swarm of people, camels, horses, oxen, mules and elephants lining up to prepare for the journey. The camping equipment was still being neatly folded. Furniture was being stacked on the carts and carriages. The heavy gear was being loaded on the elephants. Despite this flow of movement, there was no chaos. Everything was organised with military precision as if following longstanding standard operating procedures. In a few minutes, all the bullock and camel carts, horse buggies and other innumerable carriages orderly lined up. The substantial part of the city had been dismantled in a matter of hours. 'Only some people will stay behind to wind up everything, all the garbage will be buried and new saplings will be planted to replenish the trees felled to accommodate the city,' the guard told her, noticing the astonishment on her face.

The coachman waited for the signal to start moving forward. A few minutes later, they heard the sound of drums and trumpets in anticipation of the emperor emerging from his tent. The royal tent was always the last to be wound up. Suddenly, there was a flurry of activity around them. The guards and the charioteer got done hurriedly and stood with their heads bowed. Nadira stuck her head out. 'The entourage of Akbar's wife is approaching,' the guard muttered. Jahanuma also joined her daughter to look outside. They could see the queen sitting on an elephant in a pitambar, a canopied throne made of beaten gold and precious stones which sparkled even in the softness of the morning sun. Tens of urdubegis warrior women armed with spears surrounded her. Eunuchs walked along carrying silver-tipped lathis. Countless palanquins followed bearing other women, each accompanied by her retinue of slaves and servants. Somewhere in the middle of the caravan, they received the signal to join the allotted slot in the column of her caravan. From where they were, they could see neither the beginning nor the end of the column. Somewhere, far ahead, the emperor rode with his sons, she was told. What was until a few minutes ago a full-fledged city was now a moving mass of carriages, horses and soldiers on foot.

## II

The surprisingly comfortable journey on the carriage took about eighteen hours with a brief halt for lunch. On the way, Jahanuma was told that the emperor had agreed to meet her in Agra. She requested Aziz Koka to seek the emperor's permission for her to stay back in Lahore for a few days to meet Ali's aunt, his father's half-sister. The emperor granted the permission.

As they approached Lahore, a part of the caravan including their carriage were instructed to halt at the outskirts. The entourage would enter the city with a predetermined number of vehicles so as to avoid overburdening the infrastructure and causing disruption to the regular activities. When eventually ordered to move, they had to go through security checks at a number of points. Guards appeared out of nowhere, ordering them to halt, notwithstanding the royal Mughal flag their carriage hosted. The drill was most rigorous at the entry gates of the largely mud brick-walled city with many structures of red sandstone. The city itself was heavily guarded. Jahanuma had heard from her father that Lahore held a strategic importance for the Mughals and was kept adequately guarded to meet threats from attacks.

Jahanuma parted the curtain of their carriage to look outside. She was taken by the grandeur of the city. The guard gave her a knowing smile. The awe of first-time visitors to the city was all too common; that Jahanuma was captivated was evident. 'Is it true that the city has thirteen gates?' Jahanuma asked the guard. He nodded. Nadira excitedly looked out as the coach moved ahead. Her eyes gleamed at the sight of the staggering structures. 'That citadel,' the guard pointed out to her, 'is the majestic Shahi Qila.' As the coach moved ahead, she was mesmerised by the splendour of the gardens and the lush trees, the fountains and lakes they passed. It was all very lively and colourful, exactly as she had imagined the city to be from the stories she had heard from her grandparents. 'Ammi, we should wake Suraiya up, she should see this!' she insisted to Jahanuma who smiled and shook her head.

'I have heard from my grandparents that some people believe the city gets its name from the son of a Hindu God,' Nadira spoke to the guard. She loved hearing stories and even more so narrating to others what her grandparents narrated to her. 'What was his name?' Nadira paused, looking at her mother to help her remember.

'Luv,' a voice answered from the front. It was Madhur, the coachman.

'Yes! I know he was the son of Ram and Sita.'

The coachman chuckled. 'You're right. This city has seen plenty of famines and invasions since the time of the gods, but each time it has risen from the ruins as if by the blessings of the divine. This fort's foundation was laid centuries ago by Lohar Chand. It was then called Loharkot ... believed to be a marvel of its own times...'

'Focus on the road,' interrupted the guard sternly, annoyed at the coachman for indulging Nadira.

'But I want to hear more about the city,' Nadira said to the guard.

'No,' he growled back. 'All you need to know about the city is that it was built by Padshah Akbar; long live his name.'

'Why is that? Is there a law against telling tales? And why would you scream at a child? I will tell on you to the emperor when I see him,' Nadira fought back. Jahanuma gestured at her to remain quiet. She couldn't let Nadira's bluntness get in the way of their meeting with the emperor.

'Shut up,' the guard said, taken aback by the girl's directness. Turning to Jahanuma, he said, 'We are about to reach the gate. I suggest you drop the curtain of your coach as the rules require.' Jahanuma did as she was asked. The coachman nudged the horses to surge forward. Nadira sat back, annoyed. She decided she would ask somebody else to tell her stories of the beautiful city.

The coach entered the gateway and headed straight.

'What is the name of your relative?' the guard inquired from Jahanuma.

'Naaz Khatoon,' she replied.

One of the guards went inside a shop to find out where Naaz lived. She returned soon. 'She is well known here it seems.

The first shop owner I asked gave me directions to her house. It is a short distance from here. Follow me,' she instructed the coachman.

They reached the house in a few minutes. Naaz stood at the entrance of the single-storey brick house, expecting them. Obviously, the soldier's inquiry had not been discreet and Naaz already knew that some guests were headed to her house.

Naaz was the youngest sister of Ali's father. She appeared to be in her late forties. Jahanuma introduced herself and the girls to Naaz. She appeared pleased to meet her and hugged the girls warmly. After the introductions were over, Naaz led them inside into the small courtyard. A bunch of young girls sat on a mat in the centre of the courtyard, some dressed up in dancing costumes. A slightly older boy sat in the corner playing a pair of tablas. A young girl, a few years older than Nadira, stood in the middle of the room, dancing gracefully.

'This is my daughter, Asma,' she pointed to the girl.

Naaz dismissed the class for the day. Asma touched the feet of her mother and guru and bowed to the tabla player. She then stepped forward to greet the guests.

They settled on a charpoy in the courtyard. Asma went inside to fetch some sharbat. Nadira followed her into the kitchen to help. Naaz instructed the boy who was playing the tabla to take her guests' belongings inside.

'What brings you to Lahore?' inquired Naaz.

Jahanuma sighed. She could finally let her guard down. Over the next few hours, she recounted everything that had happened in the last few days. By the time she was finished, Naaz was sobbing uncontrollably, saddened by the news of the death of her brother and other family members. Jahanuma consoled her. 'You and the girls can stay here for as long as you want. Treat this as your own home,' Naaz said, pulling Suraiya onto her lap.

# The Gift of God

Jahanuma arrived in Agra three months later, leaving the girls under Naaz's care. Naaz had become fond of the girls and suggested that Jahanuma did not take them along. She feared that the emperor might renege on his promise and the girls would be disappointed if Akbar did not meet them despite having made them travel all the way. Even Jahanuma was unsure how empathetic the emperor's court would be to their tragedy or of his willingness to help them. She did not want to find herself abandoned in an unfamiliar place where she knew no one. There were many uncertainties and she couldn't risk exposing her daughters to any danger. Nadira had become good friends with Asma and did not mind staying back. Suraiya insisted on going with her mother but relented after some coaxing from her elder sister.

Jahanuma deposited with Naaz some of the jewellery she had managed to sneak away from Kabul. 'Do not hesitate to sell any of these if you need any money for their sustenance,' she told Naaz. Suraiya cried inconsolably when Jahanuma was leaving. Jahanuma was teary but did not weep. Nadira exhibited remarkable composure for her age. 'I will take care of Suraiya and myself, but promise you will return soon, Ammi,' she said to her mother. She had grown responsible all of a sudden. Her demeanour had changed as if she had realised that uncertain times lay ahead and found the resilience needed to deal with them. While Jahanuma was glad that her daughter was prepared to cope with the trying times, she was also overcome with grief at seeing a chirpy and playful girl turning into a quiet and contemplative person ahead of her age.

The emperor's protocol office in Lahore had organised a carriage drawn by three oxen to take her to Agra. Two armed soldiers were appointed to escort her and a woman attendant-cum-cook was also deputed to accompany her. The carriage was not as comfortable as the one in which they had arrived in Lahore but Jahanuma was grateful for the arrangements.

The monsoon was over and the weather was unusually good. As they travelled, Jahanuma was charmed by the verdure of the countryside, the fertile tracts of land, the imperceptibly changing landscape, lakes and rivers, abundance of trees and colourful birds. So many of those animals she was seeing for the very first time. Every now and then she would ask the attendant, pointing to an animal, what it was called. Nilgai enthralled her. It was no smaller than a horse and strong enough to overturn the cart if it came rushing in. Everything was so different from Kabul. Each village was surrounded by fields of wheat or mustard crop. The villages were mud-walled, thatch-roofed and protected by thorn fencing. Small white temples dotted the village skyline. The washerwomen beat their clothes on the stones. Buffaloes lazed in water enjoying the antics of their masters. She watched many children playing together, and in one instance a few of them excitedly ran along their carriage for a distance.

The fields were full of peasants tilling soil. Most men were bare-chested. Some wore only a cotton loincloth tied round the waist and hanging down two spans below their navels. Nearly all men wore a turban. Even in the villages she passed through, she observed all men dressed alike in white, a long shirt and a loose pyjama or dhoti. Only some, obviously affluent, carried over their shoulders shawls of very fine woollen fabric. Women were mostly tall but not as much as in Kabul and Lahore. They did not observe purdah except in some parts of their journey where she noticed that women partially covered their face using the scarf. Their sharp features were complemented beautifully by their skin shining golden in the sunlight. She was somewhat surprised to note that people living on the village outskirts were scantily dressed. Men only wore the *langota* and a cloth wrapped around their heads, not as a turban but to protect their heads from heat or serve as a cushion if they needed to carry heavy materials over their heads. Women mostly fastened one long piece of cloth around themselves, half of which was tied to their waists and the other half thrown over their heads, sometimes revealing their breasts. She looked away, embarrassed by the casual display of their bodies.

The journey had made Jahanuma less anxious about her destination. She found the countryside and the people very warm and hospitable. They took shelter in the serais when temperatures soared during the day or when it rained. Wherever they stopped, people from the village shared food and several stories with them. At night, she would invariably get invited by the local villagers to stay in their houses. She particularly enjoyed eating the chapatis of jowar and bajra, with generous portions of ghee and buttermilk served in tall bronze tumblers. By the time she reached Agra, Jahanuma and the cook were fully conversant with Hindustani cuisines and people's ways of eating. She had already made many friends whom she promised to see again on the way back.

Despite the pleasing trip, she was relieved when they approached Akbarabad, or as people fondly called it, Agra. The kotwal checked their papers at the entrance of the city and delivered a message from the emperor's court telling her to reach the serai located three kos from the Lal Quila and await further instructions. A room had been reserved for her at the guesthouse.

The serai was located in the heart of the city. It was reserved for visitors who awaited a meeting with the emperor. Rahim-ud-Din, the supervisor of the serai, was an elderly scholarly man. He also taught children, who fondly called him Rahim chacha, at the madrasa located next door. Rahim chacha lived in a small quarter behind the serai with his wife, Bano, and her teenage daughter, Mehar. Old, grey-haired Bano was Rahim chacha's second wife. His first wife, much younger, had fallen in love with a young man and had eloped, taking all their jewellery and valuables. Rahim was devastated. Bano, a part-time cook in the serai, took pity on Rahim and married him. A widow herself with a daughter to take care of, she too needed the companionship. Mehar continued to call her new father Rahim chacha even after her mother married him.

Rahim chacha was a diligent man always busy taking care of the serai and teaching in the madrasa. In his spare time, he could be found reading books he borrowed from the local library. Bano looked after the serai when Rahim chacha was away. Every day, after cleaning the serai and fetching water from the nearby well, she settled down under the enormous neem tree that shaded most of the front courtyard of the serai to sew intricate patterns on stoles with deft fingers. For most patterns Bano sewed, the colours of the threads were inspired from Rajputana, from those used by the nomads in the region. Mehar watched and learned her mother's skills. She went to school in the evening only for a couple of hours.

Jahanuma and Bano quickly became friends, connecting through their separate but similar sorrows. They often chatted for hours after Bano was over with her chores. Jahanuma learnt that the stoles Bano made belonged to

Jodha Bai, the emperor's most favoured wife. She was very fond of Bano's work.

'Jodha Bai gets plain stoles made from someone from Amer, a region her family rules, and passes them on to me for embroidery. She then sells them in Meena Bazaar.' Before Jahanuma could inquire about Meena Bazaar, Bano provided the explanation. 'It is a mela organised only for the women of the zenana. The women ... wives and daughters of the nobility of the court ... set up their shops to sell textiles, jewellery and handicrafts, among other things. The emperor and his sons are the only men allowed to visit the mela. Even Jodha Bai, the queen herself, sets up a stall. There is a fierce but healthy competition amongst the royalty to sell the most out of their stalls. Although outsiders are not permitted, Jodha Bai gets me in every year to manage her stall. It becomes quite a festive affair. It is especially nice to see royal women have unrestrained fun.'

Jahanuma was amused to learn of the work that the ladies of the zenana did.

'I have been forbidden by Jodha Bai from taking up any other client so that the designs of stoles she sells stay exclusive to her. But she compensates me adequately and even credits my work. Besides, I can't work more than what I already do. I am not getting any younger, you see. I am saving all I earn for Mehar's marriage.'

## I

Jahanuma was surprised to see the large number of people living in Agra. Although more crowded than Lahore, she found Agra better planned and administered. The Mughals were present in large numbers. The locals appeared relaxed and went about their business quietly. They were submissive to the Mughals but it did not seem as if they feared them.

Bano had been living in Agra from much before Akbar shifted his capital from Dilli and knew the city like the back of her hand. She was happily married to her first husband at the time and the two had decided to make a life in the city. Soon they were witness to Agra coming to life under the planning and administration of the empire.

'Why did he move to Agra?' Jahanuma asked Bano.

'It is said that he never truly overcame losing his father. Perhaps Dilli reminded him too much of his death. He came to Agra and the city turned around. The army, the palace staff, servants, traders, artists, everyone followed his stead. Only his mother stayed back to oversee the building of a grand tomb in the memory of her husband.'

Rahim chacha, like most other civilians, had worked for the construction of Lal Quila. He was apparently sentimental about his association with the fort and disapproved of the emperor's attempt at relocating the capital and building another fort there. 'We were all very dejected when the emperor ordered a new city to be built in Sikri next to the bed of the seasonal Khari Nadi not far from here and moved his capital there. Fortunately, he returned after a few years, troubled by the shortage of water in Sikri,' he said, raising his hands to say a prayer of gratitude.

Jahanuma was now curious to learn about Sikri. 'Why did he build the whole city and shift in the first place if he was to abandon it only in three years?'

'Don't tell me you don't know the story behind the building of Fatehpur Sikri?' Bano asked in amazement. 'Every child in Hindustan can recite the story that lies behind it.'

'Not all news reaches places like Kandahar and Kabul, Bano Bi. And Kanchani women have little interest in such news.

They are too engrossed in meeting the demands of household work and professional commitments. Any spare time is spent on keeping our dancing and musical skills polished,' Jahanuma replied, sounding a bit gloomy.

Bano thought she had embarrassed Jahanuma. 'I will let Rahim narrate the story. He is good at it,' she said, smiling apologetically. 'And also keep your bags packed and don't be surprised if we are asked to move to a new capital soon,' she added jokingly, nudging Jahanuma with her elbow.

Jahanuma looked puzzled.

'The rulers can be whimsical about these things. They treat their kingdoms and subjects as their personal assets. We have heard rumours that Akbar's team of architects are working on the design of constructing a new quila in Lahore which will be bigger than the fort here in Agra.'

Rahim chacha looked at Bano with disapproval. He rebutted his wife, 'Forts are not built out of fancy. Invariably, there is a strategic reason behind building or rebuilding a fort. They are meant to protect from enemy attacks and large enough to accommodate the army and civilian population. Their grandiose is a reflection of both the might and prosperity of the ruler. They are also symbols of the reign of the ruler of the time…'

'All right, all right, I was only telling her that Akbar may move his capital to Lahore. I have heard rumours that he has grown weary of the humidity here,' Bano interrupted Rahim chacha, somewhat irritated at his disapproving tone.

## II

After dinner they all settled in the courtyard around a fire made out of dry cow-dung cakes and some wood. Mehar was also excited as she did not know the story. She prepared the hookah for Rahim chacha and a big pot of tea for Jahanuma. She kept the pot next to the fire to keep it warm.

Rahim chacha sat quietly for a few minutes recollecting and gathering his scattered thoughts. Finally, he started speaking softly.

'The court was hit hard when Emperor Humayun passed away. Akbar was so young, and before the child could even mourn his father, he was forced on the throne. With support and guidance from Bairam Khan, his erstwhile khan-e-khanan, Akbar not only held on to the empire but consolidated it further and went on to expand it beyond what he had inherited. He acquired many wives and concubines and his harem was adorned with beautiful women by the time he turned twenty-five. Yet none of them were able to bear him a child. He was deeply saddened by the thought of not being able to produce an heir to the fast-expanding empire.'

Rahim chacha paused to take a drag from the hookah before continuing. 'Hakim Ali Gilani, Akbar's personal physician, examined the emperor and assured him of his sound health and the ability to father children. Finally, some of his partners conceived. A concubine from Kashmir was the first to give birth. She delivered twin boys. Sadly, they died soon after their birth. Later, a wife gave birth to a boy who also died after a few months. A girl was born to another concubine. She too died. The emperor was desperate for a child, a son, an heir to the throne of Hindustan. Two years passed. Akbar was suffering and it began to cost the court work. His rivals started conspiring. He lost interest in his harem. When Hamida Banu learnt of her son's condition, she invited him to spend a few days in Dilli. There, one morning, while strolling in the gardens of his father's tomb, he heard a commotion at the entrance. The guards had stopped an old deformed woman and a child from entering the tomb. The woman had burn scars on her face and could not see from one eye. She was pleading with the guards to allow them to go in. The guards were not letting her because the emperor was inside. Akbar intervened and ordered the guards to let her in.

On seeing the emperor, the woman bowed tersely and said, 'O, Humayun's son, I am glad I bumped into you...'

The guard screamed at her, 'Careful, you old wretched woman. How dare you address the emperor like that...'

He reached out to hit her but Akbar stopped him in his tracks. 'Let her speak.'

The woman continued unperturbed, 'I worked as your father's chef in the royal kitchen at one time. I had accompanied him from Kabul. As a young slave I was totally devoted to him, lovingly cooking for him his favourite dishes every day. One day a fire broke out in the kitchen. It was an accident. I was severely burnt and had to stay at home in pain for months. Not once did any one from your father's court come to see me or inquire of my condition. My husband abandoned me. He could not bring himself to look at my ugly face. My son...' She looked at the boy with affection, and continued, '...My son was only three years old then. Alone in my room I shrieked day and night in pain. I was in agony for months but bravely fought my miseries, hoping to get back to work. I wanted to give a good life to my son. I wanted to meet your father and ask him why no one from the court ever bothered to ask about my well-being when I had so diligently devoted myself to work for him. Finally, I recovered and went to the palace, hoping to get back into the kitchen. I was stopped at the gate. My services had been terminated and I had been replaced by another cook a few days after the accident. All my efforts to meet Humayun went in vain. I was shattered. I had no money. Your father paid no compensation or pension for my services. I had served him for ten long years. I was sickened at the way he treated me. A great king with a small heart he turned out to be. I have lived a desolate life in poverty for ten years, cursing your father every single day.'

She paused to catch her breath. Standing in his father's tomb, Akbar listened with patience to the old woman's grievance.

She continued, 'Last night, Allah summoned me. My time has arrived, he told me. I may be gone any day. This teenager will be left alone as an orphan in this world. I have come here to curse your father again one last time before I die.'

The boy was now trembling with fear, expecting the emperor to get angry and order them to be jailed. But Akbar was in deep thought, unperturbed by the provocation. Finally, he spoke.

'This is between my father and you. But if you believe my father has mistreated you, by all means you can swear at him. But as his son, I request you to forgive him. I apologise to you for the hurt and for the wrong you deem has been caused to you. Let him be in peace.'

The soldiers and the boy stood in awe, unable to believe what they had just heard. The old woman did not react.

The boy fell on the emperor's feet. 'Report to the mansabdar tomorrow. He will find you a job in the stable,' the emperor told him.

The old woman started weeping. She raised her hands and said a prayer. She then looked Akbar straight in the eye, her gaze a mix of pain and admiration for Akbar. Then she spoke in a peculiar voice.

'Jalal-ud-din Muhammad Akbar. Unlike your father you are compassionate. You deserve not one but many sons. On a hilltop in Sikri not many kos from where you rule lives a saint. Go take his blessings. May Allah give you a long life! May history immortalise you as the greatest emperor of this land!'

The woman fell. She had passed away.

Jahanuma and Mehar sat spellbound. Rahim chacha spoke as if he was present when the episode occurred. So engrossed were they in Rahim's account that they did not notice when the fire had almost died out. Rahim fetched some more dry wood. Jahanuma replenished her cup with tea. Mehar got up and went to get some raisins and almonds. Bano joined them. She brought a thin blanket for her husband who accepted it gratefully.

Jahanuma was fascinated and was anxious to hear the complete story. 'Who was this saint?' she prompted Rahim to continue.

Rahim smiled at her impatience. 'He *is*,' he said. 'The saint is still alive. May Allah bless him with many more years of life.' He offered a prayer for the saint, before continuing.

'Initially, Akbar did not take what the old woman had said seriously. But it kept nagging him. He told his friend Abul Fazl about the bizarre incident and sought his counsel. Abul Fazl was his guide and philosopher and Akbar did not act without his good advice. He told Akbar that as strange as it might be, it would not be proper to ignore what the old woman had said. He sought time from the emperor to verify her antecedents. After a few days, Abul Fazl informed the emperor that the old woman had indeed been employed in the royal kitchen. Humayun did not take her back as he had been advised by his doctors that she carried the risk of infecting the emperor and others. He had also traced the saint. His name was Sheikh Salim Chishti and he lived in a small hut on a hilltop in the village of Sikri. Salim Chishti was one of the descendants of the revered Khwaja Moinuddin Chishti of Ajmer.

'Arrangements were made for Akbar to travel to Sikri. Akbar rejected the suggestion of sending for the saint. If this saint could bless him with a son, he deserved to be respected and honoured, he decided. Abul Fazl accompanied the emperor.

The sheikh is stated to have received Akbar in his modest hut where the emperor sat on the floor cross-legged without even a mat underneath. They talked for hours without water or food. Akbar felt eternal peace in the presence of the saint. He sought guidance from the saint on many complex matters and was deeply impressed with the advice he offered. He felt the clouds of doubt lift. He spent the entire day speaking with the saint but not once was he able to raise the matter which had brought him to the saint. They broke the conversation only to offer namaz.'

Rahim paused to look at his audience. Mehar had already dozed off in Bano's lap. The women appeared sleepy.

'It is late. I will finish this tomorrow,' Rahim said, sprinkling water on the fire to douse it.

'Rahim chacha, can I ask you a question before you leave?' Jahanuma asked.

Rahim nodded, continuing to sprinkle water on the hot ash.

'Is there a relation between the names of Salim Chishti and the Shahzada?' she asked.

'Indeed, there is!' he answered. 'The emperor's first-born was named Sultan Muhammad Salim. The name Salim was added after the darvesh in grateful recognition of the holy saint's prayers and to ensure his lifelong blessings and protection on the prince. Akbar affectionately addresses the prince as Sheikhu Baba. Some say even that is inspired from the saint's name.'

'And was that also the reason Akbar moved his capital to Sikri?'

Rahim smiled. 'Yes. Salim was born in Sikri, next to the dargah. As soon as Akbar learnt of Jodha's pregnancy, he decided to send her to Sikri to live under the saint's blessings. Some say it was to protect her from any conspiracy to harm their child as many in his court did not wish the first-born to be from the womb of a Hindu. Others say Sheikh Salim Chishti himself had advised the emperor to move her to Sikri so that their son was born in the dargah. No one knows the actual reason behind the decision to move Jodha bai to Sikri. The fact remains that she did move there with her entourage of servants, cooks, midwives, physicians and other comforts. It is there her first child was born. Perhaps Akbar developed a sentimental association with the village. He also felt immensely grateful to Salim Chishti. No one can say with certainty why he decided to build an entirely new city but it is known to all that it was built after the saint.'

As they spoke, they heard loud cheers ring out from the outside, followed by bells and trumpets.

Bano scoffed. 'Another idol of their elephant god ready to be submerged in the Yamuna. Akbar has permitted everyone to follow their religious practices but some of these practices keep getting stranger and stranger by the day. And he doesn't stop at that. He goes on to have so many Hindu wives, letting them put up their idols in the very palace he lives and sleeps in? Don't mind me, I respect Jodha Bai, but that she wasn't made to renounce her religion despite her marriage to the most powerful ruler in the world is beyond me.' She shook her head, making no attempt to hide her disapproval of these liberal allowances made by the emperor. 'Anyway, such are the whims of the powerful; who are we to challenge them?'

Jahanuma gave her a slight nod and said nothing. She did not agree with Bano since the ways of her own family back in Kabul were no different from the emperor's. What baffled her was how Bano couldn't see what Akbar was really doing. *Isn't it admirable of an emperor to inspire peace by letting all faiths find prosperity under his rule,* she thought. But she decided it best not to contradict Bano. This was a delicate subject among people here. It seemed like while the emperor was making way for all faiths to coexist, many people just took these efforts as a challenge against their own way of life. Bano too was one of those people. Jahanuma smiled to herself as she realised the folly of their insecurity.

*'Shabba Khair,'* she said softly as she got up to leave for her room.

## II

Despite her resentment about Akbar's tolerance for other faiths, Bano was in awe of him. She kept Jahanuma occupied by recounting tales of the emperor's valour and the expanse of his empire. She learnt from Bano that Akbar was descended on his mother's side from Genghis Khan, on his father's from Timur. 'In his blood is a strange mixture of the Mongol, the rough, adventurous, cruel nomads of the steppes of Central Asia and of the Timurids, as cultured as they were brave. 'Despite the hard, fugitive, wandering and fighting in the early life of his father and grandfather, and of his own, his longing was culture, good governance, even luxury and civilization of the Turkman courts, a longing he seem to be fulfilling well,' she spoke with the authority of someone who knew the emperor very closely. Jahanuma couldn't help smiling at her in such moments as she sought Bano to know more about the man who would soon decide her fate.

Bano also told Jahanuma about the immensity of Akbar's empire. 'He has extraordinary courage, curiosity, strength, and intelligence. His shaping of the empire of the Mughals took it to heights it had never scaled before. I have heard that it takes a camel train sixty days to cross from the eastern boundary to the western one, the land between Persia and Bengal and a further sixty days to travel from the Himalayas in the north to the Deccan plain in the south,' Bano said with a hint of pride.

Back in her room, Jahanuma went over all that she learnt from Bano. So vivid were her descriptions that she could imagine Akbar sitting on his silver throne, gazing east to the very edge of the earth where his empire ended. She shook her thoughts away and thought of Ali. She missed him more than ever. Things would have been different if he was still alive. She wouldn't have to leave their daughters behind. This was the first time the girls had to stay without their mother for so long. She was particularly concerned about Suraiya who was not even five and was not accustomed to being away from her mother. Nadira worried her for a different reason. It seemed that a quiet anger was piling up inside her daughter. She was afraid that Nadira would keep questioning herself why all this was happening to her, why they were being made to suffer for no fault of their own, why her father, such a good man, had to die for defending his family. This bitterness could make Nadira reckless and turn her into a rebel. That night as she slept, she was visited by her daughters in her dreams and woke up to tears streaming down her cheeks.

# Under the Emperor's Wing

Eventually a message arrived from the emperor's office. Jahanuma was given the day and time for an audience with the emperor. She accepted with alacrity Bano's offer to accompany her. She couldn't go through with it alone.

On the appointed day they reached Lal Quila ahead of time. The fort stood like a diminutive hill of red sandstone on the bank of the Jamuna, shaped like a great bow with the string directed towards the flowing river. Jahanuma was taken aback by its grandeur. Bano was a regular visitor to the fort and was familiar with many details not known to outsiders. She had also heard many tales about it from Rahim. Noticing Jahanuma's reaction, she said, 'The original fortress comprised mud-brick walls built by the Lodi sultans. The sandstone wall was erected by Akbar. He added the watchtowers.'

They entered the fort from the Amar Singh Darwaza. The other entry points were reserved for the Mughal army which occupied more than half of the fort. The street to the diwan-i-aam was lined with royal soldiers who wore scarlet uniforms, burnished armour and were armed with swords and shields. The two ladies were instructed to stay in the courtyard where countless others waited. The commander recognised Bano and offered her a greeting. Her closeness to the emperor's wife was well-known. The guards checked the list of appointments and shouted at the soldiers to allow both the women to pass.

From here, the street sloped steeply upwards, between two high walls. At the top, the ground levelled out. Ahead of them was the pillared diwan-i-aam with its wooden roof and beaten silver ceiling. Beyond the garden, to the right, on the eastern wall of the fort stood the palace. Even from the distance it looked exquisite. 'I am told the emperor rarely sleeps in his palace. He lives and sleeps in the *bargah* pitched in the garden, that is when he is not in the harem,' Bano said, winking at Jahanuma.

'Why is that? Who would forsake the luxury of a palace as huge as this?' The more she found out about the empire and its ruler, the stranger she found it.

'They say Timur had decreed that none of his descendants should sleep under the roof of a building.'

From where she stood, Jahanuma could clearly see the enormous red-sandstone courtyard where Akbar held his public meetings. The courtyard was open on three sides. The eastern side abutted the palace. A recessed balcony made of pure white marble had been placed at a height higher than a man could reach. The balcony was decorated with inlays of semi-precious stones. On either side of the balcony were windows with marble lattice from which the ladies of the palace could observe proceedings while being hidden from public glare. Most part of the courtyard was covered with awnings to provide shelter from the sun. It was lined with an imposing guard of decorated elephants and caparisoned horses on which sat upright, alert and uniformed lancers, archers and cavalrymen. The courtiers stood in their precisely allotted places, rank by rank. The senior amirs, rajas and ambassadors stood closest to the royal balcony. The next rank stood behind them. Beyond them stood the various servants and foot soldiers. The remainder of the courtyard was filled with other officers, people seeking audience and spectators. Sentries bearing maces stood watch, keeping a careful eye on the crowd.

The banners of silk hanging in the diwan-i-aam wafted in the soft breeze. The assembly waited in patience for the emperor to arrive.

The diwan-i-aam fell silent on the announcement that the emperor was approaching the hall. Akbar emerged from the rear door and sat on the white marble throne placed in the centre of the large elevated balcony hanging from a depression in the wall. Everyone performed *kornish* by bowing deep down from the waist, the palm of their right hand placed upon the forehead and the head bent forward.

The official business started straight away with the reading of the farmans sanctioned by the emperor. Officials stamped the order with the bejewelled ink-pot insignia. This exercise went on for almost an hour. This was followed by reading out of diplomatic exchanges and gist of dispatches from the provinces. Later, the emperor received the foreign ambassador of Persia who presented a Turkish Tipuchak horse from the Shah of Persia. Noble after noble appeared with large silver platters on which reposed gifts ranging from gold mohurs, ornaments and gems to swords and daggers with delicately chased and bejewelled hilts, guns and carpets. Akbar nodded his head in acknowledgment and occasionally murmured a word of thanks or appreciation. This was followed by a few announcements which Jahanuma could not entirely understand. But it was when he was settling a confusing dispute that she became interested in the proceedings.

From where Jahanuma stood, she could hear the pleas made by the contesting parties. She could make out from their arguments that one of them, apparently a retired mansabdar, had borrowed a handsome loan from the other, who was a prominent moneylender of the area, to start a new business of making saddles to supply to the Mughal army. The borrower had promised to repay the loan within two years, with a share of the profit from the business for a period of five years after sale commenced. The former mansabdar appeared to have offered to repay the loan within six months as he had received a large order from the army. He, however, refused to pay the profit because he was prepaying the loan much ahead of the agreed time. The moneylender, however, demanded that the borrower honour his commitment to pay a share of the profit as promised and it being a term on which he had made the loan. It had ended before the emperor as efforts by the governor of the province had failed to resolve the dispute to the satisfaction of the two.

Akbar gave a very patient hearing to both. He even asked a few questions of the two. Then he inquired from one of his officers if there was a precedent of his decision on a similar dispute. It appeared there was none. After giving the matter a thought, Akbar cryptically announced his judgement.'It is clear this lender is in the business of making loans from which he makes his profit. He earns his livelihood by earning interest or other forms of returns on the loan. In this case, his return from the loan was a share in future profit. He parted with his money for two years to make an earning from the profits after two years, for a period of five years. It was not a friendly loan. If the borrower will not honour his commitment, moneylenders will be wary of lending which is not good for the market and trade. At the same time, it is true that the borrower is willing to repay the loan much ahead of two years. It would be fair to allow him to do so. The moneylender can use this money to give a loan to someone else and earn a profit from it. Yet, it has to be understood that the borrower is able to repay ahead of time because he is flush with funds and making a profit. This has been possible only because he could start the business with the borrowed money. Therefore, the borrower is obliged to share his profit with the lender. But because the lender parted with his money only for six months, and will receive the full amount back and be able to reuse it, I consider it fair that the agreed percentage of profit to be paid by the borrower be reduced from five years to two years. My decision will be followed by both parties honourably. A record of these proceedings will be kept by the concerned officer.'

Jahanuma could see that both the aggrieved parties were happy to accept the emperor's decree. Performing the way of *taslim*, they placed the back of their right hand on the ground and raised it gently till they stood erect. Gleaming with joy, they hailed the emperor for his judicious verdict: 'Long live the Padshah! Long live Zil-e-Ilahi!' All present repeated the cry. The hall thundered with the echo of the cries of hundreds present.

After that Akbar announced a daily allowance for an old widow whose only son had died fighting for the empire. She too offered her salutations to the emperor. Next in line was the audience to a small ruler from the Deccan. He had brought with him three horses loaded with precious gems, jewels, ornaments and books to be presented to the emperor as a token of his submission.

Jahanuma could no longer remain silent. She was too moved by seeing in person what she had only heard so far from Bano. 'Now I know why he is respected so much by his people. He is fair and gentle in matters which deserve to be handled with care but sharp and ruthless when he needs to be,' she whispered to Bano.

Three hours passed. The emperor addressed the proceedings one after the other, tirelessly. Finally, her turn arrived as she heard her name being announced. She was ushered into the centre of the pillared hall facing the balcony. Beneath the balcony, on an elevated marble stone in the hall, sat a young and handsome man, who Jahanuma guessed was Shahzada Salim.

As was the etiquette, she stood with her head bowed, eyes on the ground, while Bano stood behind her. Jahanuma had been warned that looking into the emperor's eyes was forbidden. But this was her only chance to get a closer look of the emperor, she thought, and from behind the safety of her veil, stole a quick glance. She was surprised to see how young the shahenshah looked. He had broad shoulders and a strong built. He was not very tall yet had a formidable, imposing figure befitting a king. His shaven face was tanned from the rigors of many battles fought and won. There was a boyish expression on his face and his eyes were wide and smiling. Unlike his grandfather, Babur and father, Humayun, Akbar didn't sport a beard and only maintained a moustache.

Akbar sat with his head held high, wearing a rather small but smart turban with a plume of herne tops. In the middle was an emerald the size of a walnut. A divine aura clung to him. He was perhaps nearing fifty in age but his face was youthful and charming. He looked imposing. His deep blue silk robe was plain except for a gold lace that traced the borders. He wore only one string of white pearls. At his elbows were armlets set with diamonds. His left hand rested on the rim of his talwar and the right on his waist. There were no rings on any of his fingers. He conveyed an authority that commanded respect of the court.

Jahanuma performed kornish. Aziz Koka stepped forward from behind the file of senior officials standing in the row left of the emperor. He was in his official attire. He too offered the customary salute to the emperor and in brief recounted the events leading to Jahanuma's appearance in the court. Akbar listened with rapt attention and nodded his head on both occasions when the names of Nazr Culi Turkistani and Aslam Khan were mentioned.

When Aziz Koka finished his report, an attendant stepped forward and produced the kilij for the emperor's inspection. Akbar lifted the kilij and examined it carefully. The assembly waited for the emperor's reaction.

'Subhan Allah!' Akbar exclaimed, swashing it in the air. He turned to look at Jahanuma. 'Aslam Khan was a loyal servant of my father. Late khan-i-khanan, Bairam Khan, who was a close confidant of my father, had mentioned Aslam Khan on more than one occasion. May Allah grant him the eternal bliss of paradise! The days of that insect Hasan are numbered.'

Jahanuma once again performed kornish but remained silent.

Akbar looked at the kilij and added. 'It is after long that I have seen such exquisite craftsmanship. Your husband must have been gifted.'

Hidden behind the veil, tears rolled down Jahanuma's cheeks. She muttered a prayer for Ali. She wished to thank Akbar but found her voice choked. She bowed once again in appreciation.

Akbar turned to look at the wazir sitting in the front row to his right. 'Let a farman be written for this woman's appointment as a servant of my aunt Gulbadan.' He then turned to Jahanuma and added, 'As has your family served my father, so shall you serve his sister. As the rules do not permit children of the women to live in the harem, the administration will take your daughters in its care. Chief sadr is directed to arrange for their education and allowance. Their safety will be his responsibility. The girls will be able to meet their mother according to the rules of the harem.'

Jahanuma was profusely moved by the proclamation made by the emperor. No wonder he was so popular and bestowed the status of the emperor of emperors. 'I remain eternally grateful to His Highness for his generosity,' Jahanuma said respectfully. She hoped she was able to convey her gratitude to the emperor. She wanted to say something but hesitated.

Her hesitation did not escape Akbar's watchful eyes. 'If there is anything you wish to say, speak now.'

'If Zil-e-Ilahi will pardon my audacity, I would be immensely grateful if my daughters were allowed to stay in the care of their grandaunt in Lahore. I have faith in the ability of His Excellency's officers. It is just a mother's worry for her daughters. The elder one is stepping into her youth and the other is too young.'

'Be that so,' Akbar said and waved at one of his officers. 'Let their grandaunt be appointed as their caretaker. Set an allowance to be sent to her regularly for the girls. If the girls convey in writing to the chief sadr that they wish to relocate to Agra or wherever their mother resides, the treasury will take care of their needs.'

'May I ask for one more favour from His Highness?' Jahanuma asked, afraid that she would be snubbed.

'Out with it, quick, there are others waiting,' Akbar said, now somewhat irritated.

'My husband's grave...'

Before she could finish her sentence, Akbar waved her to silence and turned to Koka who stepped forward. Knowing the emperor's ways, Koka could anticipate what he wanted to know.

'In deference to the shahenshah's command, on the morning after the day her husband died, as the sun rose from the east of the Mughal Sultanate, he was rested in his grave.'

Akbar nodded and turned to look at Jahanuma, sharply.

For a moment Jahanuma was terrified. She cursed herself for raising the issue. She should have deduced that the emperor would have given the go-ahead for this after she was permitted to be hosted in the camp as a guest. 'May Allah bestow a long life on the shahenshah of Hindustan!' Jahanuma said apologetically, offering obeisance to Akbar by performing kornish.

'Zindabad, zindabad! Shahenshah zindabad! Jalal-ud-din Muhammad Akbar zindabad!' The air echoed with the cries of hundreds assembled in the hall.

Akbar waved Jahanuma away, as the next person was ushered forward for an audience with the emperor.

# The Veil of the Harem

Jahanuma followed the khawajasara to the harem. She had noticed her standing outside the diwan-i-aam after the emperor dismissed the proceedings. The khawajasara had obviously been watching the proceedings from behind the jaali. She had approached Jahanuma after the audience with the emperor was over. Jahanuma had bid a hurried goodbye to Bano and rushed after the khawajasara. Her belongings kept at the guesthouse would be sent for by the harem officers, she told Bano.

She was a tall woman nearing fifty years in age and carried a pleasant sense of grace around her. *Her delicate body and alluring curves must be the envy of many women and the subject of desire of many men,* Jahanuma pondered as they walked past the Machchi Bhawan through the Angoor Bagh towards the harem.

A faint smile appeared on her face as if the khawajasara had read Jahanuma's mind. 'My name is Ruksana. I was the favourite concubine of Humayun. Even on the night before he died a tragic death by falling from the steps of his library, he had sought me with the same passion as the first time. Most of his wives were immensely jealous of me.' She smiled with a sense of pride before continuing, 'Aware of my training in the

Kamasutra and my special skills in providing sexual delight, His Majesty appointed me keeper of the imperial harem. The first time a eunuch had been so appointed. As the keeper of the imperial harem, one of my duties is to train the emperor's concubines in the art of giving pleasure so that they can keep His Majesty happy.'

As they walked past the Angoor Bagh, Jahanuma was awed by the sheer magnificence of the fort complex. Set on the western bank of the Jamuna, the fort followed an irregular, semicircular pattern. The royal apartments were located on the riverside ramparts. They overlooked a sandy ground earmarked for parades and sports for the entertainment of the royalty. Its thick walls rose high and were girded by a deep, broad moat filled with water drawn from the Jamuna. The double wall was broken by the Dilli Gate on the west and the Shahi Gate on the south. Only the walls facing the river were excluded from girding. The two massive gates were distinguished by rows of arched niches and stunning veneer in red and white marble with highlights in blue glazed tile.

Ruksana noticed the expression on the awe-struck Jahanuma and smiled to herself. 'Magnificent, isn't it? The charm of the palace – it makes you want to be useful to it. You offer yourself up to it with gratitude. It takes you in, uses and discards you, and when you are spent and your voice is no longer heard, you still mumble a praise and a prayer to its name,' she said softly, as if talking to herself.

Jahanuma looked at Ruksana trying to decipher her words. Slowly they started to sink in. And with that, the realisation of the illusions of the riches of the palace, how impossible it was for any woman not to get drawn to the enchanting figure of the emperor and want to be close to him in the hope of getting his love or a taste of power or both, knowing full well that neither was in the realm of possibilities.

'But how can an ordinary mortal be blamed for walking into the ruse created by the pleasures that come with the dominion. The enticement would be hard to withstand for anyone.' It was now Jahanuma's turn to mumble softly.

'A new mahal is coming up for Prince Salim in that enclosed area there,' Ruksana interrupted her thoughts, pointing to a massive ongoing construction in a part of the fort. Jahanuma looked at what appeared to be a massive structure nearing completion. It did not interest her much. Her thoughts were focused on Akbar.

They walked down a long corridor to the forbidden part of the fort – the imperial harem. It was surely not an easy place to enter as apart from the women of the royal family and the emperor's concubines, it also housed the incalculable treasure of the great Mughals. The corridor was guarded by the royal guards, all armed with jezails or lances. The guards did not search them but inspected the papers the khawajasara carried. Uzbek slave women formed the next ring of guards in the corridors. They looked just as ferocious as the royal guards Jahanuma had seen so many times, broad shouldered and fully armed. They were enormous in their build, giants in front of Jahanuma. The entrance to the harem was guarded by the eunuchs whose sole concern was to ensure no man capable of lying with any of the women could enter the harem. At the gate, Jahanuma underwent a thorough body search. The eunuch first frisked every inch of her body, followed by an intimate body search that left Jahanuma deeply embarrassed.

'You had better get used to this routine,' Ruksana whispered to her flushed face. 'Every time you step outside the harem you will have to go through this drill on your return. They have to carry out the search with great care. Women in the harem are fond of opium a little too much. They also stop the entry of radishes and cucumbers, you will soon understand why.'

Ruksana giggled wickedly, lifting her purdah and winking at Jahanuma. 'Now, you will have to live behind the veil in the public parts of the harem till you are medically cleared. You can take it off once you are inside your room.'

Jahanuma's eyes opened wide with bewilderment as she stepped inside the harem. There were hundreds of women. Some were basking under the sun on the beautifully manicured lawn, some swam in the pond in the centre of which a large fountain sprouted water. A few sat on the benches under the shady jamun trees, others sat on the lofty divans placed in the corridor around the harem.

As they passed down the hall, a furtive movement caught Jahanuma's eye. In a cubicle, screened from view by a curtain of fine muslin, three women lay together on a divan. They sighed and kissed and giggled like little girls. For a moment her gaze was held by the intimacy shared by these women. Others passed by the cubicle but paid no attention to what has happening inside.

She was startled by a tap on her shoulder.'Let's go,' Ruksana prodded Jahanuma to continue walking.'Even I have lost count of the number of women here. The emperor has hundreds of wives. Some he loves but most are here out of a political alliance or charity,' she informed. Jahanuma kept quiet. Although Bano had told her about the wives and some tales of the harem, the enormity of it all was striking her only now when she was witnessing it with her own eyes.

'All the women here are his wives?' she couldn't help asking.

'No, many are his concubines. Women of many nations live in this compound, one more beautiful than the other. Some are distant relatives. Those married to him live in the other part of the harem, bigger and dripping with opulence.'

Jahanuma looked around at the vast honeycomb of rooms varying in sizes. Some appeared aristocratic while others ordinary-looking tucked in the background. Anticipating the query, Ruksana spoke, 'The importance of the occupant dictates the size, design and the furnishings of the palace and quarters. Only the privileged have the luxury of large personal quarters with terrace, fountains and balconies facing the river. The emperor's mother Hamida Banu Begum, aunt Gulbadan, foster-mother Maham Anga and his wife, Jodha Bai, are granted the most spectacular and finest luxuries. As for the others, what lives they lead here is decided by their closeness to the emperor. Not all women have met the emperor here. No adult male is allowed inside the harem except him. Now you can imagine how the entire harem vies for his attention every time he visits.'

Bano's words came back to Jahanuma. She had called it a gilded cage that from the outside presented an illusion of paradise. She was afraid Bano had been right.

They reached the quarters reserved for trainees and were allotted a room which was adequately furnished. It had a small bathroom attached to it. 'Hakim sahab will arrive shortly in the *bimar-khanah* to examine you. You have to remain behind the curtain. Hakim sahab is allowed only to pass his hand through the curtain and you simply follow his instructions. After you are cleared for employment by hakim sahab, the head eunuch will meet you and explain all the rules of the harem. Only after that will you be presented before Gulbadan.'

Jahanuma removed her veil.

Ruksana paused to look at her. 'You are beautiful, Jahanuma!'

Jahanuma blushed. 'Shukran!' She felt the entry awkward as Ruksana's eyes regarded her face closely and a bit too long for her comfort.

'What about my belongings?' she asked Ruksana. 'My things are still at the serai.'

'Don't worry, a dispatch rider is on the way to bring it here. Also, a copy of the emperor's farman will be sent to you shortly.

A copy has been sent to the Lahore governor. He has been asked to inform your aunt and daughters.'

Before Ruksana turned to leave, she paused at the door and looked at Jahanuma. 'Take off your burqa,' she directed her. Jahanuma was taken aback. She felt uncomfortable, but realising she had no choice, she did as instructed. Ruksana's eyes surveyed her from top to bottom. Jahanuma felt naked under her gaze and turned pink with embarrassment. Just then Ruksana turned and left without saying a word.

## I

Jahanuma completed her formal training in a month and was assigned to assist Gulbadan Begum. She was the youngest daughter of Babur. Gulbadan's eldest sister was Gulrang, rose-coloured, and the second, Gulchihra, rosy-cheeked. In keeping with her name, Gulbadan embodied the rose. Gulbadan was popular amongst the women of Babur's household as a rose is loved and prized in the East, from Persia to Hindustan. A battery of servants assisted her and she did not feel the need to assign any specific task to Jahanuma.

The first few weeks Jahanuma spent most of the time hanging around the quarters running small errands for Gulbadan's experienced servant, Nazia. She was not comfortable taking instructions from Nazia. She wanted to do something more meaningful. She realised that life inside the harem was made of loneliness and deprivation. Although the women were pampered with all material comforts, they lived in a smouldering world of misery that too was veiled and private. Acrobats, snake charmers and jugglers were invited round the year to amuse the occupants. Musicians, jesters, storytellers and reciters from all over the country visited to entertain. These were good pastime enjoyments but didn't do much for the sad, abandoned lives of the inmates. None of it interested Jahanuma. She missed her visits to the library and the music of literature and poetry.

Once, Gulbadan spotted Jahanuma reading and summoned her out of curiosity.

'I wasn't aware you were interested in literature,' she said.

'Forgive me, Her Highness, I should have mentioned it when you interviewed me,' Jahanuma replied with her bowed to the ground.

'Never mind. Tell me about it now,' Gulbadan prodded her.

Jahanuma narrated her inclination for reading prose and poetry, even oral history, and in writing, albeit occasionally. She also mentioned how first her father and then her husband had ensured she had access to reading and all kinds of books.

Discovering Jahanuma's inclination for reading and writing, Gulbadan interviewed her for a job in the library. After intense questioning about her interest in books, Jahanuma was appointed as the assistant librarian of the harem's library. 'You must inspire everyone in the harem to read so that the tradition of our empire to pursue education is honoured. Akbar's grandfather was a learned man and accomplished scholar in Arabic, Persian and Turkish. He entrusted his public works department with the task of establishing schools.'

Gulbadan paused for a moment and then continued, 'Poor Akbar, he never got the chance to go to school. The responsibility of the kingdom was put upon him when he was just a boy. He was fighting battles when he should have been learning,' she said with a hint of both sadness and pride. 'Even though Akbar never received formal education himself, he understood its value. He promotes schooling. He does not believe in confining learning to the literature of one's own language. He has set up a translation bureau and appointed scribes, clerks, translators, theologians and pundits. A large number of texts, both well-known and obscure, are chosen for translation into Persian. These include Sanskrit texts such as the Ramayana, Mahabharata, the *Panchatantra,* known in its translation as the *Anwar-i-Suhayli.* Arabic encyclopaedias were also translated into Persian. *Baburnama,* his grandfather's memoirs scripted in Chagatai Turki, are also being translated. They are available here and in the library in Lahore. You must read them.'

Jahanuma was pleasantly surprised by what Gulbadan had told her. She had heard a lot about the rich ancient texts of Hindustan. She wanted to read them but did not know that their translations were available right here in the harem library. She also made a mental note to make sure Nadira gets to read them.

Jahanuma had since started reading the translations and found them fascinating. She made detailed notes which she discussed with Gulbadan frequently. Gulbadan was growing fond of Jahanuma. She admired her for diligently fulfilling her duties. What fascinated her the most about Jahanuma was her knack for reflection. She had the qualities of a scribe. Soon Gulbadan started seeking Jahanuma's help in recording the history of the sixteenth-century royal family.

This task had been entrusted to her by the emperor himself. Initially, Jahanuma wondered why Akbar charged Gulbadan with this salient task over a historian. But soon she understood the reason behind her election. Not only was Gulbadan blessed with a photographic memory, recording the smallest details of the eventful life spanning the reigns of three emperors, her father Babur, her brother Humayun and her nephew Akbar, she also had a remarkable ability to narrate them. Her accounts were so clear; she was certainly best poised to chronicle the extraordinary rise of the sultanate.

Jahanuma immersed herself in the writing of the book, as she heard Gulbadan recount episodes of nomadic wandering, life in the harem, her pilgrimage to Mecca and many other stories in a way which marvellously conveyed the atmosphere of the time and place. Jahanuma noticed that Gulbadan observed highest caution while writing anything about the inmates of the harem. She did not include anything which could displease the royal temperament. Akbar had given clear instructions that chroniclers were to not mention anything about ladies in the harem unless they were senior in age and played some important role in religion or politics.

Working closely with Gulbadan, Jahanuma progressively found the true ways of Akbar's harem. The reality of the harem was somewhat different from what she had observed from the outside or learnt from Ruksana. She discovered that though life in the harem appeared strange at first glance it was not as frivolous as she had initially assumed. She realised that the harem was not just a place where the emperor sought pleasure. It was an extended zenana. He had married many Hindu women, mostly as part of diplomatic treaties, but also taken others as his wife to save them from other exploitations. The harem gave them a life of safety while offering the freedom to practise their own faith. They were free to seek whatever they liked behind the veil of the harem.

While there, she learnt many management skills. It was efficiently operated. Its organisation was based on the same pattern as the administration of the emperor's household outside. The affairs were administered only by female officers and eunuchs who were divided into three main sections, *mahinbano, paristaran-ihuzur* and other staff. Several women were appointed as *darogas* and superintendents over each section, the *mushrif,* the *tahwildar* and other petty officials. Those who were clever were appointed as superintendent of harem expenditure to keep an account of cash and the stores.

As months passed, Jahanuma got accustomed to her new way of life. But she pined to be with her daughters. She had received the message from the chief sadr that the emperor's orders had been carried out. She was told that Naaz had also been delivered the first allowance. Nadira had joined a school run by the governor's office. Suraiya was struggling to cope without Jahanuma but Nadira was taking good care of her younger sister, she was told. She missed them every day. She missed Ali. She missed the world outside. Jahanuma had not met Bano even once after she was settled in the harem. She yearned to talk to her. They had developed a special bond in the few weeks they spent together. She had been out of the harem only once with Gulbadan when she went on a hunting trip. She decided the only way out was to not sulk and drown herself in work and reading. She felt immensely grateful to Akbar for having taken her in his care and for providing for his daughter's education. And she consoled herself that Eid was nearing. It meant she would finally get to see her daughters.

# The Family Reunion

One morning, as the two sisters slept in the early hours of the day, Jahanuma's soft hands grazed their faces. She was not going to shy away from interrupting their dreams so she could smother them with her love. She had been finally allowed to visit her daughters and in time for Eid. Nadira was the first one to stir awake. Once she had slowly opened her eyes and overcome the shock of seeing Jahanuma, she screamed with joy. That was enough to wake Suraiya too, and both the sisters had charged at her with hugs and kisses. Naaz had been kind enough to keep Jahanuma's visit a secret and watched the reunion of the family in delight.

By noon the excitement of the girls had settled a little and they decided they had a lot of things to talk about. They demanded their ammi make them their favourite food and declared they were not going to leave her side even for a minute, even as she cooked. Later, Suraiya sat her down and shared a list of complaints against people who had upset her. She whispered how she did not like the meals Naaz had been serving them, and how Asma was trying to get closer to Nadira.

'She is my sister. Asma should get her own sister,' Suraiya huffed while Jahanuma relished her childishness. 'Another thing I hate, Ammi, is that Naaz doesn't tell us stories,' chimed Nadira. 'If you are not around, who else is going to tell us about the world if not her!'

As a resolution to this, Jahanuma promised her to get books from the harem library the next time she came. 'Gulbadan begum wouldn't mind it,' she said. 'Do you know, girls, the emperor cannot read?'

'That's a shame; even I can read a little!' Suraiya giggled.

'Not everyone gets lucky like this, my child, which is why you make sure to do your learning properly as you grow older,' Jahanuma said.

'Tell us more about the emperor, Ammi. Did you meet him?' Nadira asked.

'Yes,' she answered. 'He is the reason why I have been granted work in the palace and money for your education and living.' Then Jahanuma had to assure Suraiya that she would thank the emperor on her behalf.

The girls wanted to hear everything about Agra and the royal court but before Jahanuma could begin, much to the dismay of the girls, Asma interrupted them with a word from Naaz. All the ladies had gathered in the courtyard and they wanted to meet Jahanuma. Naaz wanted to introduce her to some important women. She left with the promise to continue her stories in the evening.

After dinner was wrapped up in Naaz's household that evening, Asma, Suraiya and Nadira gathered around a tired Jahanuma, asking her about her life in Agra. She told them about Bano, her sweet daughter and her husband who had, with his stories, acquainted her with the emperor much before she had actually met him.

'So, Suraiya, the reason Akbar could never learn to read was because he was made to sit on the throne around the same age as your sister is now. And now his empire is so vast,' she spread her arms, 'that it would take more days than you can count to cover the distance of his empire on a camel!'

That left Suraiya speechless.

Soon Naaz joined them. Jahanuma realised the more she talked about Akbar, the more she had to say. And it didn't help that her audience too was quite enthusiastic.

'The day I was called to the royal court I understood how the Padshah had managed to do it. He has a way with people,' she looked at Naaz, 'he understands their plight without getting carried away in sentiments. He is patient; he thinks before he acts. As an emperor should,' Jahanuma said, her admiration for the king gleaming in her eyes.

'In that case, the prince must be a cause of worry for this empire. Do you know if the rumours are true?' Naaz asked her.

Nadira and Asma's ears perked up and they cut in with their questions.

'Are you talking about Prince Salim, Ammi?' Asma asked.

'And what rumours?' Nadira followed.

'I have heard some whispers about the reckless nature of the prince,' Jahanuma admitted. 'But who can say how many of those are true. However, the entire court adores the prince because everyone knows how precious he is to the emperor.'

'Why? Does the emperor love him more than his other children? That's not very nice of him,' Suraiya shared her reservations.

Jahanuma laughed. 'There is a reason behind it. The emperor may be strong now, but there was a time when he too was troubled beyond help. He wanted an heir but none of his wives could birth him a son. After years of this, he was guided to a village in Sikri, to the hut of a holy saint.'

'Wasn't Sikri the empire's capital before Agra was chosen to house the court, Ammi?'

'No. Agra was the capital but the emperor decided to relocate it to Sikri, and soon moved it back to Agra,' Jahanuma answered, seeing her own impatience with Rahim chacha's stories being reflected in Nadira. 'Now, where was I?'

'In the hut of the saint,' the girls said together.

'Yes. In the dimly lit hut, the emperor spoke, "O holy saint, I have not told you yet the real purpose for my visit to your abode." The saint is said to have waved the emperor to silence. He picked up the Holy Quran and touched it to his eyes. He then picked up the Gita, the sacred book of the Hindus, and touched it to his eyes. He then stood still staring at an abstraction on the wall representing Khwaja Moinuddin Chishti. After a few minutes, he turned and said to him, "Allah will bless you with not one but three sons. One of them will be your able successor. Go in peace, O Emperor of Emperors." It is said Akbar started weeping with joy. He cried for many good minutes holding the saint's hand.' Jahanuma's voice turned from dramatic to exultant as she continued, 'Four months later, the emperor's Hindu wife, Jodha Bai, was with child. Shahzada Salim was born to Akbar. Son of a Muslim father and a Hindu mother. Successor of Akbar and the throne of Hindustan.'

'Is he very handsome … the prince?' inquired Asma.

'I have seen him a few times but only from a distance but I have heard he is taken after his mother in looks. And, I have to tell you that Jodha Bai is a beautiful and elegant woman. Those in the harem who have seen him can't stop talking about how good looking and charming he is.'

'Enough about the prince. Tell us about the harem. I hear it has a lot of pleasures to offer,' Naaz whispered, winking at Jahanuma.

'You will be surprised. It is not like what you think. Yes, it is mainly the zenana, but it is also the place which supports the emperor in carrying out many administrative functions.

Gulbadan runs schools and libraries. The emperor reveres his mother Hamida Begum, Humayun's child bride of over fifty years ago, even though she is only fifteen years older than him. She is the energetic and powerful hub of royal family life. As a mark of honour and privilege, the emperor has conferred the most respectable and lofty title of Mariyam Makani, the Mary of both the worlds, on his mother. Another resident of the harem held in high esteem by him is his aunt. He admires her learning and ability and encourages Gulbadan to write an account of his father and his own reign. His wet nurse Maham Anga, who attended the emperor's cradle till after his accession, also holds a special status in the harem. Although Akbar is the master of his own will, he often comes to the harem to seek the counsel of these wise women on administrative matters. His wife Jodha Bai is the first among equals. She is given the title of the queen and the only wife of his who has access to all privileges. Harem is full of activity and festivities.'

The three girls were mesmerised. Were it not for Naaz, who had heard the stories enough times for them to have no effect on her, they would have had Jahanuma stay up and tell them tales all night. But on her insistence the gathering was put to an end.

Finally reunited with her children after months of staying apart for the first time, Jahanuma, as she lay in her bed, could feel her love for them coursing through her veins. That's what having a child meant, just harbouring an inevitable devotion to them, she thought. It led her to realize how difficult it must be for an emperor to move ahead, with his heart devoted to his children, but his mind always having to think of the empire. She could hear Nadira hum in the dark and realised she wasn't asleep. She wanted to know what thoughts were running in her head this late at night.

'I was wondering what it must be like to be born following a saint's prophecy that declares not only your birth but also decrees your future. With all his riches and responsibilities, is Prince Salim really fortunate or just cursed?'

Jahanuma was struck by the sincerity of her question. She remained quiet and did not answer her. Before she fell asleep, the words of the fortune-teller came back to her. Nadira's future too had been declared on her birth, and she had chosen to never tell her about it.

Nadira lay awake. Her mind struggling to find answers to the many questions that continued to haunt her. Why does Allah allow such disparities, make some so fortunate, others left to be miserable. Her thoughts wandered to the prince. Was he as nice as his father? What would it be like to meet him in person?

She turned to look at her mother who was fast asleep. She cuddled up to her, thrilled to be sleeping next to her again. She felt safe after a very long time.

# A Fleeting Affair

Jahanuma entered Gulbadan's boudoir to light the lanterns at dusk. The bedroom had all the comforts one could desire. She looked at the elevated bed on the floor made of layers of soft cotton mattresses and silk linen. How would it be to sleep on such a soft, warm and sinking bed, she wondered. She and Ali had to be content with two Kashmiri carpets on the hard floor. On nights when they wouldn't sleep, her back would ache after they'd tire from making love and even his knees would have bruises. She felt a pleasant sensation come over her at the thought of Ali and all those nights she was lucky to spend with him. This was the first time after his death that she could feel a hint of desire come over her. Suddenly she was shaken out of her reveries by the familiar sound of a woman.

'Padshah Zindabad, Padshah Zindabad,' the voice welled up gradually and it took her a while to realize that Akbar was about to enter Gulbadan's quarters. Gulbadan had gone out for a stroll. She rushed to exit from the side door but it was too late. As she reached the door, Akbar entered the room all by himself. She could not turn around as showing her back to the emperor was considered an act of insult. She stood still, head bowed and her face uncovered. It was only after a few seconds that she regained her composure and pulled her stole over her head and said, 'Her Highness is outside in the garden, Jahanpanah.'

Akbar turned and left without saying a word.

After dinner, Jahanuma lay on her bed. Normally she would go for a short walk after the evening meal, but today she wanted to lie in the dark and think. Tonight, she felt the absence of Ali even more. The glorious time they spent together in Kabul kept flashing before her eyes!

Just then Ruksana entered her quarters, unannounced. 'Bathe and get dressed. I am waiting,' Ruksana instructed her.

'Where are we going?'

'Akbari Mahal. The emperor is taken in by your beauty. You didn't tell me he saw you in Gulbadan's chambers! He summoned me and instructed he would like to spend the night with you. Looking at you, it's no surprise he wants you.'

'What?' Jahanuma was shocked by what she had just heard.

'Now don't pretend. You let him see you on purpose, didn't you?'

She was filled with anger. 'How dare you make that insinuation?' Jahanuma snapped at Ruksana. 'I am a virtuous woman. I love Ali and have never let another man even enter my thoughts. Not even after he passed away. And here you stand, nonchalantly asking me to sleep with the emperor. Yes, I am in his care but that does not entitle him to ask me to sleep with him.'

'Your naivety is not my problem, Jahanuma. It was only a matter of time that this happened. He has seen you and now he wants you. There are innumerable women he takes under his care and if he chooses to sleep with them, they don't say no. Besides, half the ladies here are desperate for his attention. They'd say you are lucky that the emperor has called for you. You are beautiful, Jahanuma, use it to your advantage. It is the only weapon this harem allows you to own.'

'No, I don't want to do this, Ruksana. I still love Ali. I can't do this to his memory. And my daughters, how will I face them?' Tears welled up in her eyes as she spoke.

Ruksana stepped forward and took Jahanuma in her arms. 'Oh Jahanuma. I will not force you. I can go back and tell him you are menstruating, but word for you will come again. He is a great man but his ego may get hurt if you refuse him again the next time. You should know that men in his position are not accustomed to hearing 'no'. You are under the care of the empire and he is providing for your girls. If it was not for him, you would be struggling to make ends meet. Why would you want to disappoint him? Honour his wish, I suggest. It is a matter of one night. Ali is dead, Jahanuma, but you are alive. You can still continue to love the memories of your husband. But don't let your principles get you in harm's way.'

Jahanuma was worried. Maybe Ruksana was right. But did she really mean what she said or was she manipulating her into submission? Jahanuma sensed it was a mix of both. By now, Ruksana probably recites this script out of memory. And why not, she thought, Ruksana was only doing her job. She had to make sure the emperor was never disappointed.

It hadn't even remotely occurred to Jahanuma that she would have charmed Akbar when he saw her in the evening. It was a fleeting moment and he barely had a look at her. But strangely, although offended by Akbar's proposal, there was a part of her which felt thrilled that Akbar was attracted to her. It reminded her that she was still beautiful enough to be wanted by a man no less than the emperor of Hindustan. She was suddenly ashamed of herself. Even this thought was a betrayal of Ali. Then her thoughts went back to the evening, when in Gulbadan's room the sight of that comfortable bed had sparked desire in her. She wondered if the emperor had seen it in her eyes.

'We don't have time, Jahanuma. Make up your mind!' Ruksana prodded her.

Jahanuma was ready. She would do as he wished. It would be a service, an act of gratitude for taking care of her daughters, she comforted herself.

Ruksana patted her face with affection. 'Go and dress up, love. I will organise some perfume and make arrangements for the evening ahead.' She winked. 'Make the most of it.'

I

Akbar admired Jahanuma as she stood before him in his chambers. She was dressed in a translucent robe, and a pink silk stole was wrapped around her shoulders. Ruksana had dressed her for the special evening. She knew Akbar's taste. She suggested Jahanuma wear no ornaments. Her breasts and the inside of her thighs had been smeared with a perfumed ointment that worked as an aphrodisiac for the emperor.

Jahanuma stood silently gazing at the floor.

Akbar stepped forward and lifted her face. Her eyes appeared cold and nervous. He wondered why. Most women he summoned were nervous but never cold. Some even were too eager. But this woman seemed indifferent, as if she had no desire to be in his chambers. His wives, concubines and even slaves longed to get in bed with him and find his favour. The thought of her indifference towards him intrigued him.

'You are beautiful,' he said, and he meant it. 'Did you ever imagine the emperor of Hindustan calling you, let alone being in his chambers?'

'His Excellency is very gracious. I am happy to be here,' she said.

This irked Akbar. Had she remained quiet, he could have taken her silence as permission to proceed. Her voice, so cold and unfeeling, gave away the meaninglessness of her words. The words were probably part of the brief she was given in preparation for the night she was to spend with the emperor. But her voice rang in his ears the implication that she did not want this and anything he did would mean he was forcing himself on her. He couldn't let that be.

'It is my duty to please Zil-e-Ilahi.' Jahanuma raised her face but kept her eyes lowered, unsure if she was permitted to look into the emperor's eyes even in the privacy of his bedroom.

Akbar shook his head. He did not have time for this. 'Don't believe everything Ruksana has told you. You don't have to do this. You can go. I will call for another one.'

Jahanuma was surprised by the emperor's words. She looked at him confused, but her gaze had lost its coldness. He was the shahenshah of Hindustan. Every word of his was a command. Yet he was giving her the choice to leave if she wanted? She was moved by this slight show of dignity.

Despite what he had said, he kept looking at her intently, waiting for her to take a step, either towards or away from him.

She could do this she was sure. He was the emperor after all. Didn't some women consider this an honour? She walked towards him, covering all the distance that stood between them. Sensing her willingness, Akbar moved to remove her robe gently. She stood in front of him, her soft skin shining in the golden light of the lamps, her hair falling by her waist. It was the right thing to do, she thought to herself, as she let Akbar take in her body. He pushed her hair away from her face. His hand brushed her skin and she felt a tinge of longing and with it, some shame. Ali was the only one who had ever touched her. She thought of the last time they had made love and felt a wave of desire overcome her, suddenly moving her to seek Akbar's body, until she could find herself melting in his arms. He smelled of wine and perfume. She frantically removed his turban and his gown, and the two let frenzy guide them to the bed where they collapsed into each other. Jahanuma was weakened from want and opened herself to him. There they lay, becoming bodies that moved against each other, their skin glittering with sweat, he no longer her emperor, she no longer a harem woman. They were nearing the culmination of this passion ... she could feel it in her belly and in the grunt that escaped Akbar. And in that moment she forgot everything, letting the wave of pleasure take over her entire being, until all became nothing and through the silence resounded her long sigh.

A few minutes later, she could hear him snore. He had fallen asleep. She looked at him, the emperor of Hindustan, lying next to her in bed. His face somehow still bore the innocence of a child, twitching intermittently it seemed from some taxing visions in his dreams. Clearly, his mind was not at rest even when he was asleep. She noticed that he had a beautiful mole on his left nostril, a sign of 'great good fortune'. *Whatever might be bothering him, he is destined to overcome all obstacles and continue to rise to greatness,* she thought. She liked the weight of his body beside her. Ruksana walked in at that moment, signalling her to leave. There was no time or reason to share goodbyes.

## II

The emperor began summoning Jahanuma every other night for many weeks. On evenings when Ruksana wouldn't come carrying the emperor's word, she would go to bed worried that finally he had lost interest in her. It was only in the dark when she'd have to sleep alone that Jahanuma would find the courage to admit that she missed Akbar. To her surprise, there'd come another night when she'd have to perfume herself for the indulgences of the king.

It had been a few days since she had been called by him. Word had spread in the harem that Akbar had fallen sick. She desperately wanted to check on his health and anxiously waited to see Ruksana.

'How is the emperor?' inquired Jahanuma as soon as Ruksana entered her chambers.

Ruksana looked around to check if anyone was around. Assured no one was listening, she said in a hushed tone, 'He is very sick but recovering. No one other than the queen and doctors treating him know of his sickness or its cause. The servants taking care of him are sworn to secrecy. They are not allowed to step out of the emperor's palace or meet anyone outside. There is a lot of speculation around his poor health. Some even suspect he may have been poisoned. Someone who has access to him, who he trusts may have put *zahar* in his wine. The emperor is tough. He can fight his way back but his will is becoming feeble. What is coming in the way of his recovery is his tormented heart that is unable to forget Salim's rebellion. He cannot comprehend Salim's behaviour or forgive him. It is slowly eating him away.'

Jahanuma was aghast. 'Poisoning!' she exclaimed. 'Who would dare to poison the emperor?' she asked.

'There are many who want to see the emperor dead. The tragedy is that Akbar suspects his own son is behind this attempt to murder him,' replied Ruksana sadly.

'Which son?' Jahanuma inquired.

'Salim,' Ruksana answered.

Jahanuma was stunned. For a moment she was not sure how to react. Then she spoke in a tone that surprised Ruksana. 'That is impossible! Akbar loves him. He sings praises for Salim and how much his son respects him. The prince would never stoop so low.'

Ruksana was startled by the manner in which Jahanuma defended the emperor. She had been so swayed by her emotions that she was calling him by his name. No one dared to do that. Nor had she heard Jahanuma address the emperor by name before. Gulbadan had once lightly mentioned Jahanuma's growing interest in Akbar to Ruksana. She had also dismissed the undue attention the emperor showed her.

'Women can mistake his attention as affection or love. Akbar is a respectful man but he knows the demands of his stature. It is always the women he momentarily attends to who turn blind to the limitations of their positions and start to see the boundaries blurring. Jahanuma seems like a wise woman; she is certainly not blind.'

Ruksana had taken it as a casual remark then. But as she stood there listening to Jahanuma, alarm bells started ringing in her mind. Gulbadan was an experienced woman. Her remarks were not a joke. There was a clear message in them. She probably even meant those to be tactfully conveyed to Jahanuma. She shrugged away her thoughts and replied, 'I agree with you, Jahanuma. From what I know of Salim, he not only admires his father but is too scared of him to attempt anything as foolish as this.'

Both of them offered a prayer for the emperor's early recovery.

The concern that shadowed Jahanuma's face worried Ruksana. She hugged her and said kindly, 'I know you are thinking about the emperor. We all are,' she emphasised. 'There are people taking care of him, you don't have to worry. You work all the time but you must think about your life too, Jahanuma. The girls will grow up, find their wings and fly away. You are still too young to live your life without a companion. I can introduce you to some interesting men.'

Jahanuma pulled away, confused by Ruksana's concern for her.

Ruksana looked at her and continued speaking softly, 'Maybe you will like someone and start your life afresh. I am sure the emperor will permit you to leave. He likes you, but don't delude yourself. Plenty of women here have made that mistake. You will never find any more space in his life than what you have now.'

'I am fine, Ruksana. My hopes are limited. I only care for Nadira and Suraiya, and I am not ready to let another man take space in our lives. I want to stay busy so that my mind and heart have nowhere to wander. But thank you for asking,' she replied politely, masking her annoyance and giving her a warm hug.

Jahanuma felt miserable. Were her feelings that transparent, she wondered. It was true that she was worried about Akbar and she missed him terribly. What had started as a service to repay her debt to the king had grown into a fondness that she had secretly begun to harbour for him. It hadn't helped that he had also started opening up to her. He would talk endlessly until sleep overcame his thoughts. She liked listening to him. The news of his sickness had disturbed her, and she was unwilling to believe that Akbar was convinced Salim had poisoned him. He had always spoken affectionately of Salim, even if he hinted at his anxiety for the empire's future that lay in the hands of his son. When he was feeling particularly frank with Jahanuma, he would even lovingly refer to Salim as Sheikhu.

However, she could sense that Akbar had been growing impatient with his son. One night, as they sat drinking wine out under the open sky, he had laid bare his dissatisfaction with Salim. He was precious to him but of a disposition that did not befit an emperor. He had called for Jahanuma after a hard day of clearing court matters. 'I am growing old, Jahanuma. I can only sustain the empire now, not expand it. If only Salim could lead the way. But he loves hunting over battle, wine over the intoxication of power.'

Jahanuma could see he was troubled and wanted to comfort him. She stroked his hair lightly but said nothing.

'I laboured hard to bring him into this world, by sheer force of my will, vows and prayers knocking at almighty's door. I groomed him to succeed me as the ruler of this great empire, but here he is, addicted to alcohol and drowned in pleasures while the great empire I have built has to wait for a brave and an able heir. You see that ruby,' he said, pointing to the magnificent gem pinned to his turban resting on the golden tray. 'My mother gifted the ruby to my son on his birth. She directed it be passed on to Salim when he was throned, a symbol of the empire finally finding its right successor. But is he one?'

'That only time will tell,' Jahanuma had dared to whisper.

'Time can both be a friend and an enemy, Jahanuma. I don't know how much longer I have left, and who knows what will happen to this empire, my bloodline and the memory and legacy of my ancestors. If I could lead the empire, rule the land forever, I would. Everything I have ever done has been for its sake. In death there would be sorrow only because it would mean I abandon my throne.'

Jahanuma did not know what to say. She thought of Ruksana and how she would know exactly how to counter the emperor's pensive mood that was growing darker with the night.

'Can I put faith in Salim?' he asked to himself, forgetting he was talking to Jahanuma, and looked at the red gemstone again. 'My younger sons, Murad and Daniyal, on the other hand, are worse, with their terrible weakness for opium. Salim is my only hope. Sheikh had cautioned me once that one might entreat Allah for the birth of a boy but there was no assurance of an heir.' He shook his head in disappointment. 'That is the cause of my worry,' he whispered.

'But what choice do you have, Jahanpanah?' Jahanuma posed the very question he had asked himself several times.

He fell silent and rose to leave for his chambers soon after. That day, for the first time, she had sensed that whatever it was that Akbar was thinking, clearly a kind of inchoate resentment was beginning to corrupt the relationship between father and son. But she knew that wasn't the end of it. There were many things that happened in the privacy of the royal chambers that she would never know or understand.

# Bold and Beautiful

Nadira missed Kabul, once the centre of her life. Kabul was like a spot of heaven in Khorasan. Years had passed. Tears filled Nadira's eyes as she recalled their imposing house on the outskirts of Kabul. Her grandmother fondly grew vegetables, fruits and flowers in their kitchen garden. They had a stable with six handsome horses. There were always relatives visiting them. Her mother would cook a storm in the kitchen every time a guest arrived. Evenings were spent listening to the tales her grandmother, a great storyteller, narrated. Books, poetry and music were reserved for discussions after dinnertime. Nadira missed her father who would take care of them, cook for them and take them to fairs; who would have given her the moon if he could.

Here in Lahore things were so different. Naaz was a kind woman but her ways of life were dull and boring. Her husband was employed in the postal department in Kashmir and visited Lahore only for a few days in the year. She gossiped with the neighbourhood women all day. The house was fairly large, comprising a courtyard, two bedrooms, a *baithak*, a large kitchen and a storehouse. Naaz and Asma occupied the main bedroom while the smaller one was given to Nadira and Suraiya. Asma shifted to the baithak when her father came visiting. So did

Nadira and Suraiya when Naaz had guests. The house was in a dilapidated state with water seeping from the roof at many places. In winter, a cold draught sneaked in through the wide gaps between doors and windows. Naaz was too lazy to make any efforts to mend the house. Her husband was even lazier. Whenever he was back, he whiled away all his time smoking opium and sleeping.

Naaz had no interest in food or cooking. She had hired an old woman who came twice to cook meals. The woman was a poor cook. Her range was limited and she prepared the same things every day. Nadira and Suraiya were tired of eating the same food, day in and day out. They missed the exotic dishes their mother churned out so regularly. Shawarma and kebab were cooked every day. Kabuli pulao and qorma was cooked twice a week. She missed the hot local breads, obi naan and lavash from the wood-fired clay oven in their kitchen. Her grandmother also used to make excellent kak, the popular wheat bread of Baluchistan.

Every two months, an officer from the governor's administration visited diligently and handed over to Naaz the promised allowance. Naaz had become even lazier after the allowance started. She did not care to inform Nadira how much money was received or pass any to the sisters. Nadira also did not ask Naaz about it. She could only guesstimate from the purchases she started making after the allowance commenced that it must be fairly handsome. Although Naaz was secretive about the allowance, she did buy them dresses and accessories. She would let Suraiya buy her favourite sweet from the corner shop every week. Nadira did not care as she was grateful to Naaz for taking care of them. She never raised the issue with Jahanuma. But it started troubling Nadira when Naaz gradually reduced the number of girls she taught to only four. She gave the governor's wife dance lessons twice a week because she received good money and gifts from her in return. She spent most part of the morning making her stock of paan for the day and the rest gossiping with the neighbourhood women, popping one paan after the other with beetle juice dripping from the sides of her mouth. Her dependence on the allowance was growing.

She and Suraiya missed Jahanuma who visited them only once a year at Eid. Though she spent one full month with them, thirty days passed by in a moment, laughing, sharing stories from Lahore and Agra and going around the city every evening. She would cook their favourite food and buy new dresses for them. Twice she had visited Lahore on an official trip, accompanying Gulbadan. While her mother did not like to talk about her place of work, Gulbadan was more forthcoming.

'When you have finished your education, you can come and visit us. Your ammi is a very hardworking woman. She is bearing the pain of staying away from you both so that she can give you both a good life. You should be proud of her.' She would encourage both Nadira and Suraiya to read as many books as they could. 'Lahore has many libraries with copies of Persian translations of some of the great Indian classics. Read about the rich history and culture of Lahore. Read about its fascinating past. For many decades, as Lahore was battered by one invasion after the other, the city's recognition as the seat of culture was lost. It is our empire that started the process of revival of the lost cultural identity of Lahore. Humayun wanted to do more but passed away too young.' She paused to mutter a prayer for her deceased brother and continued, 'But Akbar has carried on this legacy. He has encouraged open forum discussions on philosophy and scholastic theology. Cultural institutions here buzz with intellectuals and artists. Someday he hopes to give Lahore its due by spending more time here.'

Suraiya was too young to care for anything. She insisted on going to Agra only to be with her mother. Jahanuma would give one excuse or the other to turn down her pleas.

'There are no good schools in Agra. In Lahore you have the best,' her mother would try and explain every time.

Nadira on the other hand had made peace with the arrangements. She held her mother in high regard and refrained from burdening her with more issues. She had a sister to look after and a mother who doted on her. She thanked Allah for his blessings! Although she missed her mother and her advice in moments of uncertainty, Nadira had started enjoying the freedom of taking decisions for herself.

I

Though she yearned to be back in her native place, Nadira had also reconciled with her adopted city. Six years is a long time to adjust to a new place, new seasons and even new names of the days of the week. She had observed her new homeland and its way of life with keenness and was beginning to find it fascinating. It was culturally vibrant and any person who had an appreciation for the arts easily became fond of it. There were unlimited numbers of craftsmen and practitioners of every trade. For every labour and every product there was an established group who had been practising that craft or professing that trade for generations. The city was always alive with a flurry of activities.

The familiar trees, fruits and flowers helped her adjust to the new terrain and landscape. Many flowering trees had probably been brought as saplings from Persia and Kabul and planted across the city. There was a state nursery that took care of this not just in the city but also in the neighbouring districts. She loved mangoes which ripened during the monsoon. She loved mashing it to pulp, making a hole in it and sucking the juice. She also loved the unripe mango served as a condiment for meals.

Thanks to the governor's wife, Nadira had uninterrupted access to all the libraries including the royal library. She would sit there for hours and read endlessly. Jahanuma too brought a trunk full of books from the library in Agra when she visited them. Nadira finished reading them all quickly as they had to be sent back with her mother.

It was in the library that she had first met Vidya, a Hindu girl whom she had become close friends with. She was the daughter of an affluent spice merchant. Their friendship had thickened over the course of five years. The two were very different yet had a lot in common. Vidya was exceptional at designing dresses. She would sit with the neighbourhood tailor for hours, offering her suggestions on styles and even help with stitching against her mother's wishes. She wanted to do this expertly and make a living out of making clothes. But she belonged to an affluent family and was expected to pursue intellectual interests until she was married off into another illustrious family. Nadira did not have a great interest in clothes or jewellery, although she liked to dress up whenever she stepped out. Naaz would not let Nadira step out without burqa and hijab. Nadira would cover herself in black from head to toe when she stepped out to roam around the city with Vidya. Often at Vidya's house she would get rid of the black robe and they would play dress-up and put on different ensembles; sometimes dressed like a courtesan, sometimes like a man, they would laugh and play for hours. She had an entire wardrobe of hers at Vidya's house unknown to Naaz. In some ways, both Nadira and Vidya were rebels. This was perhaps one reason that brought them closer.

Nadira was immensely fond of Vidya's distinguished family. They lived in a large house a few minutes' walk from Naaz's house. One of her sisters was married in a family of famous shipbuilders in Gujarat. Her father sourced spices from the south of Hindustan and exported them to different countries. His work required him to travel for weeks and months on end. Vidya's elder brother managed the local office and shop in his father's absence. Another sister was married somewhere in Malabar. Her mother was warm and welcoming. Nadira loved the food from their kitchen. Although it lacked meat, it was still very sumptuous. The women in Vidya's household did not observe purdah. As the local rules required women from all faiths to keep their faces covered in public, they pulled the head stole to cover their faces while stepping out. Nadira had noticed that Vidya's mother held a status at home that was on par with her husband's, and he often sought her advice on a wide range of matters.

Vidya's grandmother was a wise woman. She had memorised hundreds of stories and was always eager to share. Nadira and Vidya would sit next to her to listen to the stories she told sitting royally on the cushioned cot in the courtyard as a server plied a fan made of a giant piece of fabric with the help of a rope. She loved the stories from the Hindu epics and Jataka tales. Nadira was fascinated by the tales from the Ramayana. She had read its condensed version in the library. She was mystified by the story of Rama, the crown prince of Ayodhya, and his marriage to Sita, the adopted girl of King Janaka and their decision to sacrifice the throne and live in exile for fourteen years out of respect for the wish of his father and stepmother. The stories of their adventures while in exile, in particular the kidnapping of Sita by Ravana, himself a man of extraordinary wisdom and powers, captivated her. She was baffled by the enormity of the dedication of the devoted monkey who could grow in size, fly across the ocean, fetch an entire mountain on his palm and set the whole island on fire using his endless tail. So fascinated was she by the story of Rama that she dressed up like Vidya and visited the subterranean temple located in the northern part of the fort to listen to the priest read out excerpts from the epic and then explain it in Hindi.

Nadira also liked hearing stories from the Mahabharata. She was fascinated by the character of Draupadi. However, what left her awestruck was the story of the blue-skinned Krishna and his lover, Radha. The more she heard about them, the more she wanted to know. During Krishna's stay in Vrindavan, Radha, daughter of Vrishabhanu, became his beloved friend, adviser and consort. But when Krishna had to return to his rightful throne and worldly affairs, he left Radha in Vrindavan, and Radha waited as Krishna defeated his enemies and became king. Time went by, and he married Satyabhama and Rukmini and raised a family but Radha kept waiting. The kind of devotion that Radha had for Krishna was considered the highest form of worship where she surrendered herself to him without any inhibitions.

Vidya's mother, however, was somewhat conservative in her understanding of Radha's undying love for Krishna. She saw it as the ultimate quest of a mortal to unite with the divine. According to her, the idea of Radha and Krishna as lovers had become popular only over the last couple of centuries. Poets and romantics had given this spiritual relation a physical form and distorted the original story. Like poets, writers, seers and even the common Krishna devotee, Nadira was enamoured of the nature of Radha's love for Krishna. She was sometimes the adulterous and amorous lover of Krishna and, at times, his divine consort, making her love an intriguing, immense force.

Radha was etched in Nadira's heart. It was her story that was her first brush with the understanding of love, something that she hadn't felt for any man yet. But she was convinced that pure love was unconditional. Radha always knew in her heart that Krishna would never marry her. However, that did not make any difference to her undying love for him. Her love was sacred, beyond the materialistic world and its limitations. Her romance could never fit the worldly perspective. The eternal love between Krishna and Radha was beyond human cognizance, she had realised. She decided that should she ever find herself in love, her passion would be no less fervent than Radha's.

II

Back home she would recount all the stories to Naaz, Asma and Suraiya. Naaz was a believer. She diligently followed the muezzin's calls, she prayed five times a day. She was disappointed by Nadira's keen interest in Hindu mythology and ways of life. Nadira was not deeply religious. At school, she was obliged to learn the Quran. She followed the teachings but rationalised them according to her judgement. She offered namaz regularly but she was unable to appreciate why as a Muslim she could not learn about other faiths. She disagreed with Naaz but avoided an argument over it. She was very fond of Vidya and her family and did not want Naaz to spoil that by doing anything stupid.

On some occasions, however, when Naaz nagged her, Nadira would end up in a fight with her. Once, when she had returned from Vidya's house, Naaz questioned her rudely, 'Why do you have to go to that mushrik's house every day?'

'Khaala, please, she is my friend, speak nicely of her.'

'She is trying to influence your thinking…'

'She is doing nothing of that sort,' Nadira interrupted her.

Naaz was taken aback by her retort.

'What is wrong in hearing different stories and beliefs? I am intrigued by both faiths, their exchange, similarities and dissimilarities…'

'I will tell you what the dissimilarities are.' It was Naaz's turn to interrupt Nadira. 'Do not be fooled by what you hear or read at her place. You think their faith is liberal. Haven't you heard about child marriage among Hindus, restrictions on their widows remarrying and being relegated to Benares or Vrindaban, devadasis, the tales of the wicked Duryodhana, their God Rama having suspected Sita of infidelity on overhearing a poor mortal? Don't get carried away and start questioning your own faith. When not banishing their widows, they burn them. And isn't it our emperor who decreed that if any woman was unwilling to perform Sati, the sacrifice was not to be permitted. Did he not send Udai Singh, Jai Mal's own son, to stop the immolation and save the life of his mother when she was not willing to mount her husband's funeral pyre but was being pressured to do so. It is our emperor who encouraged widows to remarry. Hasn't he also increased the marriage age? What about all that?'

'That is the problem, Khaala. Orthodox voices in all religions use the sacred texts to take away our freedom...' Nadira started to argue but Naaz cut her short and continued, 'You listen to me. Are you not aware how tolerant the shahenshah is? Is it not he who made the Sufi concept of *Sulh-e-Kuhl,* or "peace to all", a founding principle of his law? Did he not repeal the special tax on the pilgrimage of both Hindus and Muslims.'

'I agree, but if he can follow the Quran and still be tolerant to other faiths, what is the excuse to your close-mindedness, Khaala?'

Naaz was unwilling to consider Nadira's words to have any meaning. 'I am once again warning you to stay away from that Vidya who is brainwashing you. Otherwise, I will have to complain to your mother when she is here the next time.'

Nadira was fuming with anger by now. She stormed out of the room, banging the door loudly behind her in protest.

# The Confused Prince

Salim sat on the opulent balcony of his palace with his favourite pair of pigeons, deep in thought about his future and the brewing conflict with his father, the mighty Emperor Akbar. The rising sun cast a gentle glow upon his face, as if seeking to offer solace in the midst of his inner turmoil. As he stared into the distance, his mind became a whirlwind of conflicting emotions and aspirations.

Salim picked up the tumbler to take another sip of wine but found it empty. He had been drinking all night. He was about to summon his attendant when Bakshi Karim Khan walked in and broke the news to him.

'The emperor has announced that Nowruz will be celebrated in Lahore this year. He wants you in-charge of management and expects you to leave for Lahore without delay. He has also desired your presence in a meeting scheduled under the *chattri* in the royal garden in the afternoon.'

Salim was infuriated. The Nowruz celebration had established standard operating procedures and the governor of Lahore was capable of putting it together. Why had his father chosen him to run this petty errand? Was he testing him or was this a ploy to keep him away from Agra? He suspected that the latter was more likely. He dismissed Karim Khan and waved at his attendant to bring some wine.

His anxiety continued to soar at the thought of being away from Agra at this crucial juncture. He went inside and lay on the reclining divan and started contemplating the prospects of his detractors taking advantage of his absence. They would yet again step up their efforts to escalate the misunderstandings with his father, he suspected. Any falling out at this crucial time could spiral into a confrontation. Even though Akbar had proclaimed him as the emperor-in-waiting following the truce his aunt snatched from the brink of war, his elder son Khusrau openly harboured ambitions to bypass him to the throne. He was also not fully convinced if his father had forgiven him for the murder of his good friend, Abul Fazl. Did his father not realise that killing Abul Fazl was not personal and was only to serve an important political message that the emperor's heir apparent was not as soft as his father made him out to be?

Salim was dismayed that his father was mistrustful of his abilities to rule the empire. He loved his mother but felt disappointed that she did not do enough to convince his father. Rather, she sided with her husband too often.

'Your father does not consider you unworthy of the throne. He has no doubt about your abilities to rule. He is concerned about your weakness for opium and wine. And I share his concern. The ruler of Hindustan cannot afford to be vulnerable to such vices. You should know that besides being your father, he is also the emperor. The future of this vast empire and her people are his responsibility,' she would tell him every time he confronted her about his father's attitude towards him.

Salim found his mother's defence of her husband hard to digest. According to him, his father was unfair in his assessment about his abilities. It is true that Salim was fond of travelling, loved his wine and literature. He also enjoyed wandering aimlessly, north in the hot season, south in the cold, ponderously moving at an elephant's pace through the stunning landscape of his father's empire. He was captivated by the splendour of this diverse country – the mountains leaning against the sky, magnificent rivers edged by trees, blooming poppy fields, banks of ponds, customs and beliefs of the people and the enormous wildlife. Nature was at her most splendid, beautiful and vibrant in the jungles of Hindustan. But this did not mean he was not industrious or lacked interest in the matters of the empire. He carried out his imperial duties with diligence. He was the first to get on his horse and dash to the battlefield when commanded by the emperor. He was not a shirker.

He was sent to the battlefield when he was just ten. At the age of twelve, he commanded a regiment in the Kabul campaign. He had fought bravely. So much so that pleased by the victory, Akbar accorded him the highest military rank by making him the mansabdar of das-hazari. He was unable to appreciate what could possibly be wrong in balancing the imperial duties with a pursuit of pleasure. Even if he lacked his father's flaming resolve, he did possess a kind of dogged determination, a stubborn refusal to bow out of the race.

He did not think it was good for his body and mind to work round the clock. He preferred to work hard but also take out time for his interests. Constant mobility provided him the opportunity to satisfy his passion for the hunt. He loved this sport as no other. The thick deep forest with its teeming life, the cries of the falconers and the varied game thrilled him unimaginably. He was unable to convince his father that the circumstances in which he would be taking over the empire were very different from the time when the empire was forced on him.

Salim also had his own reasons for the disillusionment with his father. He felt he did not respect him enough. Salim believed that as the future king he was entitled to draw out his own vision of leading the empire. Although he held respect for other faiths, he had no doubts that Islam should remain at the centre of the Mughal way of rule. His father's deeper ventures into multiple faiths confused him. He often felt embarrassed when his friends taunted him about his father building a chapel and a guesthouse for the priests from Portugal next to his palace in Fatehpur Sikri.

He also knew that the escalation in tension between him and his father was giving his mother sleepless nights. Jodha felt helpless because most of it was only a result of clashing dispositions. Her husband and her son spoke different languages when it came to their approach for the empire; neither understood the other. It had been enough to create undercurrents of tension between the two. Jodha, along with Gulbadan, had often reminded Salim that their misunderstandings would be taken advantage of by others, and in the recent years, Salim had frustratingly watched it happen.

Salim's detractors had let no opportunity pass to sow suspicion in the mind of the emperor. It had been a prickly relationship for a while. Things had worsened when it was insinuated that Akbar's rapidly deteriorating health was on account of slow poisoning for which Salim was blamed. His father confronted him, albeit in private. Salim was devastated by the accusation. He found it difficult to come to terms with the fact that his father chose to lend credence to such insinuations. When he discovered that it was Abul Fazl who had prejudiced his father against him, he vowed to take revenge on his father's friend. Salim suspected that Abul Fazl was using his proximity to Akbar to create doubt in his mind about Salim's competence and ability to succeed the emperor. He secretly started mobilising the support of commanders, ministers, nobles and relatives who also grudged Abul Fazl for their own reasons. He was careful though not to talk ill of the emperor. Akbar got a whiff of it and sent off Salim to Persia and Rajputana. In his absence, Akbar gave Daniyal the rights to put the emperor's flags and red tents in campaigns. Khurram was taken into Akbar's household and Ruqaiah Begum became his foster mother.

Salim's wounded feelings led him to indulge in excessive drinking, on certain occasions consuming as many as ten glasses of wine. It is only after the hakim warned him of his fast damaging liver that he cut down on his drinking but could never bring himself to stop entirely. When he returned to Agra after successfully completing the assigned mission, Akbar instructed him to leave for the Deccan to help Daniyal's failing campaign against Ahmednagar. Salim saw that as yet another pretext to keep him away from Agra. This time he refused to travel. He claimed he was unwell and the Deccan summer would only make it worse.

Akbar took Salim's refusal as an act of defiance. He was the emperor and there was no way he was going to accept indifference and his son's lack of obedience. He was fed up of Salim's amateur fascination with power, without being able to appreciate the responsibilities attached to it. Hindustan does not deserve an impulsive ruler like his son, Akbar thought. If he was determined to learn the hard way, let it be so, he decided. To shame Salim, he planned to go to the Deccan himself. But before leaving, he ordered Salim to leave for Mewar, to curb an incipient rebellion, as soon as he felt fit to travel. He also made it clear that if Salim refused to obey, he would be placed under house arrest.

Salim was overcome with fury when the emperor commanded him to go to Mewar. He could no longer take the insults inflicted on him. He turned defiant. The throne was his right. His mind went to his ancestor's philosophy. Timur had once said, *Takht ya takhta*. Throne or coffin. A prince was entitled to nurture ambitions to rule, to hold the sceptre of power. He would not beg for what was rightfully his. He would claim it, whatever the consequences. If he did not get to rule, he would prefer to find peace in a coffin. His mind was made up.

As he contemplated his next move, he left for Mewar with three hundred soldiers loyal to him. The weight of the insult and hurt caused by his father's affront and slight continued to prick his heart. By the time he had travelled some distance from Agra, the ache had turned into anger. He was no longer able to think straight.

As night approached, they stopped to camp. After dinner, he decided to take a short walk hoping that the beautiful moonlit sky would help calm his mind. After he had walked a distance, he crossed two guards on duty. They were chatting loudly, unmindful of the approaching prince.

'The prince keeps drowning his frustration in wine. He doesn't seem to have the spine to take on his father. The old man is not willing to make way for the next generation,' said one of the soldiers.

Salim stopped in his tracks, enraged by the audacity of the petty soldier. But something told him to listen to the conversation.

'I think our prince is a brave man, but he respects his father. And what's the big rush? The takht is his, only his. It is just a matter of time,' responded the other soldier.

'But you have to agree, the prince seems *kamzor*, a weakling, who does not have the guts to stand up to his father; which is why nobody can imagine him as a tough, desirable king. It is also why he hasn't been able to amass people's support,' argued the first soldier.

'He can't be fighting his father...'

Salim could not bear listening any further. He stormed back to his tent. He kept tossing in bed all night, haunted by the words of the first soldier. Kamzor. The word echoed in his mind. By the time he could sleep, he had made up his mind. He was going to head back to Agra and take over the fort. He had even thought of a plan.

In the morning, he convened a meeting of his confidants and discussed the plan with them. They all vowed to fight alongside him if they were met with resistance.

But the news of his plan reached Agra before he did. Hamida Banu, who was in Fatehpur Sikri, decided to confront him. When Salim reached the outskirts of Agra, he received a message that Hamida Banu wanted to meet him alone. Salim loved his grandmother. He could not turn down her request.

He found her waiting for him a few kos from Fatehpur Sikri. She was accompanied by only two guards. He got down from his horse and walked to her. Hamida waved her guards to stay back. They complied with her order reluctantly.

Salim bowed to her grandmother but was unable to face her questioning gaze.

'I am ashamed of you, Salim! Is this how you are going to pay back your father, your mother and all of us, for loving you, for bringing you up with devotion and making you the man you are today? Are you really going to rebel against your own father?' Hamida did not mince any words.

Salim kept quiet, unable to gather the courage to answer back.

'Do you even realise how childish your behaviour is? Are you so naive that you don't realise that your father will retrieve the fort from you in a matter of hours when he returns, even if you take advantage of his absence and take momentary control of the fort? That is, if you are not killed mercilessly by his loyalists before he arrives? You will not even know what hit you. Don't underestimate your father or his men. You are no match for him. Do not take his patience with you as a sign of his weakness. There is still time for you to save your life, my son.'

'But...'

Hamida cut him short. 'Akbar would have known by now what you are up to. He would be turning back or sending the best of his men to deal with you. I will try to calm him and persuade him to back off if you follow your father's instructions and go to Mewar. Apologise to him when you return,' she directed him.

Salim raised his eyes and looked at Hamida. Her face conveyed no emotion, but her eyes were sad.

'Son, I am giving you the chance to save your life and keep alive the hope of becoming the emperor someday. If you do not listen to me, Salim, I am telling you, your dream will end today. We all love you. Your father loves you most of all. We want to see you sit on that throne one day but this is not the way you are going to procure it.'

Salim was upset that her grandmother wouldn't even listen to him. He bowed to her and turned back, more in shame than in anger.

But there was no way to go back on what he had unleashed. The arrow had left the bow. Akbar would have already decided how to chasten him. A confrontation was inevitable. Salim dropped his plan for Agra fort and decided to head to Prayag and take over the city on the banks of the Jamuna. He had very warm memories of Allahabad. He fondly remembered the lovely, leisurely cruise down this river with his father when he was a child. Akbar had given the city its new name and laid the foundations of the fort in which, with the heavy-handed irony of fate, his son, the very pearl of his prayers, would now set up a rival court.

# I

Allahabad yielded to Salim without protest; he commandeered the fort, its treasury and rushed to take over the neighbouring province of Bihar. In the ensuing weeks he gave his men titles, promotions and estates and declared himself king. This was a muted declaration of mutiny.

He expected his father to march to the city. And what better death than to die fighting in a battlefield at the hands of his own father. At least, it would make his father proud of him in his death. If a miracle occurred, he would defeat the Mughal army and sit on the throne. But it would be a bloodbath. In either case, *itihaas* would remember him with respect.

To his surprise, a few weeks later, the emperor sent an emissary to Allahabad. He read a written message from the emperor himself: 'You deserve to die like any traitor of the empire. But, for the sake of your mother, who loves you more than she is devoted to me, I ask you to surrender and return to Agra. You will be forgiven and appointed governor of Bengal.'

Salim knew it must be his grandmother and mother weighing in on Akbar to forgive his son. But he refused, digging his heels in. Not till he had settled his score with Abul Fazl, he decided. He had to prove to his father that in his veins ran the blood of the Great Mughal. The opportunity arrived soon.

A few days later, Bir Singh personally delivered the head of Abul Fazl to him.

Salim held his severed head in his hand and climbed up on the ramparts of the fort. Holding the head so everyone could see it, he spoke aloud, 'Let this be known to my enemies. This is going to be the fate of every person who stands between me and the throne.'

It was unlike him to make a display this brutal. But he could sense a sudden change in the attitude of people around him after the assassination. No one could doubt his capability as a formidable contender for the throne anymore. It had happened overnight. His opponents had received the message loud and clear that he could eliminate his enemies if he wanted, no matter how powerful and how close to Akbar. He learnt from his spies that his father had howled over the dead body of Abul Fazl. He had sworn to bring him justice.

He knew his father would have been livid upon hearing the news of the death of his close confidante and would march to Allahabad, perhaps leading his forces from the front. As expected, his father arrived in Allahabad a fortnight later leading the Mughal army. Salim climbed the highest point in the fort and looked towards the Mughal army assembled at the banks of the Ganga, holding his breath. The entire horizon was covered with soldiers, on foot or on horses or elephants, so vast that the very sky seemed part of his father's forces.

However, when they were at the brink of drawing their swords, the battle was averted because of Hamida Banu. She had taken with a sudden illness and was sick. Akbar returned to Agra. Noticing that tempers had cooled down over the matriarch's ill health, Gulbadan decided to take the opportunity to mediate and bring about a rapprochement between the father and son. Akbar initially refused to meet Salim. But with some persuasion from Gulbadan, he relented.

The meeting was scheduled to be held in the guesthouse across the Jamuna. Salim bowed to his father when Akbar entered. But Akbar refused to even look at him. Salim hugged his aunt and touched his mother's feet as he always did every time he met her. Gulbadan had planned to break the ice by asking the father and son to hug one another but realised that niceties would not make any difference in the situation. She had to act urgently.

'If we want to hold on to power, we must stay united. Whatever the differences between the two of you, they must be resolved amicably. Fighting on the battleground is not the solution. We will only harm ourselves. Only our enemies will gain from it. You cannot allow the great legacy of the Gurkani wither away because of your ego. This is the time to think of our dynasty, not your individual pride,' she said firmly.

No one spoke. Gulbadan walked up to Salim. She placed her hands on his strong shoulders. 'Tell me, Salim, what will satisfy you?'

Salim hesitated for a moment then said, coldly, 'Jahanpanah should step down and hand over the reins to me. It is time for him to rest, make a trip to Mecca.'

There was a stunned silence in the room. Everyone expected Akbar to explode with anger. To everyone's surprise, Akbar kept quiet.

'Not till I am alive,' Akbar responded after a while, looking out of the window, his back to Salim.

'How dare you, Salim...' Jodha started to say something but Gulbadan waved her to be quiet. She turned to Salim.

'There is no way you will sit on the throne till your father is alive,' she declared. 'But I am sure he would be willing to consider designating you as the emperor-in-waiting. Your coronation will take place whenever your father decides.'

She turned to Akbar for his reaction.

Tension built up in the room. Everyone expected Akbar to reject the proposal straightaway.

Finally, Akbar turned to look at Salim. 'If that is what he desperately wants, let him have it. Let him have the satisfaction of being designated emperor-in-waiting.' Although he was looking at Salim, he was speaking to Gulbadan. Salim looked away, unable to meet his father's gaze. 'But will that change his ways? A man who cannot respect his own father, how is he expected to care for his people?' Akbar turned and left the room.

Salim was confused. Had Akbar agreed to or rejected the proposal? Only Jodha was smiling. She knew her husband well. Although Gulbadan was filled with a moment of doubt, Jodha's smile lifted the air of doubt. She held Salim in her arms. 'Mubarak! Mubarak!' rang her words.

Salim was perplexed. He had not been given the chance to assert his original proposal. It had happened too fast. He was taken aback by the turn of events. It took him a few seconds to comprehend what had happened. He decided to reconcile with the situation and accept the solution. Jodha kissed him on his forehead. He bowed to his aunt. She muttered a prayer to Allah. What could have turned into a bloody chapter in the history of the empire was resolved in a matter of minutes.

Back in Agra, Salim made a sincere effort to quit drinking and stop consuming opium. But it soon became apparent to him that in his heart, his father had not forgiven him and still held grudges against his son, never losing an opportunity to humiliate and remind him of his incompetence. He went back to his drinking to drown his disappointments and pain.

Restless, Salim walked back to the balcony. His thoughts wandered back to his father. He could never understand where things had started going wrong between the two of them. Although an agreement had been reached, things did not become normal between the two. His father was still hurting and angry from his rebellion. He was rarely invited to Akbar's military council meetings. Salim did not find any change in his father; he was still as distant and cold as before.

The weight of his filial duty and the desire to carve his own path clashed within him. With each passing day, Salim's resolve grew stronger, his determination to assert his own identity and challenge the authority of his father burning like a flame within. The balcony, a place of solace and reflection, fast became a battleground where his dreams sparred with the expectations of his lineage.

II

Salim could think of nothing else. He felt lonely and sent for his best friend, Mahabhat Khan. He trusted Mahabhat with his life and confided in him. They were friends from the time they were young. His friend was the son of the emperor's trusted employee, Ghayur Beg Mahabhat. Mahabhat had been employed as a sepoy in the Mughal army at the age of sixteen under Salim's command. The two soon took a liking for one another and their shared feeling of camaraderie only grew over time. He was the only person with whom Salim expressed himself freely without feeling judged.

'Why can't he leave me alone?' he blurted out as soon Mahabhat walked in. 'Should I not be consulted before issuing such diktats?'

'Come on, Salim Bhai, do you really want me to believe you are concerned about your detractors? Isn't it that he stands in the way of your pursuit of Meherunissa that bothers you?' Mahabhat spoke to him with a familiar candour.

'Both, I think, dost!' Salim answered, sighing.

Mahabhat was right, Salim realised. In his heart, Salim was concerned about being away from Mehr, as he lovingly addressed her, the thought of whom alone could brighten his day. Only a few days back, she had relented and agreed to meet him. The rendezvous in the garden had gone really well. He wanted a companion who would adore him and offer him companionship. He was lonely and missed an intelligent partner in whom he could confide his deepest secrets and desires. He had no one he could share his problems with and expect wise counsel in return. His wives were all a result of political treaties. None was a marriage of his choice. He wanted love, the kind poets wrote about, in his life. Mehr had everything he desired in a partner. He had only recently noticed some favourable signs of response from Mehr who was his first love, who he had dreamt of winning for many years now. Although she was now a widow and free to court him, she still did not encourage his advances. He had offered to marry her and adopt her daughter. While her mother had given in to his persistence a few months ago, Mehr stayed disinterested.

Their conversation was interrupted by his attendant. 'The emperor's envoy is here, His Excellency!'

The assistant bowed and sought permission from the prince to read the order. Salim nodded. The deputy unrolled the rich textured paper carrying the seal of the emperor and respectfully read out the farman to him. He then handed it over to Salim. Salim sighed. There was no escaping the journey to Lahore. The farman of the emperor was as effective as his voice. He cursed under his breath and performed the *sijdah* as custom demanded. The assistant bowed and left.

Salim knew he was now duty-bound under law to comply with the emperor's wish, in letter and spirit. He did not have any will left to question his father. He was desperate for another glass of wine but decided against one. He did not want to go to the meeting intoxicated. Salim decided to leave for Lahore without any delay. He summoned his valet and issued instructions for his bags to be packed.

## III

The sight of the emperor's trusted men gathered in the garden waiting for the emperor antagonised him. Despite being the emperor-designate Salim commanded neither respect nor any authority over them. At the same time, he felt compelled to admire his father for his extraordinary administrative brilliance and selection of his principal officers. Notwithstanding their difference, he commended his father's genius in recognising men of talent, whatever their background, and promoting them to the office that suited their particular skills. He had an uncanny ability to judge talent in men. From the financial acumen of Raja Todar Mal, the military genius of Kunwar Man Singh, the literary aptitude of Abd al-Qadir Badauni, the administrative skill of Fathullah Shirazi and many more, Akbar promoted men through the courage of his own conviction, disregarding resentment and opposition caused by his decisions, even to his own kin. He rewarded Hindus against the advice of his Muslim advisers and Shias against the inclination of the orthodox Sunnis and stood up to the minor disagreements of the ulema, all to the glory of the empire.

His father had perfected the organisation of public services by basing it on the mansabdari system, inspired from Persia. Every important officer of the empire held a mansab or an official appointment of rank and emoluments. As members of an imperial cadre, they were liable for service anywhere in the empire. He was actively considering a proposal to classify the office holders in grades, ranging from commanders of ten to commanders of ten thousand. It was still a couple of years away as the consultation process with his ministers was ongoing. The mansabdars were paid either in cash or by temporary grant of jagirs. Appointment was made on the recommendation of military leaders, provincial governors or court officials. In addition to the mansabdars, *ahadis* were employed in posts in the palace, though they held no official rank. They were usually young men from good families, who were not fortunate enough to secure a mansab on their first try. If they showed their worth, they were promoted to the ranks of mansabdars. The existence of a single imperial cadre provided a sense of cohesion and unity to the Mughal Empire. The system had loopholes as the mansabdars did not normally maintain all the troops expected of them in lieu of salaries received. But Akbar was constantly introducing reforms to improve the administration and bring accountability.

A chair had been placed away from the emperor for Salim. It was strategically positioned so that the emperor would not have to make eye contact with his son when he addressed him. Salim nodded his greetings in silence to all present and occupied the chair.

The emperor arrived a few minutes later and sat down. The red stone bench had been layered with cushions of silk to make it comfortable. After the customary greeting, the meeting started. The emperor signalled the diwan of the administration to open the items in his agenda. The diwan was responsible for revenue and finance. He had a say in all matters of expenditure. All the imperial orders were first recorded in his office before being issued. The provincial governors, district *faujdars,* and leaders of expeditions received instructions from him before assuming their duties. All the earning departments were also under his direct control and could spend only what was allotted to them by the diwan. He had only one item to discuss. He required the emperor's approval to increase the budget for the construction of the tomb Hamida was building in memory of his father. After satisfying himself that the money was being spent responsibly, the emperor approved the increase with certain conditions. Construction should be accelerated, he ordered. The longer it took to complete the construction, the higher would be the cost, he expressed his concern.

It took about an hour for most of the official business to get over to the emperor's satisfaction. The last item on the list was the approval of the budget for the Nowruz celebration. The New Year festival was a grand affair and every year Akbar sanctioned generous funds for countrywide celebrations. While the emperor celebrated even the Hindu festivals like Shiv Ratri, Holi and Deepavali with zeal, Nowruz had the highest state patronage. The diwan presented the detailed break-up of the costs. Akbar leaned back to give the matter a deep thought.

'I approve the budgets. The festival will be celebrated in Lahore this year. I appoint Salim as the minister-in-waiting to make fit arrangements and receive me in Lahore,' Akbar announced, signalling that the meeting was over.

Everyone promptly got on their feet.

'Please be my guest for dinner tonight,' the emperor invited everyone politely.

'Forgive me, Abba-huzoor, I have a lot of arrangements to do. I will excuse myself,' Salim said respectfully.

Akbar did not care to look at Salim. He nodded curtly, his contempt transparent for all to witness. Salim looked away from the gathering, trying to swallow the insult.

Now more than ever, he wanted to get away from the court and let the taste of wine and the company of Mehr keep him warm through the night.

# The Disappointed Father

The emperor sat on the cushioned divan wrapped in a blanket, sipping wine from a golden chalice, staring out at the river. There was no moonlight and light clouds obscured the stars. A thin mist rose like steam from the Jamuna. Two slave girls lit the lamps and placed candles in the recesses. The light flickered on their faces. The palace behind him lay in pitch darkness on his instructions. He had dismissed all the attendants. Only one of them stood in the shadow holding a ewer full of wine waiting for the emperor's signal. It was one of those rare evenings when he was able to finish the court work earlier than he had expected and decided to sit back and relax rather than visit the harem. He was still angry at Salim's deplorable conduct. Not only had he rebelled against his father, he had challenged the emperor of Hindustan. He was reeling from the cold murder of his closest friend and advisor Abul Fazl while Salim had betrayed him again. How many times could he forgive him? But he had to welcome Salim back and pave the way for his succession. He cursed himself for this helplessness. The throne had offered him all the power in the world yet bound him by a difficult obligation.

Akbar prided himself on being a just ruler. That his subjects revered him was proof that he had managed to win their trust.

What Salim's actions had done was crack the image of the ruler that he had so carefully cultivated. It could push people into challenging his authority. *Had someone other than my own son rebelled against me, killed my closest confidante, would he not have met a different fate? Why have I allowed myself to succumb to familial pressures? The divine ruler is above all the pleasures and pain,* he thought and berated himself for his inability to deal with Salim like he would with any other citizen of the empire. Tomorrow, when people gather at the foot of the jharoka to see his sacred figure, how would he face them? Tomorrow, when he would sit with his ministers to discuss matters of court, would they not secretly mock him in silence? These thoughts had kept him awake each night ever since the truce was reached with Salim.

Sitting under the cold sky, Akbar gulped down one ewer of wine after the other, his mind struggling to find an answer to why things had gone wrong between him and his son. Sheikhu was a child of many prayers and he really doted on him. He thought back on the day the joyful news of his birth was brought to him by Sheikh Ibrahim, the son-in-law of Sheikh Salim. It was noon but the sky was dark from the monsoon clouds. Thunder shook the walls of the palace and heavy rain pounded its roofs. Occasionally, some flashes of lightning cracked the darkness. He was informed that a visitor from Sikri wanted to meet the emperor and had some good news to deliver. When Ibrahim announced the news of the birth of his first-born, he raised both his hands in joy and gratitude to Allah. In thanksgiving for that great good fortune, and this noble gift, he announced distribution of alms to the people, ordered release of prisoners and directed royal festivities for seven days. Poets presented him with congratulatory qasidahs. So overwhelmed was he by the news and the great fortune the village of Sikri had brought to him, he made up his mind to make the village his capital. Later, over the course of fourteen or fifteen years, he turned that hill full of wild beasts into a city containing all kinds of gardens and buildings and lofty, elegant edifices and pleasant palaces. In pursuance of a vow, he set out on a pilgrimage to Ajmer on foot to offer thanks for the birth of Salim. He sat for hours to offer his obeisance to the Sheikh.

In a break from Timurid dynastic tradition, he decided against sending Salim as a child to govern imperial appanages so that he received the best of education. He was taught Persian, Turkish, Arabic, Urdu, history, arithmetic, geography and other sciences. He had appointed Abdur Rahim Khan-i-Khanan, the renowned soldier and scholar, to teach Salim. It pleased him immensely that Salim was fond of reading classics of Persian literature and developed an interest in the works of Sadi, Hafez and Rumi. He was growing into a strong and well-built young man taller than his father. He was a quick learner of military art and his courage was remarkable. Akbar was proud of Salim. But as time passed, he noticed Salim's priorities changing; he no longer showed the expected levels of interest in the affairs of the empire. He found excuses to go wandering purposelessly into different parts of the land and spent time hunting. He also began to harbour an undue fondness for wine and that woman Meherunissa.

Akbar had worked relentlessly to build the vast empire. He knew what it took to hold on to a complex country like Hindustan. It needed a ruler with extraordinary acumen. When he tried to remind Salim of his responsibilities, he would come up with strange logic to defend himself. He wanted to enjoy his life alongside work, he would say. Akbar found those silly reasons excuses to shirk work. When he reminded Salim how hard he himself worked even till date, he would argue it was unfair to expect that his son should work the same way as him.

Soon an unpleasant equation developed between them. Salim drifted away. His drinking increased. He allowed himself, in spite of his natural goodness, to be led astray by the soft words of traitors and started openly defying Akbar. The emperor's informers frequently brought the news of Salim's misdeeds which carried shades of rebellion. He rarely attended important meetings, treated his father's loyalists with contempt, questioned the royal decrees ... the list was endless. Akbar was alarmed. His love for his elder son, whom he considered a blessing of Allah, held him back from the severity with which he ought to have chastised him. And then, the most unthinkable happened.

Akbar clearly remembered the day he stood on a balcony in the fort in Kanpur admiring his falcon. It was about noon on a day in mid-August and the monsoon would have been well under way. The sky was thick with clouds and the river below was swelling against its banks. Gusts of cool, moist air filled the fort's large balconies. He had decided to halt here for a couple of days on the way to the Deccan.

Abul Fazl brought the devastating news. 'It is my misfortune that I have to carry this news to the Padshah. Forgive me, My Lord!'

*Has Hamida passed away*? thought Akbar, alarmed by Abul Fazl's tone. She had not been keeping well and the doctors were beginning to get concerned as she showed little signs of recovery. This was the first thought that crossed his mind. He was filled with anxiety. He muttered a prayer for her good health and inquired, 'Is my mother all right?'

'Yes, His Excellency. Last I heard she has shown some positive response to the treatment.'

'Then what is it?'

'It is about Salim,' Abul Fazl stated, his voice breaking under the weight of the tragic information.

'What about him?'

'He has proclaimed himself the emperor of Hindustan and raised his own flag from the ramparts of Allahabad fort. He has ordered minting of coins in his name and issued many farmans.'

Akbar was aghast. 'Tell me you lie, Abul Fazl. You are misinformed. My son may be foolish, a drunkard and perhaps not as brave as his forefathers, but to declare war on his own father ... No, he can't do that.'

'I too did not believe this when I heard of it first. I sent my most trusted messengers and reached to our most loyal spies and officers to verify the horrifying news. They have all confirmed it. He has assembled a small bunch of traitors and proclaimed virtual independence. He has also announced distribution of land grants to members of his personal retinue and ... He even had the *khutba* read in his name,' Abul Fazl said, this time with his head bowed to the ground in shame as if it was his own son who had betrayed the emperor.

Akbar's shock had turned into rage by then. 'How dare he? No one can read the khutba as long as I am alive.' He paced in anger and frustration. Finally, getting ahold of himself, he sat down on the divan. He invited Abul Fazl to sit next to him. 'I need to know every detail of this mutiny. What is the size of his army, weapons they hold, the support he has of the nobles ... tell me everything,' he said.

For the next thirty minutes, the emperor was quiet. He listened to Abul Fazl with rapt attention, interrupting only once with a sigh that held the pain he felt from this betrayal.

'Prepare to march to Allahabad,' he said as soon as Abul Fazl had finished. From what he had heard from Abul Fazl, his forces would be able to retrieve the fort from Salim in less than a week.

He then marched to the zenana to talk to Jodha. He found her sobbing with Gulbadan and Maham Anga by her side. Gulbadan had her own informers. Apparently, the news of

Salim's rebellion had already reached her and was communicated to Jodha. Gulbadan and Maham Anga appeared unsettled. He noticed Hamida sitting on the swing in full control of herself. He paid his respects to the elderly women.

'My ancestors have been insulted; the bloodline tainted,' he started, enraged. 'A son has waged war against his father. He has pulled down my flag, the flag of the emperor of Hindustan proudly fluttering on the ramparts of Allahabad fort and replaced it with his shabby rag.' Akbar heard Jodha sob louder.

'This is the son we prayed for, Jodha. This is the son on whose birth I shed tears. He will be punished. He must be punished!'

'Calm down, my son. Let us think with a cool mind. I understand your hurt, even your anger. But an emperor must not think only like a father nor should a father judge only like an emperor in such a situation. There will be implications to how you act. Do not allow your anger and hurt to cloud your decision.' Gulbadan was the first woman in the room to speak.

'There will be implications if I do not rein in the traitor. There is only one way of dealing with a rebel. And you know it as much as I do,' he retorted, regretting his tone soon after he had spoken.

'Yes, give a rebel what he deserves. But not a naive young man who does not understand the full impact of his actions. Someone must be using him to serve his own purpose. Let me talk to him and put some good sense into his mind. Think like a father and give your son a chance,' Hamida intervened.

'Mother, I am the emperor. The court and the people of Hindustan will be watching my response. They will expect nothing but justice from me. A traitor is a traitor irrespective of his identity, be it my son, a piece of my heart.'

'Listen to your mother, Akbar. She speaks wisely. Don't do something that you will have to regret later,' Gulbadan said.

'He sets a bad example. History will not fail to record him as the first of the great Timur's race who rebelled against his father…' He made another attempt to persuade the women of the house he most respected to support him in the decision he wanted to take.

'…I beg your pardon for interrupting you, His Highness. I speak not only because he is my son but because I know he loves you and means no harm to you or to this empire. He is a misguided young man. By all means reprimand him but please do not go and fight him. I cannot bear the thought of the two people I love the most fighting to kill each other on the battleground.' Jodha finally decided to speak her mind.

'Who would know dharma better than you, Jodha? Is it not true that in the battlefield of Kurukshetra, Arjun was fighting evil and not against his blood?'

'The two situations are different, My Lord! The Pandavas had been wronged by the Kauravas, who were evil in their ways. Our son is not evil. He is a young man gone astray…'

'You look at his deeds from the eyes of a mother, Jodha. That is why you can't see him as he is – a rebel,' Akbar interrupted Jodha without raising his voice.

'If he would do anything to harm the empire or my husband, I would be the first to confront him, believe me, Jahanpanah. We must give him an opportunity to explain his side of the story. Even as the emperor, you cannot disregard the fact that you are his father. Most of his actions may be as a son who is hurt and not as the successor of the throne. You should talk to him.'

Jodha sounded convincing. Akbar turned to Maham Anga. She was the only one who had not spoken thus far.

'Is there no other way to deal with it but to enter into a battle with your own son? I ask you to fight him yourself. Don't send a general. You should not trust anyone other than yourself in such a situation. I advise you to reconsider your strategy,' Maham Anga said.

Akbar was in no mood to relent. 'I have been thinking about it from the very moment the news was broken to me.'

Finally, Hamida put an end to the discussion. 'I have to speak to Jalal-ud-din alone,' she announced. All bowed to Hamida and left the room.

'You have already lost Murad to insobriety. Daniyal too is a slave to opium. Salim is your only hope. Have you ever put yourself in his shoes and considered why he behaves the way he does? Your public display of preference for Khusrau over Salim and showering of out-of-turn affection on him are the talk of the palace. Even here in the harem, the gossip is that you have made up your mind to hand over the throne to your grandson, bypassing his father. Which father will take that insult without retaliating? He has his own honour to save. You were fortunate that you had Bairam, other loyal nobles and your father's goodwill that no one usurped your lawful right to become the emperor of Hindustan. But what if someone did? Someone your own. Would you have turned back to Kandahar and lived like a hermit? Would your Timur blood not have boiled for revenge? Would you not have reclaimed what was rightfully yours?'

'But...'

Hamida interrupted him. 'My son, you are a great emperor of a great empire. A successful and revered man. Do not be overly concerned about what people will think. Every father will respect your decision. As will every mother. Every son. Don't be pressured by the performance of right or wrong. Let me go to Allahabad and talk some sense into him.'

Akbar had calmed down by then. He saw sense in Hamida's counsel. 'You are unwell. I cannot let you take this long journey in this simmering summer,' he said as an excuse to end the conversation.

'Let me send my emissary to Salim in that case. He will not disrespect my messenger.' Hamida was not one to relent easy.

Akbar was torn between respect for his mother and duty to his empire. He always had trouble turning down his mother's advice, a trait he inherited from his grandfather. It was Babur who gave women a place in his genealogy, especially those who had influenced his life. There were a number of women who had contributed to his life and reign. The diplomatic manoeuvres of his maternal grandmother, Aisan Daulat Begum, contributed substantially to his extraordinary success. Aisan Begum was revered for her courage and integrity. From the time of the death of Babur's father, Mirza, she stood behind him, guiding his affairs with decisions and helping him overcome political crises. The real power and the control of affairs lay in her hands.

Humayun was not less fortunate in finding a mentor in his mother Maham Begum. She was educated, intelligent and broad-minded. As Gulbadan had once said, 'Maham was the chief lady of the royal household ... she was supreme, and had well-defined rights over other inmates.' Maham Begum helped in building Babur's career and exercised a great influence on him. She accompanied and stood by him through thick and thin in his distant campaigns in Badakhshan and Transoxiana.

Akbar's own mother was born to Mir Baba Dost, a Persian Shia. Through this marriage alliance, Humayun gained the support of Shia powers. This support continued to remain influential. She had suffered a lot in her youth and early womanhood, hardships, disappointments in wars and exile in the company of her husband. She was a constant companion of her husband during his exile in Sind and Persia and never left him during the dark spell of fourteen years. She stood by his father in the days of his adversity, going thirsty and hungry for days. How could then he not pay heed to his own mother's advice, he consoled himself.

Finally, he agreed. As it turned out, Hamida Banu's illness and subsequent death stemmed the rising tide of differences between father and son. But only for the time being. The rot had set in too deep.

# I

Akbar was almost drunk by now. He felt painfully lonely. He had to make his customary public appearance the next morning. He didn't want to disappoint the people who came from distant places just to get a reassuring glimpse of their emperor. He had also scheduled an important meeting in the diwan-e-khas with his four principal officers – diwan, mirbakhshi, mirsaman and sadr – after the darshan and didn't want to be late for the meeting, a trait for which he had earned respect of his council.

He tried to get up to leave but stumbled. Ruksana stepped out of the shadows to hold him from falling.

'What are you doing here? Didn't I ask you to leave me alone?' Akbar snubbed Ruksana, although his tone betrayed the gratitude he felt for her being around when he needed her the most. Ruksana helped him walk back to his bed.

'Shall I fetch someone from the harem to please His Highness?'

Akbar paused to think. He could use some company on this miserable evening. He nodded his head.

Ruksana knew her emperor's preferences for each occasion. She whispered something to the attendant who left to execute the instructions.

'I have sent for Jahanuma, His Excellency. She should be here any moment.'

Akbar seemed pleased to hear about Jahanuma. Whenever he was dejected, Akbar preferred Jahanuma's company in bed as she would quietly listen to him and also provide wise counsel. He also enjoyed her way of making love, waiting for the perfect moment during their conversation to seduce him. He needed her more than ever at this hour. He had many questions in his mind, to which he never found answers, but strangely, talking to her calmed him.

A few minutes later, Jahanuma was ushered in by the attendant only to find that Akbar had dozed off. His face appeared tense even in sleep. Ruksana appeared behind her. They exchanged glances. Both felt empathetic towards him; the most powerful man in the world rendered so helpless in the face of his duty as an emperor and a father.

# Drowned in Dance

Every day for over a decade, Nadira practised kathak under the watchful eyes of Naaz. She did not miss a single class. She had taken a liking for the form. In Kabul, it was tradition to express joy and even sorrow in the form of dance. The Pashtuns of the south had their wild and virile dances. Her favourite was the elegant Pashtun tribal dance, Attan. Attan started as a war dance that men performed before leaving for the battlefield. Over time, it made its way to weddings and other cultural festivals. Nadira had grown up watching the dance performed, starting with small and slow steps, which gradually sped up with the beats of the dhol and the sound of rubab. She loved to observe her mother dance, dressed in bright-coloured traditional clothes, in private or in the company of other women during festivals. She looked so light and happy when she moved, as if all weight had been lifted off her body. While all the women danced together, Nadira would stand in a corner, away from the eyes of everyone else, trying to imitate her mother.

When she had come to Lahore, she had brought with her the rhythms of Attan. Once, Naaz had spotted Nadira teaching Attan to Suraiya and Asma and found her movements so elegant that she had dropped everything to take her for a lesson of kathak. Naaz was a trained professional dancer and had been performing for the governor until a few years before Nadira arrived in Lahore. As her knees forbade her from performing anymore, she began teaching kathak to girls as young as eight wanting to imbibe graceful femininity.

Initially, Nadira was overcome with shock when she found in Lahore women danced in public. She had never heard of this dance form before. She found the subtle movement of the neck and shoulders intoxicating and very different from the movements she had seen back home. The throbbing of the tabla drums and the way the feet responded to it fascinated her. The tinkling of anklet bells and the synchronised music made by the heel and toe mesmerised her. She was spellbound watching Naaz dance while teaching her students.

Over time, what had begun as a pursuit in leisure soon grew into an all-consuming passion. Kathak had its origin in katha, in stories, told by ancient storytellers, kathakas, thousands of years ago. Perhaps that is what drew Nadira to learn it; she found a way of inhabiting a story and losing herself in it. It had evolved over time from a roadshow to court performances to eventually turning into an art form performed on stage. 'Now that the dance is patronised by the Mughal emperors,' Naaz told them, 'there's great benefit in learning it.'

Nadira had a natural flair for dance and it hadn't taken long for that to show. Her poise, expressive eyes and graceful movements created an atmosphere that held everyone in a trance well after she had finished performing. Naaz liked to bring people home so she could flaunt one of her best students. But she did not wish to dance for others, so it was always with great reluctance that she would perform at their insistence. Nadira also had a knack for music. She learnt playing musical instruments in no time. She could play the tabla remarkably well. She was intelligent and strictly followed Naaz's instructions. She learnt the kathas from Vidya's grandmother and remembered each story by heart. Her visits to the temples with Vidya's family and listening to devotional bhajans sitting amongst people introduced her to the holy dimensions of dance and helped her appreciate its nuances. As she learnt more, she was once again caught in the hold of Radha's fanatical love for Krishna. Radha became an obsession. In the uninterrupted quiet of her room, she would lose herself in the dance, chasing answers to the questions Radha sparked in her like a woman possessed. She would immerse herself in an illusionary love; her lover, a mirage of a man she could almost see but never touch.

Nadira once attended a festival where artists from Turkey performed the dervish dance. She was drawn to it by the transcendental similarities with kathak. She tried to find as much as she could about the dance form and did not miss any opportunity to watch the performance if she could get access to them. She learnt that in the Sufi way, the awareness of the overpowering beauty of the world fills the heart with love and opens the mind to the cosmos. The yielding of the body and mind to the powers of the earth is beautiful. In the Islamic world, movement is not just circular, whirl and repeat, but rather spiral. They grow and expand in a way that radiates from the centre out. Many forms of city order, architectural arrangement and patterns of movement, including the basic orders of music and the representation of space in miniatures, comply with such an understanding of space and time. She discovered that the dervish dance was in complete harmony with this and with cosmic movement. These influences were deposited in her subconscious. When she performed, without any deliberate effort, it was integrated in the turns and spins she would take.

I

Naaz had spotted her gift for dancing in the first few sessions. She was convinced Nadira would make a marvellous dancer. She started nurturing her talent. Soon, Nadira outclassed Asma and her teacher. Asma had been learning for many years before Nadira arrived in Lahore yet she was no match to Nadira.

One day, Naaz was woken up by the sound of ghunghroos. It was past midnight. She was irritated at her sleep being disrupted. She knew that Asma was not one to do riyaz in the middle of the night. It had to be Nadira. She decided to admonish her.

As she opened the door, she saw Nadira standing in the dimly lit room in full costume. Both Asma and Suraiya were settled on the floor ready to watch her performance. None of them noticed Naaz standing at the door.

With complete devotion, Nadira took her first delicate step, her feet making gentle contact with the floor. As if the music was playing in her mind, her body came alive, radiating grace and finesse. Her eyes, filled with passion and determination, communicated a story that could be expressed in no other way. Every movement of her fingers, every twist of her wrists, every mudra mirrored the emotions flowing through her. The intricate footwork, precise and rhythmic, filled the air with an enchanting melody of its own. Her feet, adorned with bells, created a symphony, tapping against the floor in perfect synchrony with the music. The sound resonated throughout the room, echoing the passion that emanated from each and every pore of her body.

Her body was a canvas, painting a vivid picture of devotion and dedication. Every bend and sway of her slender frame shared a tale of love, longing and joy. Her expressions, changing with each beat, reflected the depths of her emotions, captivating every element of nature around her. As she gracefully transitioned from one movement to the next, her delicate mudras, imbued with poise and elegance, spoke a language of their own, weaving a powerful narrative.

With each spin and twirl, she defied gravity, her body effortlessly floating through the air. Her energy was infectious, spreading joy and inspiration to everyone present. Her performance was not just a demonstration of skill; it was a celebration of life and love.

The intensity of Nadira's performance scared Naaz. She had completely immersed herself in the dance. She was convinced that this young girl had not only mastered the art of kathak but was also ready, through her art, to touch the souls of those fortunate enough to witness her perform.

Some of her steps and movements surprised Naaz. She had never learnt those, let alone teach. She often wondered where she had learnt those nuances and suspected that Nadira was learning from another teacher. But as far as she knew, there was no one else in the city who could teach Nadira.

## II

Zubeida had been a regular performer for the royal palace, considered one of the very best, until her ill health began to come in the way of her performances. That was when she decided to leave the court to raise a family. Her daughter Zeenat had met Nadira a few months ago and the two had become good friends.

One day, Zeenat invited Nadira to meet her mother. Nadira found Zubeida elegant and dignified. Just by looking at her, Nadira was convinced of the grace that a dancer must embody. Zubeida had been informed by her daughter of

Nadira's zeal for kathak and she had asked her to perform a few steps. After watching her dance for some time, she signalled her to stop. 'You are magnificent, Nadira. But you need to let go. Don't think and let your heart lead you. Let your soul and heart synch with your movements. I will show you,' Zubeida said, before excusing herself. She returned after a few minutes in full costume.

What Nadira observed for the next one hour was spellbinding. With every passing minute, she saw Zubeida immerse deeper in her own world. She was dancing as if no one else was present in the room. Nadira was awestruck. She did not realise when tears of ecstasy started flowing from her eyes. When Zubeida finished dancing, Nadira rushed into her arms, hugging her close as she wept inconsolably. Zubeida kissed her forehead with affection.

'Will you teach me, please? My aunt is a great teacher but the intensity you reveal I have never felt. I have so much more to learn,' Nadira pleaded.

'I am sorry, my girl, I cannot; not because I don't want to but because I get exhausted after a few minutes as my body cannot take the exertion. Dancing can be fatal for me.'

'Oh!' Nadira said, disappointment writ large on her face. She wanted to continue to plead and beg but stopped herself from being irrational and insensitive.

'I am sorry, my child, but I am sure we can talk about it, one oral lesson a week. I am sure that will help too,' Zubeida said to console and cheer Nadira.

'No, khaala, please don't be sorry. Even some tips now and then from a dancer like you will be enough to help me,' Nadira replied.

And thus Nadira came to learn from Zubeida in secret.

Nadira visited Zubeida every week for lessons. She listened to her teacher with rapt attention and devotion. After a few weeks, Zubeida instructed Nadira to perform. She wanted to find out how much of what she had taught had registered with her pupil.

Zubeida was stunned when Nadira starting dancing. She had progressed way beyond from the time she had last watched her perform. Each detail she had taught shone brightly in her movements. She was magical.

Impressed with her perseverance, Zubeida said, 'I will take you on as my *shishya*. But, wait, don't start celebrating. You will have to answer one question I ask as is customary before taking anyone as a pupil.'

Zubeida motioned her to sit on the floor in front of her. Nadira sat down on the floor, her legs folded. Suddenly, she felt nervous. What question should she expect? Millions of doubts ran through her mind.

'Why do you want to learn more than what you already know?' Zubeida asked, softly. 'Think carefully before you answer. Your answer will determine my decision.'

Nadira didn't have to think. She answered instantly. 'I am convinced that it was fate's hand that led me to dance. It is my destiny. Kathak is not just a classical dance. To me it is *ibadat*. I truly trace this divine connection to the Hindu god Krishna who, as they say, inspired one of his disciples in his dreams to preach this form of dance to celebrate him, his lover Radha and the *gopis*.'

As Nadira spoke, she appeared to gradually transform into a different person. It was as if her soul had stepped up to speak on her behalf. Her eyes glimmered with love for a divine force.

'This dance leads me to a plane where all that I don't know and am yet to experience materializes briefly; when I move, my mind in synchrony moves too, understanding love, God, the universe. I am fascinated by the eternal connection between the human soul and the supreme cosmic soul, as also symbolised by the love story of Krishna and Radha. It has moved me. The two never got married yet both represent the purest bond. For Radha, an avatar of Goddess Shakti, her lover's flute was enough to mesmerise her. Not only does their tale teach us to love but also tells us of the power of sacrifice. I want to experience that form of love through this dance.'

Zubeida was impressed. Here was this beautiful young girl devoted to dance while she should have been making friends, meeting boys her age. She took Nadira in her arms and held her in an affectionate embrace.

'I will teach you,' Zubeida announced.

Nadira was thrilled and jumping with joy while Zubeida went inside and brought a neatly folded skirt and pants and headscarf from the closet. There was a pouch containing some jewellery on the top. She offered her own costume to Nadira. 'This is yours from now as they are of no use to me. You are just about my size and they will fit you perfectly. Otherwise, I am sure your friend Vidya can help with the alterations,' she said smilingly.

Nadira was moved to tears. She bent and touched her guru's feet.

From then onwards, every week she took one lesson from her guru, keenly observing the minutest of details and diligently following her instructions to make improvements. Zubeida was a firm and no-nonsense teacher. She would watch Nadira closely and snap at her if she committed a mistake. She focussed as much on grooming her interpretation of the form, harnessing her sensuality.

Nadira did not tell Naaz about taking classes from Zubeida as she thought she might get hurt or even take affront. After her lessons, Nadira practised at Vidya's place whenever she got the opportunity.

Nadira underestimated Naaz. When she started suspecting Nadira of taking classes elsewhere, she asked Rahman to follow Nadira. When Rahman informed of Nadira's weekly visits to Zubeida's house, it became apparent that Zubeida was the one Nadira was learning from. She was angry, even hurt, that her pupil was secretly learning from another teacher, that she had the audacity to break rules and lie. But Naaz was unable to confront her because that would mean owning up that she had been tracking Nadira's movements. So she found other ways to take out her frustration on her.

'You are not paying enough attention to your reading. Your mother will be disappointed. You are not paying enough attention to your sister; she needs your time.'

She would find one or the other reason to question Nadira.

But Nadira did not let the jeering and the mocking affect her passion for dance or from doing what she cared for. Most of the times, she simply ignored Naaz, not even caring to respond. But on days she felt pushed beyond her limits, she would look at Naaz in the eye and convey her disapproval without uttering a word. It was enough to put Naaz in her place for a few days.

Naaz complained to Jahanuma every time she visited. 'Who will marry such a strong-headed girl? And if someone does, how long will the marriage last?'

Jahanuma would brush it aside. 'She will get what Allah has in store for her.'

However, Jahanuma too was worried about Nadira's demeanour. She had grown into a beautiful woman. With her doe eyes and chiselled features, buxom figure and long legs, Nadira attracted the attention of young and old men alike. Her knowledge of literature and poetry added to her sensuality. Whenever she was in Lahore, Naaz would forward many proposals for her consideration. Jahanuma had found none a suitable match for her daughter. She deserved the best. But whenever she raised the topic of her marriage, Nadira would flare up and lock herself in the room, refusing to open the door or eat anything till Jahanuma promised to not bring it up again.

# The Fateful Performance

'Nadira, my girl, the governor has appointed you to perform in front of the emperor next month,' Naaz announced excitedly one day when Nadira returned home from the library.

Suraiya was the first to begin celebrating by jumping around with joy. She struck a pose like a nautch girl, a hand on her hip and whirled around on her toes.

Asma rushed to hug Nadira. 'This is big, Nadira. It is a great honour to be invited to perform at the royal Meena Bazaar. I can already imagine my cousin dazzle the members of the royal family and nobles with her dance. And there will be many young princes too watching.' She winked mischievously.

But Nadira felt no excitement. She had never thought of performing in public. She protested. 'How can they decide without asking me? I dance for my own self, my own happiness, not to entertain people.'

'The governor's messenger came today to deliver the farman on behalf of the emperor. My contact tells me that it is the prince who inquired about the best kathak dancer in Lahore and it seems your name came up. I will soon find out who recommended your name but whoever it was has made the right recommendation. You are the best...'

'I don't care who recommended my name. They can't make this decision without my consent. I am an artist, not a performer. I am not going to dance on their demand,' Nadira announced, without waiting for Naaz to finish.

'Are you out of your mind? You should thank your stars for this opportunity. You're getting what every nautch girl ever dreams of. Don't be a snob. Have some fear of Allah!' Naaz scolded her. 'If the emperor is pleased, you may earn a handsome award; he might make you a permanent dancer in his court. Think about your future, Nadira.'

Naaz knew how intractable Nadira could be. She had to find a compelling reason to persuade her stubborn niece. 'Nadira, we may not be slaves but we are the emperor's subjects. His wish is our command, his command our privilege. This is a chance to win favour of the emperor, and it has knocked right at your door. If you refuse, the governor will be upset and the doors of the palace will shut on you forever. You are not performing for the ordinary public, you are performing for the king.'

'And you don't want all of us to miss out on the opportunity to visit the Meena Bazaar and witness its splendour, do you?' Asma said, sounding disappointed with Nadira's reluctance.

'Baji, Ammi will also be there accompanying the royal ladies. Think how pleased she would be to see you dance!' Suraiya chimed in excitedly.

Naaz was glad Suraiya had said this. She knew this was the last and only argument that could convince Nadira.

The possibilities of appreciation and being rewarded least interested Nadira but the prospect of performing before her mother was worthy of consideration. She certainly wanted to make her mother proud, she decided. She thought for some time and said, 'All right, I will perform but on two conditions.'

'Tell us,' Asma asked before Naaz could protest.

'First, Vidya will design my costume for the dance and Naaz will pay for it, and second, you will get permission from the governor for Vidya, Asma and Suraiya to watch the performance and visit Kuhs Ruz every day.'

The royal Meena Bazaar was held in the mahal during Nowruz. It was amongst the most important amusements for the royal ladies. The noble women of the harem set up their own stalls to exhibit beautiful brocades, rich embroideries of the newest fashion, fine muslin and other articles of jewellery, handicrafts and toiletries of high quality and price. The lanes were covered with carpet. Only begums, emperor, princes and some nobles could access the bazaar to purchase the goods. The earnings were given for charity. By imperial decree, the women could appear unveiled in front of a chosen audience of men. The silken masks worn all round were discarded in the evening. Sometimes, matches for marriage were seen and made here.

Naaz sat down on the divan thoughtfully. 'The second I cannot guarantee but I promise to request the governor's wife and pray she agrees. Entry of outsiders is strictly regulated. I am not certain if the governor has the power to issue invitation to outsiders. Perhaps her husband can plead with the emperor. Absolutely not for the costume; you might end up in something strange and offensive. There are rules to how a kathak dancer should dress up, and that is what they are expecting of you. I will decide what you must wear.'

Nadira put her foot down. 'I can't dance unless I am comfortable with what I am wearing. It is about me, not others. I promise you will not be disappointed. I have something spectacular in mind.'

After some pestering by the three girls, Naaz relented. She went inside and returned with a silk bag. 'This is your money, Nadira. Buy what you like.'

Nadira, Asma and Suraiya circled their arms around Naaz. The girls were overjoyed at the prospect of visiting Meena Bazaar.

'How much time do I have to prepare?' Nadira asked Naaz.

'A week. All arrangements are in place. I heard in the palace that the prince has been here for a few days now and is making arrangements for Nowruz. The emperor arrives with his entourage tomorrow. He will rest for a few days. You better start your riyaz.'

'I have so little time. I have so much practice to do. I must buy the fabric and give it for stitching. The tailor won't agree to ready the dress in such short time. But let me try,' Nadira said, seizing the pouch from Naaz. She snatched her burqa from the hook on the wall and rushed out.

I

The emperor arrived in Lahore the next day. Naaz had obtained permission from the governor's wife for the girls to watch the emperor's entourage from the roof of an office building next to the city gate. The spot provided the best view of the royal procession and a special gallery was erected for invited guests to stand and watch the grand entry from the shaded enclosure. What they witnessed was a majestic sight, with the imperial retinue and its grandeur on display. Countless military men marched in rank after rank with horses and livestock, bullock carts loaded with artillery and supplies, dozens of elephants hung with tapestry, and hunting cheetahs in golden collars wheeled in carts.

The entire city welcomed the shahenshah with the beat of drums and joyful music. Men, women and children lined the street and cheered. Nobles and beggars all cried, 'Zindabad Padshah.' Rose petals were showered on him as the king majestically rode through the city into the fort. It was a celebration none of the girls had witnessed before. At the city gate, the emperor climbed down from his elephant and kissed the soil. This had a staggering effect on the bystanders. They cheered hysterically.

Nadira was dazzled by the spectacle. She had not until then understood the magnitude of what she had hesitantly agreed to do. She realised that her selection as a performer must not have been a casual affair. The governor must have made good inquiries about her abilities and satisfied himself beyond doubt of her suitability to perform before the entire royalty on such an important day. He had never seen her perform and must have relied on the recommendation of someone he trusted. She was curious to know who that person was. She made a mental note to request Naaz to find out.

By now she was feeling embarrassed that she had reacted so sharply when she was told of the governor's decision. She felt relieved that she had relented and agreed to perform. She made up her mind to apologise to Naaz when they got back home. With her strengthened resolve, she promised herself to dance like never before, not only to not let down the governor or his wife and please the emperor, but also to make her gurus, Zubeida and Naaz, and her mother proud. From that hour onwards, Nadira immersed herself in riyaz.

## II

On the day of her performance, the Padshah arrived at the festival with the dundubhi beating, the horns blowing. The soldiers cleared the path and his bodyguards kept him surrounded. He lay languidly in the silver palanquin. Slaves hurried in the front, rolling the Persian carpets. When he rose from the palanquin, all performed kornish, offering their homage to the emperor.

Jalal-ud-din Muhammad Akbar walked steadily into the bazaar as every stall owner returned to their kiosk hoping that the emperor would swing by. Nadira rushed to the dressing room to prepare for the performance. A temporary room had been erected behind the stage for her to change. After taking a round, Akbar settled on his seat placed in front of the gigantic makeshift semi-circular stage made of large wooden planks. The stage had been covered with thick Iranian carpet. A large elevated platform had been erected for the members of the royal family in front of the stage. Akbar sat in the middle on a grand seat made of fine marble. On both his sides were set up large compartments. In one compartment sat the women of the royal family and in the other the prince, the governor and some members of the administration holding high ranks. The officials and their family members comprised the audience seated at some distance on both sides of the platform. They were in hundreds as the dance performance was the only exception during the festival when they were permitted to visit, although they did not have access to the bazaar. The stage and the seating area had been enclosed by thick fabric tied to poles.

The emperor signalled his permission to start the concert. The percussionists stepped on the stage and settled down behind their instruments. The noisy audience waited impatiently for the danseuse, chatting apprehensively about the artist whose name no one had heard.

Nadira emerged onstage looking gorgeous in a spectacular costume made of striped muslin and zarbaft. She wore as many as one hundred fifty ghunghroos on each leg. She stepped under the enormous spotlight created in the centre of the stage by hundreds of carefully arranged candles. Her costume and ornaments sparkled. She stood still, her face covered by a thin fabric donned from her head that was bowed, waiting for the chief guest's permission to commence her performance.

'Masha Allah,' the words escaped in a whisper from Akbar's lips.

'Subhan Allah! Subhan Allah!' Gasps of admiration erupted from the audience.

Akbar shifted in his seat in anticipation of the performance. '*Aagaz ho*!' he said aloud.

Nadira bowed to touch the stage and seek the customary permission from her gurus, Naaz and Zubeida, in her mind. Zubeida was not present. Her failing health did not allow her to step out of the house anymore. She had blessed her disciple's ghunghroo and granted her permission to perform. Naaz sat somewhere with the women near the stage. Nadira heard her faint voice, '*Jeete raho*,' as she blessed her boastfully. Nadira rose gracefully and folded her hands in vandana.

She then waited for the musicians to start and set the rhythm, and at the right beat of the tabla, she broke into a dance. As she continued, her dance took shape like a poem, composed of her fluid movements and rhythmically complex footwork. Her movements were delicate and steps intricate, enhanced by the sound of the ankle bells. In no time she was weaving magic. Her fast spins were delicate as well as powerfully percussive. She rendered every spin and step so fluidly that it unleashed a wave of 'wah-wahs' from the mesmerised crowd. The essence of her performance, the union of her body and mind with the realm of the spiritual and divine, expressed through her eyes, soon travelled through the eyes of her audience right into their hearts.

Akbar was captivated by the array of her movements – the pirouettes, the footwork, slender turns of the hand, diagonal gliding and the subtle statuesque poses. With every move she conveyed a sense of spatial ascent and descent lending a dramatic quality to the entire performance. He marvelled at the precise moves and a mastery over breathing techniques. He felt her gaze from behind the veil, it revealed a madness he had only ever seen in the eyes of devout artists and lost lovers.

When Nadira entered the tatkaar, the end of her performance, and the percussionist entered into the playful challenge of *jugalbandi*, the audience which had thus far sat stunned in awe broke into applause. There were rounds of tatkaar with the percussionist approximating it with his instrument. This was followed by him playing a bol on the tabla and her feet following the beats into a mesmerising choreography. Each time one replied to the challenge of the other, the venue resounded with 'Subhan Allah'. Finally, both the performers arrived at the same beat. The audience tapped their feet while seated in their positions.

Nadira had reached a state of trance now, no longer conscious of being watched and heard by others. She was unstoppable. Her flowing skirt spread like wings as she spun majestically, covering the stage from one end to the other. At one moment, she decided to improvise. She changed the order of the *bols*, inserting new ones, excluding a few and raising the tempo, emanating an energy that travelled back and forth between her and the audience. Then she added a touch of dervish. Everyone felt the atmosphere change. Loud cheers broke out from the ladies' enclosures mingled with cries of ecstasy.

As she was coming close to the end of her performance, Nadira fell to the ground gracefully. Her head bowed, she appeared to have shunned the world for a few seconds that stretched longingly in the silence, awaiting a sound to penetrate the moment they were trapped in. But nothing came. It seemed like her deep breaths alone echoed through the entire world.

Akbar was speechless. He had never seen someone dance like that. 'Subhan Allah,' he said, finally breaking the silence. He stood up. With him, hundreds of people went up on their feet, applauding unstoppably.

Nadira rose slowly. She bowed to the emperor three times and then to the audience. She turned to where she had found Naaz sitting and bowed towards her teacher.

Akbar signalled Nadira to approach him. Nadira walked confidently to the elevated platform where he sat. She paused at a distance from him and performed the kornish, her face still covered.

'What a marvellous performance! You have been blessed with a gift. Where have you been hiding?'

Nadira was still reeling from the last traces of the performance's euphoria she had been immersed in and could not understand what Akbar was saying; but she could make out that the emperor was pleased. She performed the kornish again and thanked the emperor.

Akbar pulled out one of the pearl necklaces he was wearing and extended it to Nadira. Nadira stepped forward and extended her hand to accept the gift, gratefully. Akbar gently dropped the necklace in her palms. 'Your reward. Our *durbar* may have found its new nautch girl,' he said and smiled.

Nadira was thankful for his praise but didn't like the idea of being a nautch girl for the court. She knew better than to object to the emperor. 'His Highness is merciful,' Nadira thanked Akbar and once again performed kornish. There was another round of applause from the audience.

As she was about to step back, Akbar announced, 'Henceforth, you will be known as Anarkali.'

Nadira bowed, unsure of how she felt about the title and what it denoted. Though she was aware that it was meant to be an honour, she wasn't especially thrilled that the emperor yielded the power to give her a new name and identity; she decided to express her unease about it to her mother later. Without turning her back to the emperor, she stepped back. She managed to steal a glance at her mother, whom she had spotted sitting behind Gulbadan. Jahanuma was looking at her with doting eyes and made the customary gesture to thwart the evil eye. Nadira also met Naaz's eye and saw that her face was flush with pride.

## II

Nadira rushed to meet her mother who was waiting for her outside the royal box. She ran into her arms. Jahanuma planted a peck on Nadira's forehead. 'You were outstanding. I have no words to describe it. Every single person was left hypnotised. I am so proud of you.'

'Yes, what a delightful amalgamation of dance with spiritual implications that went beyond religious confines,' complimented the governor's wife, stepping out of the enclosure to join her mother. Nadira bowed to acknowledge the compliment.

'That was one fiery performance. May Allah shower all happiness on you,' Gulbadan also appeared and blessed Nadira. 'Where did you learn this?'

Nadira offered kornish to the emperor's aunt. Before she could answer, the governor's wife pointed towards Naaz. 'From her,' she said.

It was Naaz's turn to offer kornish to Gulbadan.

Jahanuma couldn't stop smiling at all the praise being showered on her daughter. She could see this becoming a turning point in her life. She had just been conferred the title of Anarkali by none other than the emperor himself. Nadira could become a dancer at the royal palace. She would be paid well. They would be able to live together once again. This would also brighten the chances of her marrying someone from a good family ... who knows may be a nobleman too.

Her thoughts were interrupted as Nadira spoke, addressing Gulbadan. 'Her Highness, may I take your permission to leave? My sisters and friend are waiting for me to join them. We want to visit the bazaar.'

'Of course! And accept this as my blessing.' Gulbadan took out a ring from her finger and handed it over to Nadira.

Nadira accepted it respectfully. 'Your Highness is very generous.' She bowed before running out in excitement to join the girls waiting outside.

## III

Nadira was not unmindful of the significance of the title given to her by the emperor. From that day on, Nadira had another name and identity. That of Anarkali. It was laden with expectations, and she couldn't come to terms with it. She was now expected to uphold the emperor's favour by making appropriate social appearances, whenever asked. She would have to sing and dance for the royal audience especially at court festivities, whenever she was called upon to do so. All the freedom that she was able to realise through dancing was suddenly becoming a thing of the past. *Anarkali.* She was unwilling to accept it and yet had no choice.

'I do not want to be a dancing girl, Ammi. I want to be Nadira. Nadira, who loves to dance, who lives for dance but doesn't dance for an audience on command. This name feels like a lie,' she complained to her when she had found some time alone with her mother.

'It wouldn't be all that bad, Nadira. Jahanpanah's favour really is an honour. And Anarkali ... it's a beautiful name.'

Nadira had said nothing. Her mother's words were cold comfort. But her new name, Anarkali, she realised, sounded good in her voice.

# Falling in Love

Asma, Vidya and Suraiya were waiting for Nadira near the stage.

'You were magical,' Suraiya said, hugging her sister.

Asma pretended to faint. 'All the young men would be under your spell,' she said teasingly.

'Can't you think of anything else?' Nadira shot back, winking at Asma.

They giggled like little girls.

Vidya planted a kiss on her best friend's cheek. 'You were better than the best, my darling. I was watching the reaction of the emperor. His eyes were glued on you. Everyone was hooked to your performance. You looked gorgeous. And you know what, I have heard whispers that all the ladies from the palace want your dress made. Seems like I am going to be in brisk business. Thank you.' She gave Nadira a tight hug.

'Enough about the dance. Let us now go and have some fun. I am hungry,' Nadira said, embarrassed from the compliments.

'No, let us see that gift from the emperor,' demanded Asma.

Nadira produced both the gifts. 'I got another from the emperor's aunt.'

'Wow,' said all the girls in one voice, dazed by the look of the two precious pieces of jewellery.

'These are stunning,' exclaimed Vidya.

They stared at the soft, white lustrous orbs. Their shape evoked the moon.

'These are pearls, daughters of the moon,' whispered Nadira. She had gathered from ancient literature that the pearl was born of the earth's waters and the heaven's powers, fertilized by a flash of lightning. It is considered to be the daughter of the moon.

They all turned to look at her with surprise. Nadira looked at the ring closely. It had a large solitary gem planted on it.

'What gem could this be?' Suraiya asked no one in particular.

'Who cares! We will find out from mother,' answered Nadira, sounding the least interested.

'These are priceless.' Asma took the necklace from Nadira and put it around her neck.

'Be careful! It is delicate,' warned Vidya.

'You look like a princess.' Nadira hugged her cousin.

'Let us leave these two with your mother,' Vidya suggested. 'You don't want to drop them in the crowded market.'

I

There was a brief respite from the celebrations after Akbar retired to his palace. The ladies were back in their stalls to sell their goods. Stalls selling food items like kebabs, poori, dahi vade, kachoris and sweet items produced an irresistible aroma.

The girls went around the bazaar to admire the finest jewellery and silk. Finally, they stopped at the stall set up by the governor's wife.

As the girls looked at the glittering jewellery and beautiful clothes, barely able to conceal their excitement, Nadira sensed someone's eyes on her. They were insistent, wanting her to turn in their direction. She was filled with a strange feeling. She could feel their gaze caressing her. When she turned to steal a glance, she saw him through the intervening stalls, leaning against a tree in the lane beyond. She was captivated by his eyes; jet-black, longing, lonely, alight with a fire of their own. There was a childlike innocence about him. She could not turn away from him. She had never seen him before, but it seemed like he was made of everything she had conjured in her dreams. In her dreams, she had stretched out her arms to touch a man like him. She looked at him again, no longer than her shyness could let her. His companion tucked at his shoulder. He turned and walked away.

Nadira felt her heart race. Was she dreaming this moment? She could not focus on the bazaar anymore and insisted they return. Vidya agreed silently but wondered why Nadira was behaving strangely all of a sudden. The festivities would continue late into the night, and they would only get naughtier as the night progressed. Asma and Suraiya protested. They decided to stay back and return with Naaz.

The two friends didn't say a word on their way back home. Vidya realised that something had affected her friend too deeply and she did not want to break the spell Nadira was in. As they made their way back on the carriage, Nadira let the cool breeze of the night graze her flushed face. She closed her eyes, remembering those eyes that had so mesmerised here, and recalled a poem by one of the Sufi poets she most admired, Rumi: 'Close your eyes, fall in love, stay there.' She smiled to herself, almost afraid of opening her eyes ... what if all of it was a dream? What if she opened her eyes and it transpired that none of this had happened? For once, even her passion for dance seemed inconsequential in the face of this unknown craving. She would give it all up for his gaze to caress her once again.

## II

Salim sat on the terrace of his palace looking at the deserted bazaar. From where he sat, he could see that the women had retired to their room and would be back again around noon. He poured another cup of mellow Portuguese wine and sipped it slowly, thinking of the girl he had seen in the bazaar in the evening. By Allah, she was the most beautiful girl he had ever seen, and he had seen some. He could not get over her sublime beauty. Her sharp features, her large captivating eyes so deep that he wanted to drown in those twin orbs, exploring the secrets within for the rest of time and those luscious lips that mischievously promised endless delights.

He was taken in by the perfection of her body; her skin from even afar had looked soft as silk, her lustrous tresses cascaded in waves down her narrow waist, hovering over the earth on which she glided with effortless grace and confidence. Her laughter was gentle unlike the shallow laughter of the ladies in the harem. She reminded him of a rosebud yet to open its petals.

He sensed the same intensity as he had experienced when he had seen Mehr for the first time many years ago. This time the intensity was not that of a teenager in love but of a man who responds not in impulse but calmly. Soon, as the wine soothed his senses, he fell asleep.

In the morning he was woken by his valet. His mother wanted to see him to discuss some arrangements. All day Salim could not get the girl out of his thoughts. In the evening, as he sipped the mellow wine and watched the peacocks strutting and dancing as if to the tune of the water splashing in the fountains, his thoughts returned to the girl he had seen the night before. The thought of her obsessed him as nothing ever had. Somehow, she seemed familiar. He would leave no stone unturned to find out who she was. He decided and called for Mahabhat, his man Friday.

Mahabhat arrived in no time. Salim narrated the episode from the bazaar to his friend. 'Find her for me, my friend. She has consumed me. I will have no peace until I have met her,' he pleaded.

Mahabhat smiled and vanished only to return in an hour. It had been easy for Mahabhat to trace Nadira from the guest list kept by the governor's office. Only a few outsiders had been permitted access to the bazaar. One guest's name was the same as that of the dancer who performed. He had ordered his spies to ascertain the whereabouts of the girl. Soon he had all the information about her.

'Her name is Nadira Ali. She is the eldest daughter of your grandaunt's assistant, Jahanuma Ali. She and her younger sister live here in Lahore with their distant aunt. She was the one who performed that marvellous dance yesterday,' he informed the prince.

'No wonder she seemed familiar. Although no one had seen her face when she was dancing, I sensed a familiarity when I saw her in the bazaar,' said Salim, his voice full of childlike excitement. 'What would I do without you, my friend?' He patted Mahabhat on the back and smiled at him.

'Anything for you, Prince,' Mahabhat said.

Salim went to his writing desk and carefully wrote a short note. '*I cannot stop thinking of you ever since I saw you at the bazaar. Our eyes had met and that one moment was enough to cast a spell on me. You disappeared. Then I spotted you again and I felt your eyes were searching for me. Will you give me the honour of meeting you? I will wait for you in the garden of my palace in the evening. My trusted friend Mahabhat will escort you here. This is not a command of a prince but a plea from an admirer.*'

'I need one more favour, my friend,' Salim said, handing the note to Mahabhat. 'Please bring her to me only if she wants to do so of her own will.'

Mahabhat smiled and left to fulfil his friend's wish.

## III

Nadira sat in front of her mirror, applying kajal around her eyes while Asma brushed her hair. 'Are you sure I should go and meet him? That too at this hour?' she asked Asma.

Mahabhat had delivered Salim's letter to Nadira an hour ago neatly rolled inside a royal cylindrical box. Luck was on Salim's side. When Mahabhat knocked on the door, it was Nadira who opened it.

'This is a message from the prince. You may want to open it in private. He wants to meet you. There will be a palanquin waiting for you around the corner in an hour,' he said and disappeared before she could react.

Nadira was puzzled. She escaped to the balcony to read the contents of the box. The sun had set but there was enough light to be able to read. She carefully opened the box and pulled out the fine paper. She felt a tug at her heartstrings. She had been unable to get the handsome man she had seen in the bazaar out of her thoughts. Not in her wildest dreams had she imagined it was the prince of Hindustan. She had been thinking of him from the time she returned home. That he would find her and reach out was not a thought that had even occurred to her. She had made peace with the realisation that what she had experienced was a beautiful, fleeting moment. She was willing to live with it. But here was the same young man, none other than the emperor-designate himself, writing to her in his own hands and beseeching her to meet him. Such were the ways of God, she thought. Reading the letter she experienced a blend of feelings, of joy, excitement, nervousness and, to her surprise, hope. She wanted to meet him, she knew it in her heart.

She would have decided against going out but for the tenor of the letter beseeching her to meet him when he could have very well commanded or even forced her to do so. A smile appeared on her face. But she was concerned about meeting him in the night alone. She would take someone along, she decided. Suraiya was too young to come along and there was not enough time to go to Vidya's house and explain everything to her. Asma was her only option.

She looked around for Asma in the house and was relieved to find her. As Nadira had expected, she was a little too ready to accompany her for the rendezvous. 'Oh, who would have thought! Our virtuous girl is willing to meet a man, that too the prince, in the dark of the night. This doesn't happen every day! Of course I will accompany you,' she said.

As they sat in front of the mirror, Asma teased her by insinuating things Nadira was too shy to even think about. 'Don't pretend like you don't want this,' she remarked while brushing Nadira's hair.

'I am afraid, Asma. What if someone sees us? And no, I don't want this. I am only doing it because he is the prince and I don't want to upset anyone from the royal family,' Nadira insisted. 'Oh, why couldn't he wait for the morning to call for me!'

'You're no longer a child, Nadira. You know things happen in the quiet of the night; there's a reason why he has chosen to meet you now.'

That was too scandalous for Nadira to hear and she blushed. 'Don't say that, Asma!'

'You are worrying too much. Close your eyes, take a deep breath and think. Do you not want him too?'

Nadira closed her eyes and thought about the letter and the prince. A smile appeared on her face.

'See! I knew it. Your hair is done. Now come on, let us leave. We will slip through the side door,' she said and winked at Nadira, who was amazed by her decisiveness, as if she had done this many times before.

## IV

Salim stood under the canopy in his garden, waiting for Nadira, praying she would turn up. Then he heard the footsteps. He rose to look in the direction of the sound. A slightly odd-looking girl appeared. She happened to be dressed like a man. 'That's not her,' he whispered under his breath. He recognised her from the bazaar. This was the girl who was with her that day, talking and giggling into Nadira's ears, he remembered. His eyes searched for Nadira.

'She is here, don't worry,' Asma said, as if reading the Prince's thoughts. 'No decent girl will sneak out of the house at night. I had to dress up like a man so that no one would think this pretty girl was out all alone at night. I am a pretty girl myself,' she said, giggling as she unlocked her hair, teasingly.

Nadira stepped out of the shadows into the light of the lamp post. Their eyes met and he noticed a faint smile in hers. Her eyes were brown, large and intelligent. She stood at a distance. She was not frightened, Salim sensed, but her body had a certain stiffness to it as if questioning the purpose of being there. Unsettled by his intense stare, she lowered her eyes in modesty and began to bow in obeisance. It was enough to cause Salim's heart to ache.

Salim turned to look at Asma.

'Yes, yes, I will give you some privacy but don't expect me to stand here and wait in the bushes fighting the mosquitoes. Isn't there a better place to wait?' she asked, reading the signal.

Salim nodded towards Mahabhat, who was standing away from hearing range. 'My friend will escort you to my chambers. You can wait there comfortably,' he said with a smile.

'Let her stay here,' Nadira protested reluctantly.

'If you insist,' Salim agreed at once.

'You will be okay, Nadira. Don't worry. And I'm right around the corner; call for me if the prince behaves too wickedly.' Asma winked at them and walked towards Mahabhat.

'You don't know how delighted I am...'

'Why at this hour, His Highness?' she interrupted him.

'Salim. Call me Salim!' he said.

'That is not an answer,' she countered politely.

'Night is the quietest time for me. It gives me moments in which I can forget I am a prince, at the beck and call of the empire and its king. I wanted no distractions to come in the way of our meeting. And look at this garden in the moonlight, isn't it beautiful? I find my peace here, and I wanted to find you here. Thank you for coming.'

Nadira nodded.

'You can leave whenever you want to, I have a man around here who will take you and your friend home,' Salim offered.

'Thank you,' Nadira said to him, trying to relax, but her heart was beating so fast, she was afraid he would hear it. 'Should we walk?' she suggested.

Salim gestured with his hand for her to take the lead. They walked in silence, their voices not interrupting the quiet of the night. As their bodies moved beside each other, Salim slowly reached out for Nadira's hand. If she was surprised, she did not show it. She looked ahead but let her fingers playfully intertwine with his. She longed to say something to him, to make him laugh, to please him, but she could not overcome her fear. Salim, on the other hand, liked their shared silence. It seemed to have stretched the night; time had slowed down in this garden. He felt like they were the only people alive. He could live here forever.

They neared a bench and he suggested they sit for a little while. His hand rested on hers. She felt as if she had been struck by a thunderbolt. She raised her eyes and looked into his, allowing him to see past her silence and read the words she had not spoken. She felt the tremor cease. She could no longer disguise her joy. The air was cool and perfumed by raat rani. The moon looked down at them. Their breaths were charged by a yearning to embrace each other. But they chose to give it time, to let it simmer, to savour each moment and relish this longing and desire.

'How do I address you, Nadira?' Salim finally asked.

'Nadia…' She could barely hear herself.

'Nadia…' he said as he came closer and whispered it again in her ears.

'Salim…' she uttered under her breath.

They sat looking at each other. Not a word was said.

An hour flew by.

'I must leave before my aunt wakes up and finds us missing.' She tried pulling her hand away, gently. He held on to her hand, not wanting her to leave. 'Let me go, Salim, please … I've been away for too long, if my khaala finds out…'

'Will you meet me again?' he asked as she rose to leave. He let go off her hand reluctantly.

She blushed and lowered her face, shying away from saying yes but not wanting to say no. Salim came closer to her and took her face in his hands. 'I will wait for you, same time tomorrow.'

Asma appeared from nowhere, reiterating Nadira's concern about Naaz and insisting they head back home. The two started walking to the waiting palanquin. Suddenly, Nadira turned and walked back to Salim. 'Can I ask you something?'

Salim was perplexed. Before he could respond, Nadira inquired, 'Who recommended that I be invited to perform at yesterday's event?'

He smiled. 'My father had demanded that there be a kathak performance of the highest standards. I inquired from the governor. He in turn asked his wife. It appears she knows your teacher who spoke highly of your talent. I am glad she did. I must thank her. If not for her, you would not have been there in the Bazaar, and I would have never met you.'

Nadira smiled. *So, it was Zubeida!* She bowed and returned to the palanquin. Asma babbled the entire way back as she described the luxury of the palatial guestroom where she was made to wait. Nadira was too occupied by her own thoughts to hear her. She remained silent all the way, still trying to understand the feelings fluttering about in her heart. Her heart raced in anticipation of meeting Salim again. She wanted to know him; she felt a deep longing to touch him She was filled with joy and wonder and a nervousness she couldn't explain.

# Exalted Love

Time passed. Seasons changed. They fell deeply in love; she for the first time, he like never before. The taste of his lips lingered on her mouth, she missed being with him every hour of the day. The memories of the time they spent together would come to her at odd moments and she would be left blushing, trying to come up with meaningless explanations to the people around her for why she was suddenly so happy and glowing.

In their initial meetings, Nadira was nervous. Her emotions were a mix of hope and anxiety. She fumbled her words when she spoke in his presence. She still remembered how after the first time he had kissed her, she had not spoken a word through the entire evening. They had decided to meet in his garden again. There, sitting under a tree, hidden by the bushes, Salim had come closer to her, to put a flower behind her ear. He had brushed aside her hair and lightly placed the champak behind her ear. On the pretext of wanting to smell the flower, he had come even closer. He had looked at her and she had let him close his lips on her, taking soft and slow sips, like they had all the time in the world. The thought of it still made her feel as nervous and euphoric as it had that day.

From then on, she had started growing comfortable with him and more like herself. Her nervous laughter turned whole-hearted. They talked endlessly. Every conversation was a precious gift, every shared moment a treasure to be cherished. They talked of a shared future filled with love and adventure, leaving her heart aflame with the hope of a beautiful life ahead. The world had ceased to exist for them, leaving only the two in a universe uniquely their own.

His praise of her beauty and the passion with which he conveyed his love echoed in her heart all the time. She became aware of herself like never before. She saw her reflection through him. It was not that Nadira was not aware of her beauty before she met Salim. She had been mindful for some time now of men of all age eyeing her with interest. Some had even proposed to her. Many had sent her poems eulogizing her beauty. Not that those men did not interest Nadira, but her eyes were constantly searching for that one man who was able to look beyond superficialities. Someone who did not expect her looks to be the only crowning achievement of her life. She waited for the one who matched the look and charm of the prince of her dreams. Someone who was like her father, as brave in battlefield as he was gentle. Her wish list was endless. She wanted to love a man who understood how passionate she was about her dance and admired her for it.

Vidya often mocked her for dreaming of the perfect lover. 'You will only meet the man you love in your dreams because no such man will ever walk the face of the earth, Nadira!' she would say. She was in love with the younger brother of her sister's husband in Gujarat. The boy worked with his uncle as a silversmith. He was saving money to open his own shop in Lahore. He had promised Vidya that he would ask her parents for marriage as soon as he had saved enough money to relocate to her city. She was happy to spend her life with an ordinary man as long as he loved and respected her and of course let her run her boutique.

Nadira, however, was unwilling to compromise on the idea of her ideal man. She was willing to wait. Occasionally, she would let some boy flirt with her but it never meant anything to her. Until Salim entered her life. She had never felt attracted to any man the way she did to Salim. And it happened in that one moment when their eyes met in the bazaar.

She had also unexpectedly discovered the extent of her desires. Every time they kissed it seemed like lightning that lit the skies in the monsoons had touched them. She wished to be near him, skin to skin. The very thought of it set her heart beating like the drum of war. She did not know how long they could hold themselves from each other and eagerly awaited the moment when their bodies would know no restraints in the face of blazing desires. She blushed at the very thought of making love.

She also felt embarrassed of the yearnings her body felt for Salim. Only a few weeks before she met him, she had questioned Asma on the propriety of having a physically intimate relationship before marriage.

It had been a hot and humid night. Nadira was sleeping in the courtyard. Suddenly she woke up feeling thirsty and went to the kitchen to get some water. She could hear Naaz snoring loudly in her room. While returning to her room, she heard a muffled giggle coming from a room near the entrance of the house. The room was used for dumping inessential things of the household. Hearing a faint voice of a man had made her stop in her tracks. But no man lived in this house. For a moment, she dismissed the voices as a figment of her imagination. She was willing to believe that her half-asleep mind was playing tricks on her. But when she heard the giggle again, she decided to check, and she tiptoed to the room. She placed her ear against the door and tried to listen.

A man and woman were talking in hushed voices inside. She pushed open the door gently, careful not to make any noise. The room was dark. As she stood still and acclimatised herself to the darkness, she could hear the voices coming from the far end of the room. A faint light fell out from a door of another room that was left ajar. Nadira didn't know there was another room inside. She stepped forward to have a look. In the soft light of a diya, she saw two bare bodies on the bed, shining with perspiration, perhaps from the intensity of their recently concluded lovemaking. Now they lay engrossed in kissing each other. Nadira froze. She was about to turn back when the man suddenly turned slightly.

It was Rustom. Nadira was shocked.

'You are delicious,' she heard Rustom say to Asma as she started to walk away. She heard Asma giggle in reply before her voice faded.

'What the hell on earth do you think you were doing with Rustom last night in that storeroom?' she confronted Asma the next morning.

'What the hell were you doing peeping in there?' Asma snapped at her cousin. She sounded neither shocked nor surprised.

'I am sorry about peeping in. It was unintended. But aren't you ashamed of what you were doing?' Nadira asked.

To her surprise, Asma giggled. 'No, I am not,' she replied, quite unfazed. 'We love each other. We have surrendered to all its demands – making love is just one of those, a blissful experience marked by our want for each other.'

'Shouldn't there be any boundaries?' questioned Nadira innocently.

'There are none in the minds of lovers. Boundaries are created by society. It is the reason we have to meet in the dark of the night ... to hide from people because they won't understand.'

'You are being stupid, Asma,' Nadira said and started to walk away.

Asma stepped in her way. 'I will remind you of this conversation the day you fall in love,' she said, looking Nadira in the eye. 'Also please don't tell my mother about this,' she pleaded.

'How would I ever mention such a shameful thing to her even if I wanted to,' Nadira said, pushing Asma out of her way.

Nadira felt embarrassed recalling the conversation. Now that she was in love, Asma appeared to not just be right but also justified. Nothing mattered in love. She felt the same way now. Salim's touch made her succumb to an emotion she had never known before. The warmth of his flesh sparked millions of desires. She longed for him and wanted nothing more than to lose herself in him and experience the heady pleasures of that union.

When she was not with Salim, Nadira was either singing or dancing. She danced and danced in the divine circle of the Rasa every night till dawn. It too became a means through which she found she could embody and express her love for Salim.

The sudden spring to her step did not miss Suraiya's attention. She had never seen her sister spend time in front of the mirror, but lately, every time she passed the mirror, she would stop to admire herself and strike a pose, humming her favourite song.

'What is happening? Are you hiding something?'

'I am in love,' she whispered. She had been thinking of telling Suraiya about Salim soon.

'What? Love? Who?' her sister asked, pleasantly surprised.

'The prince.'

'Prince? Which prince? Why are you talking in riddles, Nadira?'

Nadira recounted to Suraiya her meeting Salim in the Bazaar and the many romantic rendezvous that had followed in the moonlit palace garden. She told her everything, holding back only details of his caresses and kisses.

Suraiya's eyes opened wide as Nadira spoke. Seeing the look in her eyes, talking about Salim, there was no doubt that her sister was madly in love. And with none other than the prince who would inherit this vast empire and its riches. She was delighted for her sister. But she was also disappointed with her for breaking rules and secretly slipping away in the night to meet her lover. Did love make one do such outrageous things? She also felt hurt that she had chosen to confide in her cousin and not her own blood sister.

Nadira hugged Suraiya, sensing her hurt and scepticism. 'I am sorry. I wanted to keep it a secret because I was scared. I wanted to be sure that it was real.'

'Is it now? Do you think he is going to marry you?' Suraiya asked.

'He says he will. But how does it matter, Suraiya,' Nadira replied, annoyed at how her sister was probing the same way Asma did. 'The love we share is what is essential to our being, and that's all I need.'

Her words disturbed Suraiya. 'Are you being fearless, Nadira, or is this just plain recklessness?'

'Love demands I be both, dear sister.' Nadira laughed off her question.

I

It was like other nights. Nadira slipped out of the side door to leave for the palace. She felt much more confident now that she had Suraiya to provide her with an alibi if needed. She was escorted to the guesthouse inside the palace complex. She was surprised to find it lit with lamps. Bouquets of flowers greeted the eye wherever she looked. A carpet of petals had been laid. The bedroom was decorated with flowers of all colours. The room was heavy with the fragrance of flowers, and she was filled with excitement. This was special. Salim entered the room from another door. Both the doors were closed gently behind them by the attendants. Nadira ran into his arms. Salim held her warmly.

'For you, my love, for you,' he spoke in a whisper, suffusing her with the longing to be held like that forever. The ornaments in his waistband hurt her. She stepped back and took it off him and flung it aside. Salim lifted her in his arms and carried her to the bed. The two lay down. The curtains swayed from the gentle wind that was blowing outside. It put out the lamps one after the other. The room was filled with moonlight and the desire of two lovers. Salim undressed Nadira languidly and admired her skin that was glowing from the soft light of the moon. Her long black hair reflected its silvery radiance in every curl as they wound down between her full breasts, along her waist, like a river flowing in the night.

Nadira brought her lips closer to his. They were entwined in an embrace and kissed each other endlessly before he took her willingly. She had resisted him for weeks, but that night she surrendered. It was a frenzied celebration, a declaration of their love for each other.

The first ray of the morning sun found the two lovers sleeping as one on a cushion of colourful flowers. The twitter of birds woke Nadira. She looked at Salim who was in deep sleep. Even in sleep, there was a faint smile on his face. She found herself naked but suddenly it did not matter. The birds outside seemed to be singing different songs – songs of joy and celebration. A soft drizzle added to the romance in the air.

She went to the bathroom for a quick bath. When she returned, naked, wiping herself with the softest towel that had been placed for her, she found Salim awake. He looked at her, admiring her in the light of day. Surprisingly, her state of undress did not bother her. Looking at her, he felt no lust or greed, only love that wanted to cherish her body and being. Nadira blushed. He signalled her to join him in bed.

## II

It was time to share the news with Vidya. She had not confided in Asma about the details of her meetings with Salim after the first two meetings. Asma was also distracted with her own matters and did not have much interest in Nadira's affair. Rustom had decided to quit the job and leave for Agra in search of new opportunities so that he could make a decent living when they got married. Asma was unable to make sense of his decision even when though he was acting in her interest. Asma needed Nadira to listen to her predicament rather than hear the tales of her blossoming romance.

Vidya was so delighted to learn the news that she broke into a dance. Like a true friend, not once did she question Nadira on why she had not confided in her earlier. Nor did she express any concerns or apprehensions about the relationship. She was excited.

'Have you slept with him?' was the only question she asked mischievously.

'Yes, I did,' Nadira answered without any hesitation or shame. She had no qualms sharing it with her best friend. 'I have no guilt, only happiness to feel. It wasn't indecent, it was an act in testimony of my love. It was sacred.'

'Silly girl, you don't have to justify it to me. But I want to know every single detail of how it happened. And don't you dare censor anything,' she said with a wink.

The friends sat on the roof and talked for hours with Vidya listening to her friend as she narrated the story from the time their eyes had first met to how they had so completely and wildly fallen in love with each other. When Nadira finished, Vidya looked at her, feeling a surge of warmth for her friend. She was immensely proud of what she embodied – fearlessness and a fervour to experience life and love with an open heart.

# Crimes of Passion

It was more than a year since Salim had left for Lahore. He had met Meherunissa before leaving, heavy in heart. 'I will miss Agra,' he had told her in an obvious reference to her. 'I will be back soon after Nowruz.'

Meherunissa had merely nodded. The emperor, and with him the city, returned three months after Nowruz. But Salim had stayed back, she learnt. He delayed his return on one pretext or the other. She had received only one message from him a few days after he had left. He had to travel to Kabul and would return to Agra soon. He had since remained elusive.

She was beginning to wonder if he had got tired of her stubborn refusal to respond to his persistent advances and eventually lost interest in her. That worried her because she did not want to lose him. She had decided to defer her decision till he was promulgated emperor-in-waiting but he had stupidly defied the emperor and compromised the prospects of his succession. She had been delighted to learn of the truce between the emperor and Salim and of his declaration as the emperor-designate. But she decided to delay her acceptance of his proposal so that he did not link it with the elevation in his position. But he left for Lahore before she could convey her acceptance of his proposal. She loved him, she always had.

But she had no intentions of marrying a prince who was out of favour with the king and may have to be on the run. She was not willing to choose a life in oblivion, away from power and pleasure.

His drinking habits also bothered her. She often blamed herself for that. Perhaps if she had married him back then, she could have controlled his vices.

Salim had first seen Meherunissa at the harem where she often visited with her mother. She was only sixteen then. Once, he accidently saw her when she was without her veil. He was transfixed. He could not get her off his mind and longed to marry her. Although he had been married to many women in quick succession ever since he came of age, not one of them was owed to love. They were all a result of his father's political stratagems. He respected his wives but could never bring himself to truly love them.

One day he landed in her house. Ghiyas Baig extended warm hospitality and invited the members of the house to introduce them. While introducing Meherunissa, he informed Salim that she was engaged to Sher Afghan Ali Quli, a nobleman. Salim was devastated to learn of the marriage. He was by then madly in love with her and could not bear the thought of another man in her life. Salim went straight to his mother and requested her to plead with Akbar. Akbar refused his plea outright, claiming it would be improper for him to ask Ghiyas Baig, knowing she was already engaged. 'He expects his father, the emperor, an honourable man to commit such a disreputable act. Ask him to stay away from her,' he told his mother in plain terms. Her mother relayed his father's advice to him adding her own counsel along similar lines. Salim retired to his chambers, abashed, and drowned himself in wine for days.

A few days later, he found her alone in the harem. High on wine, he caught hold of her hand and expressed his love for her. He begged her to call off her marriage with Sher Afghan. She remained quiet, staring at the ground but made no attempt to free her arm.

'I won't let you go, Mehr,' he said forcefully.

She raised her eyes and looked at him through the fine muslin. 'Shahzada, we must obey the emperor. I beg you to let me go. If someone saw us, we will be in trouble. My family will be in trouble,' she replied softly and left.

The emperor learnt of the episode and reprimanded him in the presence of his mother and brothers. He instructed Ghiyas Baig to marry off his daughter immediately. Meherunissa became the wife of Sher Afghan. As soon as the wedding took place, Akbar granted Sher Afghan land rights in Bengal and dispatched him with his wife to that distant province.

There was a moment when Meherunissa got carried away and was tempted to call off her engagement and accept the proposal of the prince of Hindustan. She wanted the dazzle and enchantment of precious gems and cascades of silk. But her mother talked her out of it. She feared the emperor. Her husband and many other members of their family were dependent on the emperor. Mehr's father was a loyal in Akbar's court at Agra. He was hardworking and had risen rapidly in the imperial hierarchy by sheer merit. He held the important position of the diwan of Kabul. Her brother was also employed as a courtier and was a junior member in fiscal administration. He held the potential to rise higher in rank. Both of them would have fallen out of favour of the emperor if Mehr created trouble over the marriage. She loved her daughter and did not want her to be one of the many wives of the prince. Unless she was to be made the first among equals, being a wife of the prince was of little significance.

Mehr married Sher Afghan, and they departed for Burdwan in the distant eastern province of Bengal. She left her father's haveli with her new husband and began a new life in a land rich with rivers, far more verdant, lush and wild than her childhood home. Sher Afghan was a good man and she remained loyal to him through their marriage. With her marriage, she stepped over the threshold, entering the world of the householder. Like her mother, she took charge of her own home. Her husband and father allowed her enough liberty to patronise cultural activities, and she utilized her time and resources well. While other Mughal men too gave their ladies freedom, some used the opportunity to pursue religious and literary activities, while others passed their time in music, dancing and fine arts, considered the best sources of entertainment. Mehr took up the opportunity to learn about administrative and military affairs by engaging in long conversations with her husband and her father. Over time, she acquired administrative skills and the art of marksmanship and military strategy.

She was very attractive and pursued by handsome men younger in age but she stayed loyal to her husband, allowing only Salim to venture into her thoughts occasionally. Sher Afghan was busy with his duties and had no time for romance. She often missed being the subject of the prince's pursuit.

Suddenly, Sher Afghan died and her fortunes changed. In the meantime, Ghiyas Baig had also fallen out of favour with the emperor after he was caught accepting a bribe. Akbar was unforgiving of corruption. Gulbadan invited Mehr and her daughter to return to Agra and live with her in the harem. She assured her that in time she would persuade Akbar to forgive Ghiyas Baig and re-employ him. Mehr returned to the Mughal court with her daughter. In her heart, she hoped to meet the prince again, hoping his love for her was still intact.

When she reached Agra, she discovered that Salim still felt passionately for her. Gulbadan told her that Salim had never been able to get her out of his mind. The moment she saw him, her dormant interest in the prince sparked back to life. It was as if it was only yesterday that he had proposed to her. She had aged but only grown more beautiful. Her desire to become his lover returned with full vigour. She started charming him subtly.

He too found one excuse or the other to meet her. She was polite to him but also somewhat indifferent. She did not dissuade him from visiting her but showed no signs of reciprocating his feelings. She let him speak about the books he had read or the poem he had written, politely listening and responding, but when he tried to steer the conversation towards his feelings for her, she would find some excuse to end their meeting abruptly. She did not want the emperor to think she was seducing Salim.

But Salim appeared determined. He refused to relent. For many months he continued to persist, hoping she would give in some day and agree to become his beloved. Just before he was to leave for Lahore, she had asked Salim to meet her. She wanted him to know that she was willing to consider his proposal.

I

Another three months passed and there was no news of Salim. She was now alarmed that something was terribly wrong. Had he found another woman? After all, she was a widow and not young anymore. The chances of the prince falling for another woman could not be ruled out. The thought troubled her. She could not afford to lose Salim. In her mind, she had already started thinking of herself as the next queen of Hindustan. She regretted not having been more direct in conveying her feelings to Salim when he visited her before leaving for Lahore.

Mehr had always been immensely ambitious and liked to be in control. She knew that once she married Salim, she would be able to dominate him not by her charm but her counsel. She had no plans to become another indulgent queen and spend her life in the comforts of the harem.

She decided to find out what was going on in Lahore. Mehr knew the most trustworthy source to provide some intelligence in the matter. She had found out that Mahabhat Khan's wife, Nafisa, had returned to Agra with the emperor's entourage. She was the wife of Salim's best friend. She would certainly have some information to share, Mehr was sure and sent her a message that she wanted to visit her. Nafisa returned the message, offering to visit the harem. But Mehr insisted on visiting her house. The harem had no privacy. Only the royal family could take visitors in their quarters. She would have to meet Nafisa in the guesthouse under the prying eyes and ears of the guards which posed the risk of exposing her plan.

Mehr arrived at Nafisa's house at the appointed hour with her attendant whom she instructed to wait outside. After they had exchanged pleasantries, Mehr presented a dupatta from her collection to Nafisa. Nafisa was pleased to receive the beautiful garment. They had food prepared by her cook from Kashmir. After lunch, they settled in her courtyard to drink tea.

'Why did you not stay back longer in Lahore? I have heard it is beautiful in the winters,' Mehr asked casually.

'Mahabhat wanted me to return with the emperor's entourage. It is safer to go back with his troupe, he said. Crossing some of the parts between the Indus and the Sutlej can be dangerous with rebels having taken refuge there.'

'That was a sensible thing to do. But why did he not come along,' she asked. She did not want her inquisitiveness to arouse any suspicion.

'He wanted to return with us but he could not have left Shahzada Salim behind alone. Those are the orders of the emperor. And Shahzada wanted to stay back in Lahore.'

'There must be work to finish now that he is the heir apparent performing many duties delegated by the emperor.'

Nafisa looked straight into her eyes. 'You can ask me directly what you want to know, Mehr. Why go around in circles?'

Nafisa knew about Salim's interest in Mehr. She knew the purpose of her visit and had anticipated the question.

Mehr held Nafisa's hand. 'Will this stay between you and me if I ask, Baji?'

Nafisa took a deep breath. 'Yes. But promise me you will also tell no one about this conversation.'

Nafisa sighed. 'The prince is in love. She is beautiful. She is a dancer and performed at Meena Bazaar. I do not blame him. She would have that kind of effect on any man.'

Mehr felt the ground shift under her feet. Her worst fear had come true. She nearly fainted. Nafisa rushed to get some water.

'Are you okay, Mehr?'

Mehr nodded. She felt shattered. She lay on the divan for some time to regain her composure. After some time, Mehr politely excused herself and returned to her quarters.

## II

For the next few days, the only thought that dominated her mind was how to reclaim Salim. She was taken over by a sense of entitlement; feelings of sadness, competition and anger possessed her. She knew she had no reason to be angry at the girl. Salim had every right to be with the girl of his choice. She had rejected him for far too long. But she was envious of the girl and envy knows no rationale.

To reclaim Salim, she had to get him back to Agra and do it promptly. She started thinking of a way to get him away from that despicable daughter of Gulbadan's servant. Once that was done, she would find a way back into Salim's affections. The prospect of Anarkali becoming the wife of the future emperor of Hindustan was too unbearable to contemplate.

# Turmoil

Meherunissa rolled out the first act of her plan without any delay. She met Gulbadan and convinced her that Anarkali was seducing the prince, luring him into marriage. Initially, Gulbadan did not pay her any heed. A prince was entitled to his indulgences. At the same time, she had met Anarkali. She didn't seem to be the greedy or plotting kind. Her mother was dignified and their ancestory was respectable. But Meherunissa persisted. Eventually, she succeeded in sowing a seed of doubt in Gulbadan's mind. Could it be that the two had got married secretly? Could that be the reason why Salim was not returning to Agra? More than a year had passed and Salim continued to stay back in Lahore ignoring his duties. He seemed to have forgotten about the throne. His father was also getting impatient. A fling wouldn't hold him back from returning to Agra for so long. There appeared to be some substance in Meherunissa's suspicions that Salim was hiding something from her family. There was merit in her suggestion that Salim be summoned back. She should act before things went out of hand, Gulbadan decided.

# I

Akbar stormed out of Gulbadan's chambers into the lashing rain. His attendant struggled to hold the umbrella up against the fury of the strong wind. He reached his palace fully drenched and stood shivering, not with cold but with rage.

As he entered his quarters, four slave girls appeared with towels. Two carefully patted him dry. The other two helped him into his nightgown.

'Taqliya,' he announced, demanding privacy. The girls disappeared after bowing to the emperor. He signalled for a cup of wine. An attendant appeared out of nowhere with a silver cup and a vase of wine. He poured wine into the cup and stepped back into the shadow. Akbar settled down on his favourite divan in the balcony. Rain lashed the fort with fury. But his mind was still raging at Salim. To have married without telling his parents and make a dancing girl the empress of Hindustan was absurd.

How dare that ungrateful dancing girl show the audacity to seduce my son into marrying him and dream of becoming my daughter-in-law? And that mother of hers whom I gave shelter to when she was in deep trouble ... did she conspire and plot this to rise and become a member of the very royalty she serves as a servant? She was boasting a few weeks ago of how good a dancer her daughter was and that she should be in Agra so her talent could be used to entertain the royal family and visiting dignitaries. Akbar had got the hint that Jahanuma wanted her daughter to be employed in the palace. He saw nothing wrong in a mother desiring her daughter live close by. He was even considering appointing her. But now he could see that the suggestion was not an innocent longing of a mother but a conspiracy to bring her daughter in close proximity of the palace.

How could she dare to do this? Her daughters had grown up under his mercy. How could Jahanuma be so ungrateful? But for his care, she would have been selling herself in a brothel every day. He had given her so much respect. He had spent nights talking to her, sharing even his deepest secrets. She was the only one he had spoken to about his feelings for his children. She had taken advantage of the trust and set her girl after Salim. How dare she dream of making her daughter his son's wife? He was infuriated. He wanted to send an order to Lahore straightaway to arrest the girls and put them in prison. He was hurt and angry at Jahanuma, he could not bear to see her face. He wanted her to be brought to the court first thing tomorrow and shame her publicly before throwing her in a dungeon to be left to die. He wanted to summon Salim and reprimand him. He would strip him of his title of Shahzada if he did not fall in line.

But Gulbadan had firmly counselled him not to act in haste. 'Arresting the ladies would be inexpedient as it will enrage Salim who will do something imprudent, even declare a revolt once again.'

'How can I be a mute spectator to such outrageous conduct of those lowly women? They must be taught a lesson.'

'Don't act in haste, my son. Salim is under the spell of that girl. He will have to be handled with care. A mutiny under him will not be good for the empire at this stage when your health is failing,' she advised him.

'Why can't this boy ever let me live in peace. He aspires to the throne but refuses to change his ways.'

'I can understand your pain but it will be sensible to act discreetly. We should prioritise getting Salim back in Agra and deal with the situation with utmost care,' Gulbadan said, trying to pacify him. 'I suggest you send for Salim immediately on the pretext of urgent administrative work. But don't let him get a whiff of the reason behind summoning him.'

He signalled for his cup to be refilled as he gulped down the last sip.

How could Salim even think of making that girl the empress? How could he be so immature? When would he grow up? First, he wanted to marry a girl promised to someone else. After her husband died, he started chasing the middle-aged widow for marriage and now suddenly he wanted to marry this dancer? Why was he bent upon shaming his father? When would he understand his responsibilities? His thoughts went back to their most recent confrontation which had brought them to the brink of war. He could have taken Salim prisoner for life. But he had been merciful and had even declared him future king on his assurance that he would mend his ways. But he refused to learn from his past mistakes. *What a foolish man! Completely unworthy of being the emperor of Hindustan,* his thoughts concluded.

By now Akbar had drowned a few cups of wine. The cool wine had somewhat calmed his mind. Ruksana appeared as if she had sensed his state of mind. 'Does His Highness desire Jahan...'

'No, never,' Akbar snapped at Ruksana. 'Anyone but her,' he added under his breath.

Ruksana was taken aback. He seemed furious with Jahanuma. She wondered what Jahanuma had done. She waited for the emperor's instructions but none came. He waved her away.

After contemplating for some time, he made up his mind to distract himself from these undercurrents of hostility and bitterness. He decided to make a pilgrimage to Ajmer, as he had done so many times in the past decade in gratitude, hope and prayer.

## II

Jodha was alarmed when she learnt that preparations were being made for the emperor's travel to Ajmer. She knew her husband did that when he was dejected and was looking for guidance to take an important decision. He would take the turbulence of his thoughts to this mystical spot to find answers to the many questions that haunted him. Gulbadan had come to Jodha after telling Akbar about Salim's affair with the nautch girl. While she did not doubt her motives, she was peeved with Gulbadan for poisoning her husband's mind against Salim and Anarkali without hearing their side of the story. It was a delicate matter which could get out of hand rapidly and deserved to be handled with care. She had tried talking to her husband but he refused to discuss Salim with her. He was sulking and had shut himself inside his chambers.

She feared Akbar might overreact as he was still holding a grudge against Salim. Even a small provocation could blow out of proportion. Father and son were sitting on the keg of a dynamite of tension. A confrontation would be disastrous. Her husband and son were both headstrong, not willing to give up their perspectives easily. The wounds from the murder of Abul Fazl at the instance of Salim, and the latter's rebellion, were still fresh. She feared for her son. But she could not think of a way to reason with her husband. He would expect her to stand by his side, preferring him over her son. She knew that the two loved each other but were also disappointed in each other. Akbar thought Salim was not aspirational for the expansion and consolidation of the empire. He thought he did not pay enough attention to the affairs of administration. This was not entirely incorrect but Akbar's reaction was often disproportionate. Even she was saddened by her son's fondness for wine. But that did not mean the father and son should be at each other's throats. Surely there was a better way to bridge this lack of trust.

She had pleaded with Hamida and Gulbadan to intervene. They had reasoned with Akbar and eventually negotiated for peace. Salim was declared as the emperor-in-waiting. But it didn't take long for everyone to realise that the truce was only temporary. Tension continued to simmer between them and erupted frequently into disagreements and arguments. Gulbadan was thinking more about the empire's legacy than about Akbar and Salim.

Jodha knew both her husband and son better than anyone else. She feared that if not handled with care, this development could turn into a cause for a major conflict. She lit the evening diya before Krishna's idol and sat down to pray for the matter to get resolved in a way that would keep everyone at peace.

## III

Gulbadan also did not want to take any extreme steps until Salim was back in Agra and she had heard him out. She was fond of Jahanuma but if her daughter had indeed done what Meherunissa claimed she had, there was to be no redemption for either of them. The mother seduces the emperor and the daughter woos the prince? This was sheer betrayal and taking advantage of the generosity the royal family had shown them. She succeeded in coaxing Akbar to summon Salim on the pretext of an administrative exigency and was relieved that Akbar agreed to hold any other action in the matter.

Gulbadan felt no remorse about telling on Salim. She had not disclosed to Akbar that it was Meherunissa who had discovered the affair and not her spies as she had falsly represented to Akbar. She had also tactfully painted Anarkali the villain and Salim as a vulnerable fool who had allowed himself to be seduced by her. She had certainly exaggerated the insinuations of seduction. She was mindful that she had conveyed to Akbar the unverified and unsubstantiated accusation that Anarkali was manipulating Salim into marrying her and making her the future queen. But she did not feel any regret. She was aware that Akbar would be disappointed if he found that she had acted on Meherunissa's behest. But she would cross that bridge when they arrived there.

She felt sad about conspiring against and betraying Salim to Akbar. She loved him from the bottom of her heart and only wanted him to find his happiness in becoming an effective ruler who could deal with the complexities of being the emperor of Hindustan. For that he needed a wife capable of aiding him and offering wise counsel in good and bad times. There was no other way of salvaging the great empire. Otherwise, it was sure to slip out of their hands and begin to crumble.

Gulbadan was also conscious that Meherunissa's motives were not entirely bonafide. She was aware that Meherunissa dreamt of marrying Salim and becoming the queen of Hindustan. She also suspected that she had incriminated Anarkali out of jealousy. But she did not make much of it, not because she was fond of her but because she would make a good wife and queen. She had been pleased when she learnt of Salim's renewed interest in her after Sher Afghan's death. She encouraged Salim because she could see Meherunissa had all the qualities to be the next queen of Hindustan. She would be of immense support to Salim in the discharge of administrative and military duties after he assumed charge of the empire. Gulbadan saw all the qualities in Meherunissa that were needed in the wife of Hindustan's future emperor. She was not only beautiful but also a woman of immense talent and acumen. She had mastered Arabic and Persian and studied arts, literature, music and dance. She was learning Sanskrit and other languages of Hindustan. Her insight into monetary and fiscal policies, matters of welfare of the subjects and the duties of a ruler impressed Gulbadan. She was a woman of remarkable strength and courage, qualities which in her perception defined manliness. She was convinced that Meherunissa would make a strong queen to Salim.

Salim was a man with a golden heart but he did not possess the talents of his father, qualities needed to rule the country as complex as Hindustan. This vast empire was created through the military genius of Akbar and settled by his acute understanding of human nature. It needed the skills of Akbar to not only defend his empire after his father's death but expand the domain too. Akbar disregarded all the old rules of warfare and invented his own. He used speed, fury and firepower to bend the forces of nature to his will. Battle after battle, he crossed deserts, forded rivers and led men across the land. His feats were deemed almost miraculous, leaving his enemies awestruck. His acts were not just physical bravado, they were carefully planned tactics. He showed fierce intelligence and a willingness to evolve constantly. Instead of spending his childhood practising calligraphy and learning astronomy, mathematics, history and philosophy, Akbar honed his physical strength and courage. He learned to ride and tame wild bull elephants. At the same time, he recognised that military power alone could not make the country subject to his dominion. He needed a tolerant milieu. Although his family was Sunni, Akbar made the Sufi concept of Sulh-e-Kuhl a founding principle of his law. With a mixture of political pragmatism and a genuine interest in Hindu tradition, Akbar sought to protect freedom of religion for everyone in the areas he ruled. He displayed remarkable respect for their faith. He repealed a special tax placed on Hindu pilgrims who visited sacred sites and, in later years, completely repealed the jizya. What he lost in revenue by these acts, he more than gained in goodwill from the Hindu majority of his subjects.

Salim, on the other hand, lacked the fire in the belly needed to rule an empire as vast as Hindustan. He was surrounded by advisors who were determined to undo all that his father had built brick by brick. His friends were intolerant. Akbar believed his son was not deserving of the throne. He wanted to overrule his right to succession. But Hamida, together with Gulbadan and some powerful imperial nobles, convinced Akbar that the customs and laws of the Chagatai did not permit that. They also told him it was not politically expedient to deny Salim his right. Akbar had reluctantly acquiesced to their advice.

But this new episode had angered Akbar and he was once again contemplating his decision on succession. Gulbadan was willing to plot to get her godson his legitimate right to the throne. She would not let Salim be deprived of the throne for a dance girl, she resolved.

## IV

Having been successful in ensuring Salim's return to the palace, Meherunissa now focused on the second act of her plot. She would have to draw Salim to herself and revive his love for her. She would also need to think of a way to get Anarkali out of their way, poison Salim's ears against her if need be.

She knew that Gulbadan visited the library every day for an hour. One day, she pretended to enter the library when Gulbadan was getting ready to leave. She bowed as she crossed her path. 'If Her Highness has a moment, I have something important to share.'

Gulbadan smiled to herself. *This girl is determined,* she thought. 'Sure, follow me.' She led Meherunissa to her quarters. After signalling for tea, the two settled down on the cushioned bench in the garden.

'Tell me, Meherunissa, what is it that you wanted to say.'

'What I am going to say may upset you, Her Highness, but...'

'Say what you want to,' Gulbadan cut her short, irritated by the mystery Meherunissa was attempting to build.

Meherunissa hesitated and then spoke softly. 'I have heard that the emperor had a while ago discussed in a meeting with his council the need for appointing a permanent kathak performer in the palace. He had directed that a panel of popular dancers be prepared. I have heard that Anarkali's name was added to the list on the emperor's instructions. And...' Meherunissa paused. She seemed hesitant to continue.

'Go on, tell me what you know.'

Encouraged by Gulbadan, Meherunissa continued, 'There have been rumours that the emperor is enamoured of Anarkali's beauty and that her ungrateful mother, Jahanuma, has been telling the emperor how much her daughter admires Jahanpanah and wants to perform for him, only him, whenever and as many times as he desires. The emperor appears to have fallen into the trap. Both the mother and daughter are up to something nefarious.'

Gulbadan did not believe all of what Meherunissa had said. It seemed implausible. She found Meherunissa's tact amusing, but she knew Akbar was not that naive and hence, found her claims laughable. She had been noticing for a long time that Akbar gave undue attention to Jahanuma, who seemed to be in awe of him. She could certainly use her access to Akbar to get him to bring her daughters to Agra. But that could be to get Anarkali to be around Salim but surely not the emperor. There was no merit to what Meherunissa had shared. Yet her mind went back to the way Akbar had taken the news of the affair. Could there be more to his anger than Salim's misconduct? She decided to stay vigilant.

Having set her second plot in action, Meherunissa turned her thoughts to her next move – how to get to be around Salim. She had to somehow find a way to get Salim's undivided attention. She had never felt the need to unleash her seductiveness until now. Men had one weakness: their insatiable desire for sex. A woman could always toy with that. But once she gave in, the man was back in control; and if she withheld sex, he could simply look elsewhere. What good was a power that was so temporary and frail? There were some women, though, whose hunger for power was too great, and who, over the years, through much shrewdness and creativity, invented a way of turning the dynamic around, creating a more lasting and effective form of influence. Meherunissa aspired for that kind of power. It would be tragic if Salim brought that dancer, Anarkali, with him to Agra to make her the queen. She would not allow that to happen, she vowed. She would go to any extent to prevent that.

# The Royal Summons

'Nadia, my love. I have been summoned by the emperor for a pressing matter. I don't think I can avoid going back this time. I don't wish to get ahead of myself,' Salim said, barely able to conceal the excitement in his voice, 'but the messenger hinted that an important royal announcement is under way. I think my father may finally have decided to step down. I have been ordered to leave for Agra tomorrow.'

Nadira was distraught. She expected him to leave some day but hoped against hope that he would stay on forever. In all this time together, they had not once discussed their separation. Now, in a flash, many thoughts raced through her mind. What if he was consumed by the court and forgot her? They had not discussed the prospects of marriage. Marriage did not matter to her as long as she was by his side. But what if his parents forced him to marry another woman worthy of becoming a queen? Would he continue to love her?

Seeing her slowly getting lost in her thoughts, Salim pulled her into his arms and kissed her. She did not respond, still unnerved by the news he had just broken to her. 'I will be back soon, Nadia. I will be. I can't stay away from you,' he said to assure her. 'I will talk to my mother about us. She is a fine woman. She will be able to convince my father to let us marry.'

Nadira was not listening. She was filled with anxiety and sadness. But she held back her tears; she had to be happy for Salim. The prince was finally getting what he wanted, she couldn't ever come in the way of that, she reminded herself. Her thoughts drifted to Radha and her selfless love. A touch of madness fell upon her as she recalled Radha's pure love for Krishna. She started muttering something but Salim could not make out her incoherent words. She was talking to herself now. He could only understand a few words ... *Krishna ... Radha ... immortal love...* Salim felt her stiffening. He was a little alarmed.

Nadira freed herself from his embrace. She held his face in her soft hands and looked into his eyes. 'I was thinking of Radha. She reminded me that love is immortal. I have no reason to worry. I know you will return. My love for you is eternal, Salim. I would love to be your wife, to give you children. But my love will sustain and grow and it will blossom without all of that too. I will love you even if you're far away from me. I just want to be in your thoughts, as you will be in mine; always, forever, till the end of my days.'

Salim embraced her. He kissed her. He confessed his love for her a thousand times.

While the thought of Salim going away clouded her mind, Nadira also felt happy for him. He seemed so thrilled at the prospect of finally ascending the throne. Hopefully, this would bring to an end the emotional turmoil he had been in for years.

She took his waistband and brought it close to his bosom. 'Can I keep this, Salim?' she asked, kissing the silk fabric. A tear escaped her eyes.

'Of course, Nadia, you can but you have my heart, my soul, my life. I too am taking a piece of you with me here,' Salim said, placing a palm over his heart. 'And, I will be back soon.' His eyes were moist too.

Salim picked up a box kept on the table and handed it to Nadira. 'Open it,' Salim said softly. She looked puzzled. 'Go on,' he prodded her. She opened the box carefully. It was as beautiful from the inside as on the outside, with a mirror on the inside of the lid. Tucked in the cushion of rich green velvet lay a nose pin with a sparking solitaire.

'I can't accept this, my love. It must be too expensive. I don't need this; a piece of your cloth and fond memories of our time together are enough,' she said, offering the box back to Salim.

He smiled. 'This has been made for you, only for you.'

Nadira let out a quiet sob. Salim put his arms around her and kissed her.

'You will get my letter every week through the pigeon post,' he assured her.

After Nadira left, Salim's thoughts went back to earlier that morning when the farman was read out to him. For a moment he thought of inventing yet another excuse and replying to his father that he would be delayed but decided against it. There was something about the tenor of the farman that brooked no disobedience. He sensed if he did not obey, his father might end up taking some unpleasant step. Salim did not want any trouble at this stage. He had also been thinking of returning to Agra and concentrating on his responsibilities. He had discovered true love in Nadira and spent the best days of his life with her. He was going to miss her. Never before had he met a woman like her. Her fragrance lingered on him every moment of the day. He was also keen to talk to his mother about Nadira and request her to intercede on his behalf. He wanted to make Nadira his queen.

Unmindful of the fate that awaited him, he left for Agra the next morning.

# I

Each day of separation intensified Nadira's feelings for Salim. She ached to be with him but did not allow her longing to agonise her. She was not unsure of his love for her. Doubts did sometimes rise in her mind if his becoming emperor would change him in any way. But she did not let such thoughts linger for long. The prospects of becoming the queen and living in the royal palace excited her but it was the desire to live close to her lover that enthused her more. Whenever such thoughts entered her mind, Nadira shrugged them aside. She was wary of entertaining thoughts of becoming the queen. She knew life had a way of coming in the way of dreams.

She intensified her dance practice to overcome her yearning. She found the evenings particularly difficult to get through as they reminded her of their trysts in his garden and later, in his bedroom. To distract herself, she also took to reading. Initially she would find it difficult to concentrate as her thoughts escaped her to reach out to Salim but soon literature absorbed her. She engrossed herself in the endless stories of ancient literature. She befriended the elderly librarian who translated some for her.

Nadira was fascinated most by the female characters from the epics. The most unexpected characters fuelled her. Many of these characters actually shaped the epics. But they seemed to have been sidelined or pushed to the fringe, deprived of due space and credit. It made her realise that the silencing of women was a practice as old as civilization. Women were portrayed as weak, wallowing in grief, harbouring vengeance, and waiting to be rescued – reduced to a mere symbol of coyness. The reality was different. Some played important roles in statesmanship – contributing as mothers, daughters, wives and sisters or impacting as queens, sages or subjects. She discovered that womenfolk had the economic, political, social and intellectual freedom in Vedic period. Many Vedic hymns were composed by rishikas. She read about many women seers – Gargi, Maitreyi, Lopamudra, Ghosha and Sulabha – who possessed indomitable intellect. These were perhaps the very first women who expressed and spoke for themselves.

She read with intensity the accounts of formidable women, unmindful of how they were shaping her and how that would play out in her life in not too distant a time.

## II

'You have been invited by the emperor to perform in Agra on Gulbadan's birthday next month,' announced Naaz. She had just returned from meeting the governor's wife.

Nadira was overjoyed. She couldn't conceal her excitement at the prospects of meeting Salim. 'When do I have to leave?' she asked.

'I will go with you!' said Suriaya before Naaz could answer. She was excited by the idea of visiting Agra and seeing her mother.

'A week from now,' she answered. 'A carriage and escort have been organised. And one more thing ... your performance is a surprise for Gulbadan, so you can't tell anyone why and when and where you are going ... not even Vidya. I have been instructed to tell you in no clear terms that this remains under the wraps till the day you perform.'

Nadira didn't care. She was too excited to worry about such trivial matters.

## III

The horse carriage moved at a leisurely pace on the dusty levelled road with trees growing on both sides, their branches locked in a tight embrace. Nadira and Suraiya were captivated by the countryside which kept changing every few miles. The rain fell intermittently from the time they left Lahore. When it stopped, the earth smelled heavenly. They kept stopping to appreciate the splendour of nature. During the day they rested in dak chaukis and serais, at night they stopped in the houses of people with whom her mother had made friends. All of them welcomed the girls warmly.

Nadira was impatient to reach Agra. The journey to Agra appeared longer than it actually was. She couldn't wait to be in Salim's arms. Her excitement knew no bounds. Salim had said he would show her the city and take her to Fatehpur Sikri and other places of interest around. She had heard from Salim of the royal band that played at dawn and dusk. She wanted to see and hear the instruments used in the band. She had heard they were different from those used by vocalists for accompaniment at the court and were also carried into the battlefield, to sound the battle cry. She was curious to visit the royal library, which she had learnt contained over twenty-four thousand volumes in Sanskrit, Persian, Greek, Latin, Arabic and several south Asian languages.

Finally, as they entered Agra, the girls saw, imposing itself on the horizon, the fort. Its sombre red sandstone seemed to paint the clear blue sky in its hue. The sisters watched the great fort, sighing in awe at its size and splendour, unable to imagine what it contained within. The fierce soldiers guarding it dressed in scarlet and shining armour made it a spectacle.

They were taken to the same serai where their mother had stayed when she first visited Agra. Bano and Mehar were delighted to receive them. Bano told her that according to her sources, the prince had gone hunting with her aunt and a few others and was expected to return soon. She took them around Agra. The sisters were bewildered by the grand city. The believers at the mosque raised their white heads towards the sky. The minarets pointed to heaven, indicating, as it were, that God is all high and one. The kerosene lamps lighted the streets but they were not enough. They saw men and women who looked different and dressed up differently. They heard countless languages they did not understand, saw people from lands they never knew existed and watched, hour upon hour, the great camel caravans arriving and departing burdened with goods from Persia, Bengal, Samarkand, Kashmir, Rajputana. Nobles and princes passed them by, afloat on howdahs, trailing soldiers, and women in palanquins with servants in their wake. They saw bazaars selling the riches of the world: porcelain, gold, silver, ivory, silk, rubies, diamonds, spices, slaves, elephants, horses and weapons. The bustling city dazzled them, made them dizzy.

Every morning they were woken by the dundubhi beat announcing the presence of the emperor at the jharokha-i-darshan. One day they decided to join the hundreds gathered on the maidan between the river and the fort, to catch a glimpse of the Great Mughal. Nadira couldn't help wondering when she would get a personal audience with the emperor.

A few weeks later, a royal messenger arrived. They had been directed to move to the guesthouse across the Jamuna.

## IV

Salim was lying in his tent. He couldn't sleep. The night seemed intolerably hot. The punkah swinging slowly back and forth over his bed barely disturbed the heavy air. Yet he knew what was keeping him from sleep was his longing for Nadira. He missed her.

They had been out hunting for a few days now. He was surprised when he learnt that Meherunissa had been invited by Gulbadan to be a part of the entourage. Initially he did not make much of it – he was aware that Mehr too was fond of hunting. But when Gulbadan started making obvious efforts to put Mehr with Salim when they split in the morning to go into different directions in search of game, Salim began to feel uncomfortable. She had even got Mehr's tent pitched next to his. Soon it became obvious that Gulbadan had conspired to bring Mehr along so that she could be around him and they could bond. And now Gulbadan refused to return. Salim found that odd too. She was fond of hunting but to spend that long in the jungle was unlike her. Meherunissa's presence in the party was obviously why she was prolonging the hunt.

'Mehr is a good hunter for a woman, isn't she?' she said to Salim one day.

'She must be, if you say so,' he replied briefly. He wanted to be polite but needed to convey his disinterest in having a conversation around Mehr.

'She is well read. She knows her poetry. You both must talk about it sometime.'

'Yes, I will. Now, if you will excuse me, I would like to leave.'

Even Mehr behaved oddly, he sensed. She showed a lot of interest in him unlike before. She would visit his tent on one pretext or the other vying for his attention. He didn't want to continue dismissing her efforts but he had no choice. Nadira was all he could think of. His discomfort had grown by each passing day. He was starting to suspect something was amiss. He wanted to return to Agra as soon as possible.

He raised the matter with his aunt. 'I think we should return. It is getting unbearably hot here. I don't want to fall sick.'

'We will leave in two days if you insist; although I am enjoying myself. I will instruct the staff to start packing. Why don't we have dinner together today, you, Meherunissa and I, in my camp?'

Salim was in no mood to have dinner with the two ladies. He wanted to be by himself and his wine and dream of Nadira. But out of respect for his aunt, he decided not to decline the invitation.

In the evening, after dinner, they settled under a star-studded sky to drink kahwa. Mehr brought up the topic of the upcoming Nowruz celebrations.

'What special entertainment are you arranging for Nowruz this year, Salim? I believe the one in Lahore was incredible. That dancer ... what is the name the emperor gave her...' Mehr pretended to recall her name. 'Yes, Anarkali, she was amazing I hear.'

Salim felt annoyed at Meherunissa for bringing up Nadira. Surely, it was not unintended, he suspected. He wanted to leave but before he could excuse himself, Gulbadan spoke.

'It will probably be her again dancing at the Nowruz. What a marvellous dancer she is and stunningly beautiful. Do you remember her?' Gulbadan looked closely at Salim to read his reaction.

He nodded slightly, fixing a vacant gaze on the ground.

Gulbadan continued, 'It appears that Akbar is going to appoint Anarkali as official dancer in the palace. She is an ambitious girl, of course she would want money and fame. Apparently, she was also floored by the compliments the emperor gave her after her performance and has been pestering her mother to seek this favour from Akbar.' She turned to Mehr. 'By the way, I don't know if you are aware, Anarkali's mother is an assistant in the harem library and is summoned occasionally to please Akbar in his bed.' Mehr pretended to be surprised. 'But her daughter is a good dancer and deserves that recognition. I will be happy to watch her perform here.'

Salim's eyes had narrowed and his body stiffened. He got up abruptly. 'Goodnight. I must sleep now.'

Back in his tent, Salim poured himself a generous cup of wine. What he had just heard had left him perplexed and confused. He was shocked to learn that his father was going to appoint Nadira as the official palace dancer. But what bothered him more was the insinuation that it was Nadira who had sought this position using her mother's influence in the palace. He knew Nadira was passionate about kathak but she hated performing in public. She had no interest in compliments or rewards. For her, dance was a way to connect with the divine. His heart refused to believe that she was seeking the status of the court dancer. Nadira had no desire for fame. She just wanted to be by his side. At the same time he was surprised to know of his father's interest in Nadira and her mother. He felt restless. He couldn't sleep. He sat on the bed, sipping wine till sleep came over him.

# An Obstinate Daughter

Jahanuma stood shivering before Gulbadan, her head bowed in shame. She couldn't believe what Gulbadan had just told her. Her own little Nadira luring the shahzada into love and dreaming of becoming the queen of Hindustan. She had been meeting him secretly in Lahore, without letting Naaz get any wind of it. And did that wretched Suraiya know? Why was Ruksana's informers not able to get a scent of this? Tears filled her eyes. She had worked so hard all these years to save money for the marriage of the two girls. She had been looking for the right match for Nadira. She had never imagined things would turn out this way. All the dreams she had for her daughter were crumbling before her. Gulbadan told her that Akbar was enraged and that Jahanuma should be prepared for the worst for her daughter and herself. It would be an exemplary punishment, she was warned.

'Tell me honestly, Jahanuma. Did you know about this or not? Don't lie because I will find out the truth any which way.'

'Her Excellency, believe me! I did not have the slightest clue. Even in my wildest dreams I wouldn't have the courage to imagine that my daughter would try to seduce the shahzada. I have served you with honesty and respect. You have been kind to me. I will not deceive you for anything, at any cost. I am ashamed of my daughter and apologise on her behalf. I plead for your mercy. I will go back to Lahore tomorrow itself and we will all leave for Kabul. I will get her married off as soon as I reach there. I promise she will never look in the direction of Agra. For the sake of my husband's family who served the emperor's father with distinction, I beg your mercy for my daughter. But if the emperor must punish, please let me plead with him that he have my head instead. I beg you to take pity on us!' she pleaded, falling to the ground on her knees and placing her head on Gulbadan's feet.

'It is beyond me, Jahanuma. The matter is now in the hands of the emperor. No one other than him can decide what fate awaits you and your daughter.'

'Can I meet His Highness once?' she implored.

'No, leave now,' she commanded.

'I beg you, Her Excellency. You are the only one the Padshah will listen to. He will not refuse your wish. I will take Nadira away. No one will ever know of our whereabouts. Please...' she begged, refusing to move away from Gulbadan's feet.

'I couldn't help you, Jahanuma, even if I wanted to. Pray to Allah if you expect the emperor's mercy.'

Gulbadan turned and left the room. Two guards entered and led Jahanuma out.

Ruksana stepped back in the shadow. She noticed from a distance the guards pushing Jahanuma into her room and taking position outside. She had been placed under house arrest.

I

They walked in the shadows, circling around the quarters to reach the guesthouse across the Jamuna. Ruksana led the way, pausing occasionally to confirm they were not being followed.

Jahanuma was deeply moved by Ruksana's gesture. She had put her own life in danger by arranging for Jahanuma to meet her daughters. After she had been detained, Jahanuma lay on the bed crying inconsolably when Ruksana entered from the door that led into the courtyard behind her room. She placed a finger on her lips, signalling her to stay quiet. Holding her hand, she led Jahanuma into the bathroom and whispered in her ear, 'Gulbadan lied to you. Your daughter and the prince are in love with each other. But Gulbadan and Meherunissa are conspiring to get the prince and Meherunissa married. The prince loved her at one time. Gulbadan has poisoned the emperor's ears with all kinds of misinformation to show your daughter in a poor light. I have heard even Jodha has bought their lies. She also agrees with Gulbadan that Meherunissa is the right match for her son.'

Jahanuma was relieved to learn that her daughter was innocent. But she was filled with anger now. Gone was her respect for Gulbadan. She also felt betrayed by Akbar. 'I don't care who the prince marries but why punish my daughter? She is a young girl,' she whispered.

'Nadira is here in Agra.'

'What?' Jahanuma said, unable to keep her voice down.

'Shh...' Ruksana said, her wide eyes asking her to stay calm. She continued, 'Gulbadan has summoned Anarkali to perform on her birthday. Your daughter has no clue about what awaits her. Salim has no inkling of the conspiracy Meherunissa and Gulbadan have hatched. Gulbadan lured him away from Agra on a hunting trip and took that manoeuvring Meherunissa along so that she could seduce the prince and corrupt his love for Nadira. They returned to Agra two days ago. Salim doesn't have a whiff of what is happening. He does not even know Anarkali is here. No one is allowed to meet him or Nadira. He has been sleeping in his palace all day and drinking through the night. He has no idea what his godmother is plotting. They propose to humiliate Anarkali by making her dance in front of everyone, in his presence. The prince himself may be arrested so that he does not challenge the emperor. I am sure they have thought through all the eventualities.'

Jahanuma was shocked with what she had heard. She could not think properly.

Looking at her confused state, Ruksana decided to offer some counsel. 'Jahanuma, my advice is that you talk Nadira out of this love affair. We are common people. Our lives hold no value for the emperor. If he is angry with Anarkali, he will not rationalise it. I am sure Akbar is more disappointed with Salim for ignoring his duties because of Anarkali than angry at your daughter. Gulbadan won't let Akbar hurt Salim. But your daughter will get caught in the crossfire. They know Salim is stubborn and getting Anarkali out of his mind forever is the only way to get his attention back to the empire. You must plead with Anarkali to seek forgiveness from Gulbadan and beg to spare your lives. The ways of the royalty are strange. She must accept the reality. We don't know if Gulbadan will relent but that's our only hope. Ask her to tell Gulbadan that the three of you will go away without telling anyone about your whereabouts and never contact Salim or anyone again.'

Jahanuma hugged Ruksana. 'My daughter has a mind of her own. She is stubborn but I will try. If she is truly in love with the prince she will stand her ground against the might of the emperor without caring for her life.'

'You will have to manipulate her somehow. Ask her if she wants to be responsible for the death of her mother and sister for no fault of their own. That is the only thing a possessed lover might consider.'

## II

Ruksana's confidant waited at the hidden exit to the banks of the Jamuna. He stepped out of the shadows to unlock the door. A boat was waiting to take them across the river. The boatman rowed them across swiftly, careful not to attract the attention of the royal guards.

The guesthouse was in darkness. Ruksana signalled Jahanuma to go in through the rear door. 'You have an hour. Be back in time. I will return to take you back to your quarters. Keep your voice low when you talk. If you are caught, all of us will lose our heads,' Ruksana said, moving into the shadows.

Jahanuma stepped inside and closed the door gently.

Suraiya sat next to a lantern, reading a book in its light. Nadira lay on the bed looking at the roof, rolling her locks around her finger, humming a song. Both were startled when their mother entered the room. She dimmed the light and sat down against the wall, facing her daughters. The two girls jumped with excitement and rushed to hug their mother. The three wept with joy.

Jahanuma wiped tears from her eyes and turned to Nadira. 'Why did you do the forbidden, Nadira?' she asked, her voice trembling out of fear for her daughter even as she whispered.

'Did what?' Nadira looked at her mother with surprise.

'Don't pretend. I am talking about your affair with the shahzada.'

Nadira was taken aback by the tenor of her mother's questioning. 'Who told you about it?' she asked anxiously. 'And why do you say it is forbidden?'

'It does not matter who told me. The emperor knows about it. Gulbadan and Jodha know about it. This foolish sister of yours knows about it, I am sure,' she said, giving Suraiya an angry look. 'Only I don't. And in a few days the entire city will know of it when Akbar confronts you in open court after your performance. The emperor has been made to believe that you have been seducing the prince because you aspire to become the queen of Hindustan. What trouble you have got all of us in, Nadira?' She started crying.

'This is ridiculous, Ammi. You know your daughter better than that, don't you? Do you really think I will stoop so low?' She took a deep breath and continued, 'I did not fall in love with a prince or the future emperor or his position or stature. I fell in love with Salim. Yes, I love him, Ammi. I really do but not because he is the prince. Salim is the man of my dreams. He loves me too. We have been with each other for months in Lahore. I have told him endlessly I have no interest in his wealth or his empire. I have told him I dream of living a simple life with the man I love, not in a palace surrounded by hundreds of people. I am aware he has many wives but I also know he does not love even one of them. Suraiya is my witness, ask her. Salim wants to marry me. He knows he will have to convince his family but he does not foresee a problem. You are doubting the intentions of your daughter, Ammi? You would rather believe these rumours ... these rumours that sound like whoever let them out wants to sabotage the love Salim and I share!'

Nadira fell silent. How could one convince another of the love between two people? That's something only those fortunate enough to experience love would know. And even they would not find the words to express themselves. How could she tell anyone of the magic of that moment when her eyes first fell on the man she loved? When she had no idea of who he was. What is it that made her fall in love with Salim? Her mother called it forbidden. In the eyes of everyone around her it was that, she knew. But how could she tell anyone about how she had grown in love and through love? How it had given her wings and taught her to be selfless. She felt it in her bones – this extraordinary empathy for the world. How can something that made you grow, that made you fearless be forbidden for the soul? Yes, it was bad for the social order she and Salim inhabited. But she did not feel any resentment towards anyone for that. That is what love had given her. It was the fearlessness that love had imbued her with that made her unafraid of the consequences. In any case, she did not desire a conventional marriage – her love was like that of Radha's. She sought love without the pursuit of its conventional fulfilment. She had cherished the privilege of being in love. Becoming one with him in spirit had been the ultimate goal – which she had achieved.

Jahanuma broke into her thoughts. 'I know you speak the truth. But it does not matter what you or I or even the prince thinks. Gulbadan and Jodha are not in favour of your liaison with the prince. Gulbadan wants him to marry Meherunissa. The emperor will abide by their wishes. Their mind is made up to put you out of the prince's life. We will all be imprisoned or killed. Our lives do not matter to anyone. And before that you and your mother will be humiliated in front of everyone. We will be labelled ungrateful, even traitors responsible for tarnishing the reputation of your forefathers. No one will even mourn for us. We will be forgotten the next morning. The prince will rave and rant for a while, but he will find himself helpless and eventually give in and marry Meherunissa. He will do it in the interest of taking the legacy of the Mughals forward.'

Nadira hugged her mother warmly. 'Mother, you are overthinking. Salim will sort out everything. Salim is on a hunting trip. The guards tell me he will be back tomorrow. I have left a message for him and I am sure he will come rushing to see me.'

'You are naive, my child. Salim is already here. He has been here for a few days. They will not pass your messages on to him. No one is allowed to meet him. He will not know you are here till he sees you walk into the hall to perform. He will be confused, even angry. He will protest in open court. That is what Akbar wants to do ... provoke him. If he misbehaves in court, it will be an act of defiance. It will show him in poor taste in front of his family and members of the senior administration. Akbar will then get a right to bargain with him for the throne. Can't you see how well this has been plotted? This is not about you or Salim, Nadira. It is about the prince. It is about Hindustan. It is about the future ruler of the empire. It is about the throne. Howsoever much Salim may love you, he won't forgo the sceptre of power for anything, not even for you. Do you think you are more important to anyone out there in that palace than the throne, stupid girl?'

'I do not doubt his love for me, Ammi. I definitely don't expect him to choose me over the empire he is promised. That would be foolish to even suggest, but I am convinced he will find a solution. He does not need to abandon me or marry me. I can love him all my life just living by his side.'

'Shut up! What a hopeless romantic and idealist you have become. Do you really believe your notions of love will convince the emperor? You are such a bright girl; why are you behaving so foolishly in love? We have only one way out of this. Let us beg Gulbadan for mercy tomorrow. Tell her you will not come in the way of the prince and Meherunissa. Tell her you will walk out of Salim's life.'

'I will not do that, Ammi,' Nadira replied bluntly. 'Why should I pretend? Why should I beg for mercy? I love Salim. He loves me too. Why should I seek forgiveness for loving him?'

Jahanuma turned to Suraiya helplessly. 'What do I do with her?'

Before Suraiya could say anything, Nadira shot back, 'As a child I worshipped you because you were the bravest woman I had known. Now you are telling me to surrender my love to save my life. What is the point of living if my pride is dead? I am sure the emperor will relent; he can't be that cruel, but if he has made up his mind I am not the one to be afraid of punishment. I have the courage to stand up for myself.'

'You may not be afraid of dying for the sake of your foolish ideals but what is the fault of your sister,' Jahanuma said, pulling Suraiya into her arms. 'I too don't care if I die. I have lived my life. But both of you have your entire life ahead.' She started sobbing again.

Ruksana had been listening to the conversation outside. She stepped into the room. 'We have to leave now,' she said, addressing Jahanuma. 'There is a lot of commotion in the palace. Apparently, the emperor is agitated and throwing tantrums. He might ask for me.'

She turned to look at Nadira with respect. She certainly was made of steel. But the poor girl had no clue of the ways of the palace. She put her arms around Nadira affectionately and whispered, 'I have spent my life around women claiming or believing to be in love. I have been that woman myself. I have no doubt that your feelings for the prince are pious. But you must know, my girl, that the court's ways in the matters of throne and women are merciless. It has shaped the lives of generations of princes. All decisions and actions are influenced by the politics of succession and often, women. To rule, to hold the sceptre of power is expected to be the only ambition of a young prince. Salim is no different. He has nurtured the dream to sit on the throne from the time he learnt to walk. He will not give it up for anything. He will also not let you go. He will disobey and rebel. There will be a fight. A lot of blood will be spilled. Do you want to be responsible for all the bloodshed, for the death of so many lives, making so many women widows, so many children orphans? Do you really expect him to give up everything and live an ordinary life? He may even be persuaded but that won't last too long. He will be ridiculed by his own people for being a coward, a weakling. Would you rather have a husband who gets his due place in the annals of history or one who is mocked as a misguided lover and a coward who did not fight for the throne which was rightfully his? Akbar is old. He will not be able to hold on to the reins for long. Rebels will get emboldened. This great empire he has built with so much hard work will disintegrate. Both Akbar and Salim will die every day watching it crumble. The very love you speak of will become a poison. You don't have to learn the hard way, Nadira and make it difficult for you and your family. I am giving you my sincere advice – forget Salim; ask for Gulbadan's forgiveness. She might relent. Try convincing Jodha you will disappear and never contact the prince again or let him find you. She will be sympathetic. She is herself a devotee of Krishna. Perhaps she will be able to prevail over Gulbadan and let you go. Else be prepared for the three of you to rot in jail for life.'

Nadira was listening in silence. The look on her face changed as Ruksana spoke. There was no fear, sorrow, anxiety or regret. It turned cold. Finally, she spoke like a girl possessed. 'The earth is testimony to our unshakeable love. Like Radha loved Krishna, I love my Salim…'

'Have you lost your mind, Nadira,' interrupted Jahanuma. 'Fairy tales are fine but…'

Ruksana waved at Jahanuma to keep quiet.

'…Radha is no fairy tale. It is no myth. It is real. Her love is pure, unconditional and unmatched. It transcends to a spiritual and divine level. Their love is a metaphor for the love between a devotee and the divine characterized by complete surrender, selflessness and eternal longing. Like Krishna is to Radha, my every thought, word and action revolves around Salim, constantly seeking his presence and craving his affection. I have no guilt and only happiness to feel. My love for him remains unwavering, unchanging and boundless even in the face of death. I see it as a union of two souls, not just bodies.'

Nadira paused for a moment. Suraiya hugged her sister. Jahanuma looked away and started sobbing inconsolably at her daughter's brazen and unashamed claim of her love. Ruksana was moved. She felt the pain in her voice. She wanted to help her but felt helpless. She resigned Nadira to her fate. Her pain was for her to bear, Ruksana thought. Love, joy, even sorrow, can be shared and experienced with others, but pain is a demon to be fought alone. It will not be coaxed away; it clings to us with a strength of its own, she thought. She had herself lived with it for years.

Nadira turned to Ruksana and asked, 'Can I meet Salim once, just once … please, khaala?'

'It is impossible,' replied Ruksana, politely but firmly, touched by the way Nadira addressed her. She hugged Nadira again. 'Even if I manage to reach out to the prince, he will want to come rushing. The spies will inform Akbar at once. You will be taken away and imprisoned before he reaches anywhere close to the guesthouse. Don't even try anything like that. You can't imagine the power of the emperor.'

As the two older women turned to leave, Nadira spoke. 'I will do as you ask, khaala,' she addressed Ruksana. She then hugged her mother. 'I love you. I won't let you down.'

Jahanuma knew her daughter well. She was no damsel in distress to shed copious tears. She would not give up her love. Like her father she would prefer to die defending her love even in the face of the empire's might. She would not compromise on the dignity of her love even if she was not able to get her way with the emperor. She was not one to express regret for a love she believed to be divine. Jahanuma knew they were doomed.

# The Manipulated Decision

Nadira wrote a letter to Jodha Bai the next morning and requested the guard to deliver it. She refused.

'There are strict orders. We are not allowed to do anything for you. The orders come from above,' she said.

'But it is just a letter, to the queen herself, the wife of the emperor. It is very important that it reaches her. If she learns that you refused to take this letter to her, she will be furious,' Nadira reasoned with the guard.

The guard was hesitant but finally decided to deliver the letter. A messenger arrived a few minutes later. The queen had agreed to meet her and was arriving in the guesthouse shortly, he announced.

Sometime later, Gulbadan walked in followed by Jodha Bai. Nadira was not expecting Gulbadan but did not reveal her disappointment at seeing her.

'*Salgirah mubarak*,' Nadira addressed Gulbadan, bowing in respect but not performing a kornish.

'What do you have to say, Anarkali?' Gulbadan said, ignoring Nadira's wishes and taking charge of the conversation, underlining her status by addressing her as Anarkali.

Nadira refused to be provoked.

'Her Highness is so very powerful. You could have imprisoned me in Lahore. Then why summon me here and embarrass your own great-godson?' she asked with her head still bowed.

'You do not deserve an easy punishment. It has to be exemplary so that no one else ever dares to conspire like you have. You will know soon.'

'Pardon me, Her Highness, but how is loving someone truly a conspiracy? And will Her Highness keep her hand on her heart and say if I have...'

'How dare you?' Gulbadan thundered. Two soldiers from the harem came rushing in, but Gulbadan waved them away.

'Forgive me, Her Highness, but I love Shahzada Salim and he too loves me dearly. If he tells me to get out of his life, I will leave without a word. Let it be his decision.'

'I cannot let him decide a matter which affects not just him but the whole empire and its future. Not when he behaves like a young boy blind in love. He can fall in love with whosoever he wishes but the marriage of a prince is not his private affair, it is a matter that concerns the state. His marriage is not just a romantic liaison. There are many questions attached to that decision and choice. What does she bring to the empire? Wealth? Power? Land? A political alliance? Will marrying her make a friend of an enemy? We must gain something out of his marriage. I have no objection to him being in love with you or you loving him back. But love does not sustain the empire. You are a nautch girl, a slave of his father. He has a number of young girls to please him and you're just one among them. He cannot marry everyone he sleeps with. How foolish of you to even consider that!'

Nadira remained unperturbed by the provocation. She argued respectfully, 'I am aware I am an ordinary person, Her Highness. But I make him happy. Is that of no significance? Does it not matter at all? Is there no value to Salim's happiness?'

Gulbadan snapped back. 'It might make him happy but you don't realise the pain and hurt it will bring with it. He is distracted by your beauty and has been ignoring his duties. He has been spending time playing with you for months and shamelessly overlooking the affairs of the empire he has to inherit and administer. That is reason enough to remind him that this affair must be put to an end.'

Nadira turned to Jodha, her lover's mother whom Salim praised endlessly. She looked beautiful and had a regal air around her. True to her name that meant a warrior, she held her chin up. She had a sense of elegance and authority around her which came from her position in the court and not being the emperor's wife. For a moment their eyes met. Nadira detected a faint sadness in them, not for Nadira but perhaps for her son. There was kindness in her eyes but behind them she perceived the glare of strength.

'Her Highness, you are his mother. Don't you care for him? Do you also put the court's needs before the needs of your son?'

'Maybe your love for my son is genuine,' Jodha said with a sense of authority but a tinge of regret laced her words, '...and which mother will be unhappy if her son finds true love. But this is not about my son, it is about Hindustan and the future of this great land. The emperor has ushered in a semblance of order and unity in his empire. Salim's father is a military leader of genius but he is also an able ruler who has earned the trust of such a vast country. If anything threatens the foundation of all that he has struggled to build, no one in the royal palace can abide by it. It would amount to treason. Nothing is of more value than the word of the man who sits on the throne, not even my son's happiness.'

Nadira listened with rapt attention. Jodha continued, 'The emperor is agitated. He thinks you have lured his son, the heir to his seat, and holds you responsible for distracting him from his duties. In his anger, he might order your arrest or even execution.

He may harm Salim. That could lead to a whole world of problems. Without a capable heir, the safety of the empire and its people is at risk. It is not only the two of you who stand to lose, Nadira.'

Before Nadira could respond, Gulbadan said, her tone more compassionate this time, 'Not only does the empire need the full attention of the king, it also needs a queen who can be of assistance to him. Look at Jodha. She shares the emperor's responsibilities, looks after trade and commerce. She is one of the only four members of the royal court to have the rank of 12,000 mounted warriors. Salim is a man with a gem of a heart but it is also true that he does not have the qualities to match his father. A mother's heart may find it hard to accept but I have no hesitation in admitting that Salim is not his father. He will need support to manage the affairs of the empire. He needs a queen who can share his responsibilities, who knows the ways of the empire. You will only be a distraction of which his detractors will take advantage. The empire Akbar has built with his blood and sweat will wither away. Salim needs a formidable woman well versed in the ways of administration and military as his partner.'

Jodha stepped forward and placed both her palms around Nadira's face with affection. She looked into her eyes and said lovingly, 'My child, I remind you once again, if his father denies Salim what is rightfully his, I know Salim will wage war against his own father. Salim can't defeat Akbar. And Akbar won't spare his son this time around, for the mutiny. There will be blood in this palace and out on the streets. One of the two will die. Likely, your lover, my son. Do you want to be responsible for the death of the man who you say you love so much, and who you claim loves you equally? Do you want to deprive your lover of becoming the future ruler of this country?'

Nadira found her world falling apart. Her only hope was Jodha Bai, and she too was convinced the affair must end.

Nadira saw the logic in Jodha Bai's reasoning and for the first time a sliver of doubt made its way into her heart. She felt torn between her longing to spend the rest of her life with Salim and her inner voice that nudged her to act in his interest and that of Hindustan even if it meant sacrificing her own desire.

Her legs felt weak and she could barely stand. Jodha held her and helped her to the divan.

'Think about it with a calm head and heart, my girl,' Jodha said, offering Nadira her shoulder to rest her head and cry.

'I have only one wish,' Nadira said, suddenly getting up on her feet. 'I want to see him once…' she pleaded '… one last time. I will walk out of his life after that.'

'No. We cannot allow that,' Gulbadan replied before Jodha could say anything.

Nadira turned to Jodha. 'I assure you. I promise I will not tell anything to him. I won't mention our meeting and conversation to him. Trust me! I just want to spend a few hours with him before I go away. I swear in the name of Radha and Krishna I will not say a thing to him. You are yourself an ardent devotee of Krishna. You know how Radha felt for Krishna. My love for your son is no different. I promise you I will go away and live the rest of my life loving him from a distance, never to see him again. Please,' she pleaded.

'Let her,' Jodha said politely, looking at Gulbadan. There was something about the way she said it that made it impossible for Gulbadan to overrule her. She left the room without saying a word.

# The Stubborn Lover

Salim jumped out of his divan when his qorchi informed that one Nadira Ali from Lahore wanted to meet him. 'She is putting up in the guesthouse across the Jamuna and claims you know her well. She says it is urgent,' he said. For a moment, Salim couldn't believe he had heard the message right. He asked his qorchi to repeat it. 'Are you sure she said Nadira Ali?' he inquired.

'Yes, His Highness, that is what she said her name is,' the qorchi replied, surprised by the prince's reaction.

Salim discarded all thoughts about Anarkali wanting to become a dancer in her father's court. In any case, he had never been able to bring himself to believe any of those accusations. At this moment, he did not care about them at all. He just wanted to be with his Nadira. If he felt the need, he would clarify it with her when they met.

Salim gulped down the remaining wine and called for a mirror. His eyes looked tired but proud. His moustache had overgrown and dominated his face. He had shaved only in the morning but could see hair already sprouting on his face. He placed his turban and adjusted it sideways in his typical style. His face gave away no signs of anxiety. It was the face of a general tanned and scarred in battle yet glowing in pride and self-esteem. He picked a cup and splashed some water on his face.

At the riverbank he handed the stirrup of the horse to his attendant and boarded the royal boat to take him across. He could see from the distance Nadira and Suraiya sitting on the steps of the rest house waiting for him.

Nadira came running into his arms when she saw him get off the boat. 'What are you doing here? How...' he asked her.

Suraiya blushed looking at the two of them. She went inside, leaving them with some privacy.

'I have missed you,' Nadira said, melting into his arms. She looked at his face and ran her hands through his unmanageable locks and kissed him, disregarding the shocked guards. Strangely, Salim felt the same nervousness he had sensed when they had kissed for the first time.

The sky darkened. It looked like it would rain. She gazed towards the palace visible between the trees.

'Isn't that your palace? Take me there,' she said, almost whispering. Salim found her behaviour a bit strange.

He helped Nadira get on the boat. The guards helplessly watched their prisoner walk away. They sat down with Nadira clinging to him, unwilling to let go. With great difficulty she had been able to extract permission to spend one night with the love of her life. She was going to make the most of every single moment of it. Salim was perplexed with Nadira behaving quite unlike herself.

His palace lay further up the river. It was a spectacular building resembling a waterfall flowing down in steps to the edge of the river. The entrance was at the highest level. Each step had gardens filled with flowers. Nadira showed no interest in them. Salim realised she was not even looking at anything.

Taking her arm, Salim led her inside the palace – a dazzling cornucopia of silver candle-sticks, gold cups, silver plates and mirrors, tubs of coral, topaz, boxes of necklaces and rings, Turkish and Chinese porcelain. Nadira did not give any of it even as much as a glance. None of it interested her. She had no desire for such wealth. To her the palace seemed like a golden cage from which no one ever escaped. It would be hard for love, loyalty and trust to survive amidst such wealth.

Inside his bedroom, his strong and steady hand guided her to him. Before he could speak, she kissed him deeply. His lips tasted of wine. The feel of his breath healed her. She paused. Looking into his eyes she whispered, 'Make love to me. We will talk after.'

He was taken aback by her brazen demand for lovemaking. He could sense Nadira was in a frenzy. On other days, it would have been appealing; but today, seeing a cloud of unexplainable resolution and sadness loom in her eyes, he was concerned.

The soft glow of the lamp illuminated them. He de-robed. His silken wrap fell away as he knelt and then lay on the bed. She undid the fastenings of her dress, and wriggled from it like a beautiful snake sloughing off its skin. Salim admired the soft pearl-like sheen of her flesh. He could not take his eyes off her. She walked towards him. His eyes searched for the birthmark on her side, a little mark beneath her breasts. It was an unevenly shaped circle, dark red in colour that almost appeared brown on her skin. He had discovered it the first night they had spent together and loved it ever since.

She lay beside him and felt his body. It had changed a little but it was still firm and muscled. She took his hand and placed them on the hard tips of her nipples. She held his other hand and ran it down over the rich swell of her hips guiding it between her thighs. Salim kissed her mouth, then the velvet hollow between her breasts, and the flatness of her belly, sliding down to the lush flesh of her rounded thighs.

It had been long – how long? Months now that they had made love. He sighed her name as he kissed her neck and caressed her breasts. Her skin felt just as he had imagined, warm and yielding. Nadira's body ached and yearned to have him inside her. It was her turn to say his name. 'Salim,' she whispered in his ears. Salim barely heard her. Her body beneath his felt slippery with sweat. As Salim entered her, she let out a moan, and he went in deeper and deeper until the night was drowned in their shuddering sighs.

He rested by her side. 'You have only grown more beautiful, Nadia,' Salim turned to speak to her. 'What is it that bothers you, my love. What sadness has consumed the light in your eyes?' He leaned across and kissed her eyes. 'Today, you look at me as if you will never see me again,' he said, looking into her eyes.

'You are even more handsome than I remembered,' she said, ignoring his question. 'Your face is tanned. Where have you been?'

'I was out hunting. The sun was too harsh. Forget that, tell me, how come you are in Agra suddenly, unannounced?' he inquired.

'No, I only look at you so intently because my eyes are not large enough to see all your loveliness. I want to look and keep looking,' she replied in answer to his earlier question.

'What's bothering you, Nadia, my darling? You are hiding something, aren't you? I can sense something is wrong. Tell me what it is that is troubling you. Why are you staying in the guesthouse and not with your mother?' He blurted out all these questions at once. What Gulbadan had said also resurfaced in his mind.

'I am here at the invitation of your father to perform at Lady Gulbadan's birthday to entertain his guests,' she said, her voice choking.

Salim sat up. 'What? Why didn't you tell me earlier? I won't let you dance in front of everyone. You are my beloved; you are no longer Anarkali. You are the future queen of this empire. I will talk to my mother first thing tomorrow. She is very sweet. She will be embarrassed and ask my father to make some alternate arrangements. I can't understand why no one mentioned this to me. I could have stopped this.'

Salim looked at her closely for any trace of lie. He found none. Her eyes only carried love for him.

*How innocent he is,* thought Nadira, *having no idea of all the plotting by his own family.*

'No, Salim, promise me you won't. I am an ordinary person; I don't know the ways of the royals but I don't want the emperor to take offence at a refusal of his request. He may take it as a defiance of his order, an insult to his aunt. This is not the time to tell him or your aunt about us. We must wait for the right moment. I am yet to tell my mother about it,' she said, looking away pretending to adjust her earrings.

'I can't let this happen, Nadia. My future wife will not dance in front of everyone tomorrow,' he said, getting up.

Nadira held his hand. 'You are not going anywhere. I am still not done with you,' she said, pulling him back to bed.

She had to stop him somehow from leaving. Tears rolled down her cheeks into the hollow of her neck. Through the tears she felt his mouth on hers. It was not gentle but harsh with passion. They made love again, forgetting everything else. Breathless and spent, both lay in each other's arms. Salim felt relieved. All the doubts created by Gulbadan had lifted.

Looking at Salim as he fell asleep, Nadira felt a deep longing to etch every detail of his into her mind. She embraced him. The day seemed charged with a sense of unutterable sadness as she tried to comprehend the inevitability of their separation. She reminisced about their shared moments, trying to find solace in the comfort of past joys. In her sorrow was the quiet acceptance that she would have to let him go.

Nadira embraced him for a final time, savouring the closeness, before reluctantly releasing her grip. She got up and quietly left the palace.

## III

Back in the guesthouse, Nadira settled down on the steps and stared at the rising moon. She felt a profound sense of loss. A breeze wafted from the river. The sun was setting on the horizon and the cattle were returning from their grazing. She could see in the distance the dust raised by a herd of cows returning home. A time when lamps were lit and plants watered before the sun disappeared. A slave girl arrived and lit the lamps and placed candles in the recesses. The light flickered on her face. She smiled at Nadira. Nadira smiled back.

Nadira thought of the following morning, of her performance. A determined smile appeared on her face. She would give it her all, she decided. She would dazzle and enchant the emperor and all those who wanted her out of Salim's life. She performed riyaz all night, determined to outclass herself in what she feared might be the last dance of her life.

# The Defiant Dance

Nadira stood in the middle of the Palace of Mirrors. Her figure reflected in all the mirrors that lined and covered the sheesh-mahal. There were several jharokhas with latticed screens. The small mirrors reflected the light filtering through the jali screens and created a dazzling effect. She wore a tight scarlet bodice that revealed the slenderness of her midriff and the muscled flatness of her belly and the wide, many-pleated dancer's skirt in emerald green silk edged in gold braid that fanned and flared outwards when she whirled. She wore around her neck the pearl pendant Akbar had gifted her in Lahore and the nose pin Salim had given to her the day before he left for Agra. She stood in perfect poise. The entirety of the hall was covered in her reflection.

The emperor sat on an elevated throne. The punkah of peacock feathers stirred the air in his face. He seemed to have aged swiftly in the last three years. She had heard that at court the seniority, influence or proximity of officers and relatives to the emperor could be measured by the protocol of seating arrangement. But this was a private event for the family with only select guests. To the left of the emperor, on a chair placed on a platform at the same level as of Akbar, sat Gulbadan, upright and alert. Her eyes gleamed with the prospects of a mission on the verge of being accomplished. Jodha Bai sat on the right of her husband, sad and exhausted. Others sat on rows of chairs arranged on both sides of the hall, leaving space in front of the emperor vacant for the performance.

At the far end, the musicians were seated on the floor facing the emperor. She could also see her mother amongst the many servants standing behind the royal women, her head held high and the look in her eyes blessing her. There was no shame or fear in those eyes. A faint smile appeared on her face. She felt no fear.

She noticed Salim sitting on the first chair in the front row. His presence reminded her of the cool and soothing taste of his mouth on her from last night. It was the first time she saw him dressed as a prince as required by protocol. He wore a turban of scarlet silk from which sprang a long plume of nodding heron feathers. On either side of the feathers, set in claws of wrought gold, were a ruby and a diamond, each the size of a walnut. In the middle, holding the feathers in place, was a brooch set with a great, glittering emerald. Around his waist, he wore a belt of gold studded with diamonds and rubies. A three-strand pearl necklace hung about his neck. His fingers too were weighted with rings. But his face was sad. He looked with disapproval at his father and aunt.

Their eyes met as she looked at him through her thin veil. His eyes were full of love and longing for her. She gave him a reassuring look even though she was aware this was probably the last time she would see him. He nodded, unmindful that those looking at any mirror would have seen the trade of affection.

Akbar nodded. A woman made an announcement about Anarkali, her talent as a dancer, emphasising that the emperor had given her the title of Anarkali and that she was officially a palace dance girl because of her title. Salim flinched at the insult inflicted on her lover, but Nadira did not care.

She performed kornish, first to the emperor, and then to Gulbadan, in gratitude of the title and the opportunity to perform before them. They did not acknowledge her. Nadira looked at Jodha and bowed. She lightly nodded her head.

Gulbadan gave Nadira permission to start dancing. 'Nacho,' she said.

Gasps of surprise escaped some women in the hall at the insult hurled on the girl. The customary respectful word used to invite an artist to start a performance is '*aagaz ho*'. Gulbadan had deliberately chosen the disrespectful way because she wanted to pull down Anarkali's performance to the level of an entertainment. She did not want to give her the pleasure of elevating her dance to the status of art.

Nadira was infuriated. She had been willing to overlook her own insult but to belittle the divine art was deplorable. Her anger, supressed so far, was ignited by the disrespect inflicted on the art she considered as godly. She performed the customary rituals remembering her teacher, Zubeida and this time, also Radha. A faint smile appeared on her face.

She turned towards the musicians and bowed. She signalled to them. The three nodded their heads in acknowledgment. Nadira raised her arms and began to sway. No music accompanied the sinuous motion of her body, only the clash of her heavy bracelets and anklets. Her nimble form moved effortlessly across the hall. Her movements became free and wild. She began tossing her head from side to side and then started to spin, bare feet stamping on the white marble as she turned. All the guests watched mesmerised. She danced to the music of her soul. Such was her energy that everyone in the room could imagine the music she was dancing to.

Then one of the musicians started playing the tabla, followed by another and then the third began beating on the tabla before him with his fingers. The rhythm was thunderous as she whirled faster and faster, arms outspread. Her body swayed to the rhythm of the music. Her delicate arms and fingers traced patterns in the air, as if painting a masterpiece only she was able to see. Her delicate footwork, twirls and spins created a mesmerising rhythm and even as her feet made contact with the glittering marble floor it was as if she was floating on air, defying gravity with her supple movements. Her flowing attire, adorned with intricate embroidery, mirrored the magnificence of her surroundings, catching every glimmer of the golden sunlight that bathed the room. The glass walls, glistening like a thousand diamonds, reflected her every motion, amplifying the allure of her performance. Each twist, each turn revealed the raw emotion that encapsulated her dance, evoking a myriad feelings in all those witnessing it.

Not once did she face or lock eyes with Salim. She effortlessly weaved through the room, her gaze locked on an invisible partner, as if engaged in a conversation with the music itself. The melodies guided her with their enchanting charms, and she reciprocated with her own artistic interpretation. Every movement exuded a sense of passion, melancholy and unyielding strength.

The guests, awed by her beauty and skill, could not help but be captivated. Time seemed to stand still as she continued on her celestial journey, a solitary figure casting an ethereal glow in the heart of the shimmering palace. She captured the hearts of all those who watched, drawing them into her world of grace and boundless emotion. They had never witnessed anything like this before. She danced like a woman possessed.

For a moment even Akbar forgot his dislike for Anarkali and allowed himself to immerse in her concert. Her dance was even more elegant than what he had witnessed in Lahore but Akbar could sense undercurrents of defiance in it. With each graceful turn, her dance was unfolding like a story, a tale of devotion, love and rebellion. She was like a vibrant flame determined to burn in the midst of a turbulent tempest. In the palace of glass, her undying spirit danced with a fervour that commanded attention. Her dance reflected in every direction that Akbar turned to. Anarkali held the palace hostage to her craft. At one point, he met her eyes. She saw him in a mix of anger and shame, and what, for a fraction of a moment, she thought was admiration. He looked away.

Nadira was unstoppable. It was as if she was etching her performance into every mirror of the sheesh mahal for all times to come. Like the story of her beloved Radha, she was determined to become part of legend. Posterity would talk of this performance and not know if it was myth or reality.

The interplay between his father and Nadira did not escape Salim. Nadira had more courage than him, he thought.

Nadira noticed someone tap Salim on his shoulder and whisper something in his ear. Salim rose and left after bowing to the emperor. She was exhausted. She entered the final act of her performance.

As she whirled, she approached the dais where Akbar and Gulbadan sat and dropped slowly to her knees while continuing her movements. She improvised her dance and pretended to slit her with a dagger and looked at Akbar as a direct challenge. At that very moment, drained from her own madness, she fell on the floor, unable to stay on her feet any longer.

Gulbadan was livid. She saw how Nadira had succeeded in turning the tables and emerged triumphant. She had made Akbar feel like he was standing in the volatile space between his son and his lover. This could complicate things, she thought. Nadira had successfully played with Akbar's mind. Akbar was fuming by now. He stood up. With him stood everyone else in the room. There was no applause. All awaited the emperor's next move.

Had he taken a moment to think, perhaps Akbar could have forgiven Anarkali. He admired her craft. He was, after all, a lover of arts. But in that room stood an Akbar who was enraged at his son, who was furious at the future emperor for being so reckless. Most of all he was angry at the impediments like Anarkali that came in the way of his blood's legacy. He also couldn't forget how her mother had betrayed him. No woman could ruin the empire that he had so painstakingly built. There was no way she could take away the prince from his father and from the throne. His anger also stemmed from the way Anarkali had expressed her defiance and challenged him through her dance. He felt dwarfed.

*'Zinda deewar main chunwa do,'* he bellowed, commanding Anarkali's death. He was the emperor and the lives of his subjects were at his mercy. Impulse governed the emperor, and it disallowed forgiveness for Anarkali. A deafening silence fell in the hall, broken only by the muffled sobs of Jahanuma.

# Confrontations

Salim was enraged at being tricked by his father to step out of the performance just before he ordered Nadira to be arrested. He was told there was an emergency as a theft had taken place in the tahkhana of which he was in-charge and the emperor wished him to investigate it at once. As soon as he stepped out, he was escorted to his palace by a contingent of armed guards and confined there. The guards had been ordered to not let him leave the palace at any cost. Mahabhat came to meet him after some time and informed that Nadira had been arrested in open court, chained and dragged out. Arrangements were being made to confine her in a dungeon in Fatehpur Sikri till she was tried for treason.

Salim was infuriated. 'Treason? Has my father lost his mind? Is loving me treason?' he shrieked. Salim was angry at himself. He could have prevented today's catastrophe if he hadn't listened to Nadira last night and met his aunt instead. If he had made an effort to stop the dance. But he had overslept. He couldn't have slept for so long after just one glass of wine. Was something put in his wine to make sure he slept long, he wondered. He was woken up by his valet with some effort and told that he was required to be seated in the hall before his father and the chief guest of the day, her aunt, arrived. He was expected to follow the protocol.

He gulped down another cup of wine. Every word of disapproval and humiliation that his father had ever hurled at him raged in his mind. He remembered the letter his father had sent him during his aborted rebellion in Allahabad.

*My son, son of an unfortunate father, you challenge the authority of the emperor of Hindustan, an empire your ancestors and father have built with their sweat and blood. You impatient and foolish man, you shame the great race of Timur who have never killed their own. You make your mother miserable who has only but fed you her milk and loved you selflessly. I am here only to defeat you and drag you back to Agra so that all may see the fate of a traitor. I would have taken you down before sunset tomorrow but your grandmother has, in her illness, given you a few more days of freedom. I must return to attend to her. If you feel the faintest of remorse, surrender and return to Agra. Seek forgiveness in your prayers, if you have not forgotten how to pray in your greed for a throne that was yours to earn and not snatch. If you do not surrender, I will be back to serve you justice.*

Every word his father had ever said pierced his heart like a burning knife sliced through the skin of a tender dove. He buried his face into the soft pillow and howled like a child. He missed his grandmother. If Hamida was alive, this day would not have arrived.

There was commotion outside. A moment later, Gulbadan walked in followed by Jodha Bai. Jodha hugged Salim.

'You have lost weight. Haven't you been eating on that hunting trip?'

He remained quiet, angry and defiant.

She continued. 'Sheikhu, my child, why do you do this? Defying your own father every time. He took many pilgrimages and made many sacrifices to bring you into this world. He did not let you leave his lap for a minute. He loved you like nothing else existed around him. Why do you have to keep hurting him like this?'

He was puzzled, still unable to fathom how falling in love was an act of defiance. Before he could ask, Gulbadan stepped forward and raised his face gently by putting her palm beneath his chin. 'Look into my eyes and answer. Do you not love any of us? Are you so blinded by your love for that dance girl, daughter of a slave, that you have forgotten your responsibilities to the empire, your family, your dynasty? Are you blind to how this compromises your case for inheritance?'

'She is not a dance girl; you have forced her to become one. She never wanted to be a performer. And her mother may be your attendant but that does not make her your slave. We love each other. Don't I have the right to choose my life partner? Didn't my father marry whoever he wished?' Salim retorted, controlling his anger but his voice trembled with rage and hurt. 'My father has spared no opportunity to humiliate me since I was twelve. I have swallowed my pride and ignored his insults. But why is Nadira being punished for all this? Why humiliate her like that? Why make her wear that cheap dress in the presence of so many people and make her look like a lowly nautch girl? Why arrest her and involve her sister and mother in this? This is between my father and me. Keep her out of this.'

'Every girl on this earth dreams of becoming your wife because that will make her the queen of this rich land, of the treasures you will inherit. Look into the depths of the love that has swayed you and you will find it's not as pure as you think it to be, Salim,' Gulbadan said firmly.

'What a pity! You think everything is governed by the motives of power and rank and riches? Nadira is different. Her love for me is pure. My feelings for her may waver but hers are etched in stone,' Salim answered.

'You have been shirking your duties. This is not *mohabbat*, it is madness. You sound like a foolish lover, not like an emperor-in-waiting of a vast empire he has to run when he takes charge. Your love is dangerous. Take her as your concubine. But don't wish for more. Be prepared to become a *sanyasi* otherwise, and wander the land in a sackcloth with your beloved. Love is not for princes and emperors. You can only marry a girl befitting the heir of Hindustan. Do you not want to succeed your father? Your father will be more than willing to reopen the closed subject, to reconsider his decision of making you his successor.'

Salim was enraged. 'Why does my father assume that I will not be able to rule the empire? When did I fail to prove my abilities? Is it my drinking? Is that reason alone to deprive me of the throne?'

'You have no control on your drinking but leave that aside. We do not doubt your abilities. You fail to appreciate what we say.'

'I see no reason for us to discuss this further. If the battleground has to be covered in the blood of our own men on both sides, so be it.'

His mother stepped forward and took Salim into her arms. 'Sheikhu, your father is devastated by your behaviour. You misunderstand your father. Even today he loves you like he did the day you were born. He forgave you and accepted you back. It is still not too late. I plead with you to seek his forgiveness. He will forgive you. He loves you too much. There is no way you can win a war against him. He will not hesitate to kill you on the battleground. If nothing, just think of me, Salim, your poor mother. I cannot lose my husband or my beloved son.'

'You have no choice, Salim. I say it again. It is in your interest, even Nadira's, and of this great empire that you forget her. Keep her as your concubine. But marry you must a girl who we think is best suited for you. Concentrate on your duties as a prince – as the successor of this great empire,' Gulbadan added, determined to change Salim's mind.

However, Salim was beyond all persuasion. He was angry and let that alone be his guide. 'I am not afraid to die. To die fighting, at the hands of my brave father, will be an honour. I am willing to seek forgiveness for my mistakes in the past, but I will not apologise for my love. I will not let go of Nadira,' he said and stormed out.

I

The royal trumpeters announced Salim. Jodha followed him, hoping to calm him down as he headed to his father's chambers. Akbar's bodyguard frisked Salim for weapons and took his ruby-and-gold-encrusted dagger. Salim did not protest. Satisfied that there were no more weapons, he let him in.

Jodha opened her mouth to speak but Akbar waved her quiet. She stepped back. No one could dare to disobey the emperor. Not even his wife. Akbar looked at Salim with piercing eyes which seeked answers from him to many unspoken questions. Akbar maintained his silence, giving Salim the chance to say his piece.

'Why are you using Nadira as a means to punish me? What has she done?'

'Punish you?' Akbar smiled at the absurdity of Salim's accusation.

It infuriated Salim even more and he launched into a tirade. 'Why have you constantly tried to deprive me, your eldest son, of the right to succeed you, breaking the Chagatai and Timurid tradition of succession? Why did you pitch others to compete with me? You let Abul Fazl speak ill of me. Are you so naive that you believe your own son would poison you? You humiliated me in front of all the members of the court, the family, everyone.'

Akbar remained quiet, but his expression was cold and Salim suddenly realised the weight of the words he had just spoken.

'My son, have you now forgotten how to talk to your elders?' Jodha rebuked him before he could say more. 'How dare you talk to your father like that? Remember, it is you who crossed the line when you decided to rebel. You have defied your father too often, Salim. And now you stand here accusing him,' she thundered.

Finally Akbar made a move. He walked up to Salim and spoke in a low, heavy voice. 'You have wanted to sit on the throne as if you are entitled to it. But have you ever considered if you are worthy of it? If you are not wasting your time getting drunk, you are out chasing dance girls. When have you ever focused on the duties given to you? I have had no prejudices against you. I have watched you to assess you. When I prayed for your birth, I was praying for my successor. And all you have shown me are half-hearted efforts ... It embarrasses me to even call you my son.'

Salim stood in silence, his eyes stone cold but filled with tears. Akbar knew he had hit his mark. He moved away from him and spoke calmly.

'I am willing to put all of this behind, for one last time, for the sake of my blood that flows in your veins, and give you my throne but on one condition. You will marry Meherunissa next week and from then on you will work closely with me and perform all the duties demanded of a prince.'

Salim realised how his father lacked all feeling. He had no regard for love. All he could see was his own way being followed by everyone, his son included. That is all that mattered. Salim decided this was not the time to stay quiet.

'I speak to you as your son and only as your son, Father ... as a son who has grown up in your arms and under your care. A son to whom you gave the best education, whom you taught to fight men and cheetahs, learn many languages, read books, appreciate the beauty of poetry, whom you taught to stay tolerant of the faith of others, to respect elders and above all to be the proud son of Akbar. I am even grateful to you for what you did not give me even when I asked. I am convinced you turned me down only in my best interest even though my reaction then may have been naive in the face of your refusal.'

Akbar listened, his face refusing to give away what was going on in his mind.

'But it is unacceptable that you treat with so much contempt a helpless girl and humiliate her in court. With no consideration for the fact that this is the girl your son loves. What is her fault in all this, Father? She only fell in love with me. It is not her fault that I happen to be the prince.'

'Is that all you have to say?' Akbar asked.

'You have been an idol for me, Father, for I do not know if there walked another man on this earth as great as you. You were so busy expanding our borders and establishing the vast empire you have built that I never had the opportunity to sit around a table and hear from you what your vision for Hindustan was. Yet I learnt so much observing you from a distance. You ordered and we obeyed. I learnt the art of negotiating treaties and winning over adversaries but not how to talk to my father. I could never discuss my feelings, doubts, dilemmas and anxieties with you. This void reflected in my actions. But I must speak up now because I love Nadira. Please leave us alone. She will be a great wife, a great daughter-in-law and an even greater queen.'

Akbar started prowling from one end of the room to the other, his hands clasped behind his back. He paused to look at Salim. For a moment, the prince saw a hint of love and admiration in his father's eyes. He was sure his own eyes would have conveyed his love and respect for his father.

Akbar paused. He looked his son in the eye. 'I pity you; I really do. My son, the shahzada of Hindustan, on his knees for a woman. Whatever happened to your Gurkani blood? Where is your manliness? Has that woman made you so dumb that you can't see the daylight around you? Don't you realise what it takes to expand or even hold on to this empire? All you care about is that woman and wine? Is that the man who will hold the reins of this great civilisation?'

'Pardon me, Your Highness, you talk to me as an emperor while I speak to you as your son. Does the emperor have no place for love in his heart? Can the emperor not be human?'

'You disappoint me. You always have ... a weakling...' Akbar said, his voice expressing his disgust.

Salim was angry now. His father continued to insult and provoke him. He could not hold himself back anymore. 'Is that so? Then why trick and arrest me? Why not fight me like a brave man, why show might on that helpless girl who came to Agra at your invitation? Does it behove of a great brave king to trick a young girl? It is your blood that flows in my body. I will fight for my own honour. I would rather die at the hands of my father, the Padshah, than let down my true love!'

'What honour do you talk about? Is it honourable to declare war on your father for the throne? Is it honourable to confront your elders like this for a dance girl? Is it honourable to put this great empire at risk for a girl?'

'What should have I done then? Stay a mute spectator as you mocked me, humiliated me all these years?'

'How dare you talk to me like that?' Akbar roared in anger.

Silence fell in the room. No one dared to speak when the emperor was angry. Salim looked at his mother. Her eyes pleaded with him to stay quiet.

Akbar turned and stormed out of the room. Jodha shuddered. She looked at Salim.

'Think hard about what I said, my son. You have a duty to your ancestors, to your elders, to your people. Don't let love cloud your judgement. I like Nadira. She may make a great wife and daughter-in-law, but she cannot be the queen you need by your side.'

## II

Back in her palace, Jodha settled down in her prayer room. It was not the first time she had sat in front of her Krishna, praying for clarity and guidance. To her, Krishna was the embodiment of love and compassion, and by connecting with him through prayer, she received his blessings and wisdom. Today, she asked her lord why he was repeating history. As a young girl, her father had made her sacrifice her love in the interest of a larger good. And today she had asked her son to forgo his love in the interest of the empire.

Jodha was reminded of her childhood spent in the picturesque palace of Aamer. It was not a very luxurious palace like the one she lived in Agra but it was beautiful in its own way. As was the practice, her marriage was arranged when she was a child, with Ajabgarh's Rajkumar Rattan Singh. She was barely eight at the time. She had accepted him as her future husband. As she stepped into her teens, she was in love with him, waiting to be by his side. But by then the empire had expanded and reached her doorsteps. Her father was aware that there was no way he would be able to defend his little fiefdom from the mighty Akbar. He thought it wiser to extend a hand of friendship to the emperor and proposed her hand in marriage with him in exchange for sparing his kingdom.

Jodha was shattered. She had only dreamt of marrying Rattan Singh. She was angry with her father for using his own daughter as a pawn to save his kingdom. Her mother tried to reason with her father but to no avail. She even suggested Jodha elope. Jodha thought of consuming poison. But soon she realised that her father had not made this difficult decision to bail out the kingdom but to save the lives of hundreds of soldiers in battle and to rescue the women of Aamer from death by jauhar. She was heartbroken but she was not a coward. She relented and agreed to marry the Mughal king. But she placed two conditions before Akbar before agreeing to the marriage. She should be allowed to continue to practise her religion without any restrictions. And she should be allowed to carry the idol of her Krishna with her and be permitted to install it in a temple in her living quarters. Much to her surprise, Akbar had agreed.

After her marriage, he extended to her full respect and privileges. He never questioned her way of life based on her faith. Time passed and she became a seamless part of his life. Whenever she looked back, she realised that her marriage, though the result of a political alliance, had in fact been a happy one. She had no complaints. Akbar had proven to be a great husband. She witnessed building of the entire empire, from city to city, monument to monument. She had no regrets. She had lived her life with dignity as the queen under the kingship of its greatest ruler, Akbar the Great, and she could only thank her father for that. She realised the importance of political exigencies and why sacrifices had to be made for the larger cause.

The only thing which troubled her was the tension between her husband and her son. Over time, they had developed a complicated relationship that oscillated between deep love and extreme dislike. The father made it apparent with his actions. Salim responded by indulging in heavy drinking and opium addiction. Jodha fasted and prayed for things to get better between the father and son. But her unflinching loyalty had to remain with her husband. When Salim revolted, she stayed back in Agra to be by her husband's side, which, as Krishna guided Arjuna, was her Dharma.

She concurred with Gulbadan that if the empire was to remain with the Mughals, it needed a strong leader after Akbar. Sadly, Salim did not have the qualities of his father. He needed a strong wife by his side, not a romantic lovebird. Meherunissa was the right choice for Salim if he was to rule successfully as emperor. She was a woman of immense talent and acumen, and also remarkable strength and courage. Her marriage to Salim was not only in his interest but also that of the empire.

But at the same time, she could not bring herself to accept a young girl being punished for falling in love or Salim being treated harshly for loving an ordinary girl. She had allowed Hamida and Gulbadan to counsel her husband but she decided it was time for her to confront him as the queen and as a mother.

## III

Akbar had just finished his dinner and was sitting in the veranda mulling over the events of the day when a messenger walked in.

'Forgive me for interrupting your thoughts, Jahanpanah! The subedar wants to meet you. He says it is urgent.'

Akbar nodded his head and the subedar was let in. 'I am afraid it is bad news, my lord! The prince escaped from his palace a few minutes ago. He held a meeting with a few generals in the outskirts of the city. They are planning to march to Fatehpur Sikri to free Anarkali.'

Akbar was enraged. He thought for a moment and then said decisively, 'I want to meet my military council in the diwan-e-khas in one hour from now.'

As the subedar left, Jodha walked in, unannounced. She had also learnt of Salim's escape. Akbar looked at her and said, 'Look what your son has done again. He continues to test my patience.'

'Akbar, calm down.' In the privacy of their bedroom, she always addressed him by his name. 'We must not let this escalate. I want to talk to you about something important but promise that you will listen to me with restraint,' she pleaded with him.

'Not now. I have to go for this meeting...'

'No, you must listen to me,' she said, firmly this time. 'You have to listen to me. I am your wife and the mother of your son. I am your queen. I have a right to participate in any decision that concerns our son,' she said, assertively.

Her tone made Akbar stop in his tracks. He sighed and sat down.

'I will go and meet Salim now. I have already sent my trusted guard to meet and inform him that I am on my way and that he should hold any action till I come and see him. I know he will wait for me and not disrespect his mother. I will persuade him to reconsider his decision to march to Fatehpur Sikri. I want you to promise me you will wait for my return and not take any decision until then.'

'How can you trust him after knowing all that he has done?'

'I speak not as Salim's mother but as your wife, Your Highness. And I am determined to leave now. If you must stop me, ask your guards to arrest me,' Jodha said, defiant. She had never interrupted him before or spoken in this.

Akbar thought for a moment. After a while, he said, 'I will wait for you to return but only on one condition – that nautch girl must die,' he announced his decision.

'Let me talk to him,' Jodha said as she summoned her runner and commanded him to execute some instructions.

# The Dungeon

Nadira lay in the dark unable to see anything around her. Her wrist and ankles hurt from the heavy chains around them. The stench in the dungeon was unbearable. She had not been able to wipe the vomit from her mouth, unable to lift the weight of the chains. She was parched. She could feel dried tears on her face. Her stomach hurt from hunger. The guard had left some rice and curry but there was no way one could eat in that stinking room. Two large rats polished off the plate within minutes of it being left there. She had not slept a wink. She had to be awake to ward off the rats from biting her.

She was still reeling from the shock. Till only about a few days ago she had everything going for her, soaking in Salim's love and dancing away in ecstasy. She dreamt of meeting Salim and spending time with him. She dreamt of their marriage, their walks in the garden, looking at the moon holding hands, making love. She thanked Allah every single day for blessing her with so much love and good fortune. She was so excited to go to Agra when she first heard the news that Akbar wanted her to perform there. She was elated. Vidya designed three extravagant dresses for her. She presented them as a gift, refusing to take money. Naaz, who hated cooking, spent two days in the kitchen making snacks for their long journey. They turned out to be delicious. Nadira and Suraiya realised that she was not as poor a cook as they thought. It seemed she could cook really well when she wanted to. She was so excited that she kept count of every single hour that stood between her and Agra.

But everything had changed so suddenly.

She was still unable to fathom why things had turned out the way they did. Not once did she think of becoming the queen. She just wanted to be a loving wife and a good daughter-in-law. Yes, she did feel happy that her mother and sister would be able to live a good life when she and Salim got married, but that was not why she wanted to marry him. His being prince did not matter to her. In fact, it was only frustrating as it kept him away from her. She wanted him to spend as much time with her as he could. She never thought that it would be perceived as a threat to his role as the future emperor.

Nadira was not afraid of death. She was only anxious of the unknown. It unnerved her that she did not have access to any information. She feared for her mother and sister. She missed them all. She missed the warmth of her mother's cuddle, her father's loving kiss on her forehead, Salim's embrace of love, even Vidya's hugs. Nadira wanted to weep but her tears seemed to have dried up.

# Speech of Love

Fatehpur Sikri was deserted. A palace that once buzzed with soldiers, slaves, courtiers, wazirs, musicians, singers, and servants, was desolate. Akbar sat on the divan thinking. Suddenly, he rose, an old lion staggering to his feet. 'Fetch her,' he growled at his soldier.

Jahanuma appeared, pushed into the room by two bulky harem guards. She stood at a distance, her head bowed, not willing to look the emperor in the eye. She was afraid that the ire in her eyes might provoke him further. She was furious at being dishonoured and shamed by Gulbadan. Her arrest had been kept a secret till the day of Nadira's performance. She was ordered to be released only to be humiliated by being made to stand and watch her daughter's arrest in the cruellest manner. Her loving daughter was chained up in front of everyone as if she were a hardened criminal. Till that day she had believed that Akbar had no knowledge of what was going on, but now she realised that even her arrest had the emperor's approval. She was filled with fury and pain.

Jahanuma was willing to overlook Gulbadan's actions, knowing that the old woman had fallen to Meherunissa's conspiracy. Her suffering came from the knowledge that Akbar had believed the insinuations made about her by

Gulbadan. That he believed she had plotted the prince's seduction by her daughter. How could Akbar be so gullible? How could he even believe such preposterous accusations? He should have known her better. Did he not once feel the need to clarify with her? They had developed a loving companionship. How could he take such radical decisions without even giving her an opportunity to explain? He was the Emperor of Hindustan. How could he allow himself to get carried away like this?

Her heart was wrenched with hurt caused by the man she had admired so much and had also begun to love. She refused to look at him also because she did not want him to see the pain in her eyes. She was still a proud Pathan.

Akbar sat down and turned to look at her. For a moment his heart melted. She was still the same beautiful Jahanuma. Was she really capable of such treachery? The question had haunted him every day over the last few weeks. His heart refused to believe what she was accused of by Gulbadan. She was too proud and honourable to indulge in such plotting. But he had no reason to disbelieve his aunt. Why would she lie? Why would she implicate Jahanuma and Anarkali? What did she have to gain out of it? Gulbadan was like his mother. A son would not question the motives of his mother. He had nothing against Anarkali but somewhere deep within he was unable to accept that Jahanuma had no knowledge of her daughter's liaison with Salim. He had decided to overlook his own doubts and follow his aunt's counsel.

The moment of weakness passed. The arrogance of a powerful emperor took over. How could she encourage her daughter to woo the prince? If she wanted wealth, she just had to ask him. After Jodha, she was the first woman outside his blood to whom he had extended so much respect. He had never treated her only as an object of pleasure.

Jahanuma raised her hands to the sky in a plea for mercy. She petitioned the emperor, 'Zil-e-Ilahi, you are the most benign and benevolent of all. You are the Badshah, the Shahenshah of Hindustan, of this vast empire whose borders know no bounds. My girl is only a child, a naive girl who has lost her way. She has not grown up enough to understand the consequences of her act. I beg you to forgive that foolish mortal! I beseech you to have mercy on her.' Her voice quivered. 'I promise His Highness I will take her away to Kabul or even farther.'

Akbar did not respond. He looked away pretending to be disinterested. The mother in Jahanuma was not willing to give up. She recounted the innocence and purity of her daughter, painting a heartfelt portrait of a young life still untouched by the trials of the world. She described her child's laughter, her curious eyes and the dreams that resided within her tender heart. She pleaded he spare her daughter for the sake of her hopes and her dreams, to let her live so that she could witness the radiance that was yet to unfold. As she spoke, her voice softened with the weight of a mother's love. With each word, she appealed to Akbar's humanity, urging him to see beyond the political machinations and to show mercy. She implored him to see beyond the confines of his royal responsibilities and recognize the worth and potential of an innocent life.

Exhausted, she fell on her knees. Akbar remained unmoved. She couldn't see his hands clutching the arms of his seat. With every plea Jahanuma made, his fingers dug in the rosewood, blood draining from them. Jahanuma's words faded as pain clouded his thoughts. However, once again, he found a way to deny himself the voice of his heart.

'Bring that dance girl,' he barked at a soldier.

A heavy silence silence prevailed as the emperor stood waiting for Anarkali to be presented before him. Jahanuma lay on the ground, on the verge of fainting.

Nadira emerged from the door that connected to the dungeon somewhere below. She walked like a ghost. Her eyes refused to open in the bright light after many days spent in the darkness of the dungeon. She was bound in chains. Her clothes were filthy, dirt caked her body and face. Skin clung to her bones as she had not eaten for days. She stumbled. A gasp escaped Jahanuma's mouth. Two female soldiers held Nadira from falling and dragged her forward.

Jahanuma stood up, helpless, tears flowing from her eyes. She wanted to cry out aloud, hold her daughter and comfort her. She wanted to scream at the emperor for his cruelty.

For a moment, even Akbar was taken aback by how frail the girl had turned. Looking at her, he experienced a mix of emotions – of anger, betrayal and hurt, and most of all, doubt of the possibilities of her innocence. He was unable to decipher where these feelings stemmed from. Was he angry with Anarkali or Salim? Was he punishing the girl or penalising Salim by killing her? What had this girl done that could justify this? What was so unacceptable about the entire episode? Was it his bloated ego hurt by her final dance that defied him without uttering a single word? She was playing with his mind but no one other than Gulbadan knew about that. Why did he feel so offended then?

He looked at her. He was willing to consider sparing her life, but the plea of mercy had to come from the accused and not her mother. But in spite of the indignity, Nadira remained calm. She did not look up once or utter a word. Not once did she ask for mercy, for her life to be spared. Her demeanour intrigued him. He wanted to hear her side of the story but was too proud to ask. The intensity of her silence unsettled him. But the ego of the emperor stopped him from making the first move. The appeal for forgiveness had to come from her. But Nadira too was not one to denigrate her love by asking for forgiveness. She sat down on her knees, unable to hold the weight of the heavy chains. She continued to look down, refusing to utter a word.

Akbar glanced at Jahanuma hoping she would catch the hint. Akbar turned to look back at Anarkali. But that brief moment was enough for Jahanuma to read his thoughts. She had spent enough evenings with him to be able to read the look in his eye. She saw a gleam of hope appear before her. She seized the opportunity. 'His Highness is the master of this universe. The world swears by the largeness of your heart. I again beg for your mercy, Jahanpanah. This inexperienced girl does not know right from wrong. She has sinned by falling in love with Shahzada Salim. Her mother begs you to forgive her. Please spare her life,' she appealed.

Nadira looked up. The sound of her heavy breathing made their heads turn to her. Akbar looked into her eyes. There was a defiant gleam in them. It made Akbar nervous. She turned to her mother and spoke: 'Please do not insult my love, Ammi, by terming it a sin. God is my witness. I have done nothing wrong. I have only loved Salim and asked for nothing in return. I will not let anyone insult the sanctity of everything we have shared, in proximity and in distance. I prefer to die than call my love a mistake and beg for forgiveness.' Her voice remained respectful yet unwavering.

Nadira then turned to Akbar. 'Even in the face of death I don't regret loving him. I have no remorse, no shame. I was never interested in his wealth or his power. If at all I wished for anything, it was to live by his side even if it was in a small hut. A child can only crave for the moon. Can the moon descend on the earth? My heart always reminded me that he may not be able to marry me but it did not matter to me. I felt love for him like Radha did for Krishna, pure and divine. The disappointment I feel is not for what lies in my fate but for your failure to understand your son. Few souls like him are sent to walk this earth. His humility and compassion are unmatched ... not even you can aspire to those standards...'

A soldier stepped forward, threatening her with his sword for insulting the emperor. Akbar waved him back.

Nadira continued to speak fearlessly,'... Salim has a tender heart but he also possesses the strength of ten elephants. His courage is no less than yours, only his ways are different. He holds you in high esteem. His eyes fill up with pride every time he talks about you and with sorrow when he is reminded of the hurt he has caused you. He is sincere and so full of life. There's no one who wouldn't love Salim. I am only fortunate for I could express my devotion to him in flesh and breath,' she paused, exhausted and overwhelmed by the intensity of her feelings.

Akbar stood motionless. He could hear his heart racing. He waited for her to continue. To Jahanuma's amazement, Akbar was not agitated. In fact, he signalled for some water. A servant appeared with a tumbler. She accepted enough to give her the strength to resume her speech. 'You are the king of kings – Shahenshah-e-Hindustan. You reign over the most powerful kingdom on this earth. Hindustan must get a worthy successor. Shahzada is the most deserving inheritor of this empire. My life is a paltry cost to pay to serve this cause. We must prevent bloodshed. I offer my inconsequential life so that Salim can become the emperor. Jahanpanah, I give to you the next emperor of Hindustan. I give you my life. But my love for him I will take with me to my grave, even to my next life.'

Nadira looked at him, her eyes compassionate and forgiving. He turned away, thinking: *She is truly a magnificent creature*. Afraid that his voice may give him away, he waved the soldiers to take her away.

## I

Back in Agra, Akbar stood on the roof of his palace looking at the majestic Jamuna. Anarkali's words echoed in his mind like the waves of the river striking the shore below. The flare of rage had disappeared. He felt calm. For the first time in many years, he felt he could think with clarity.

As he paced from one end of the roof to the other, his hands folded behind him, he mulled over his next step. Suddenly, as if his mind was made up, he waved for his qorchi standing in the far corner waiting for his master's instructions. The attendant came rushing. 'Run ahead and tell the queen I am on my way to meet her.' The attendant bowed and rushed to comply with the directions.

## II

Over the next two days, the missives flew thick and fast between Salim and Akbar with Jodha acting as a mediator. Akbar had suggested a solution to Jodha which he thought was a reasonable middle ground for all parties. His only condition was that no one other than Jodha, Salim and he should know about the agreement. Jodha had personally taken the offer to Salim. Salim, however, was still raging with fury. Sticking to his earlier position, he refused to discuss any compromise. He demanded he be allowed to marry Nadira and be appointed emperor straightaway. Jodha hoped against hope that the two people she loved the most would come upon a resolution.

# An Enduring Passion

The layers of brick rose around her. Nadira wrestled with fear, sorrow, grief and rebellion, the loss of her dreams, her aspirations and her love. But even in the face of such overwhelming despair, she remained dignified, defiant. Her spirit refused to be extinguished. She conjured every ounce of courage she possessed, declining to let her captors get the satisfaction of witnessing her defeat. She looked at the walls enclosing her as physical representations of the barriers to prevent her from embracing the love she so fiercely held. She was more than just a woman entombed; she was a symbol of resilience, challenging the very foundations of power and authority that sought to silence her.

Reconciled to her destiny, Nadira contemplated the darkness that awaited. She thought of the world beyond the confines of her earthly existence. She wondered if she would meet her father in the other world. A sense of anxiety engulfed her: Would he judge her for what she had done, her decision to sacrifice her life and for putting the lives of her family at risk. Will he be disappointed with her for jeopardising the family honour or be proud for upholding the dignity of a Pathan? His opinion was all she ever cared for growing up as a child in Kabul. She closed her eyes in that moment of deep reflection. She saw her father appear before her eyes, looking at her reassuringly. Her thoughts travelled to her home in Kabul. Memories from her childhood flashed before her – the way her grandfather placed both his hands palm down on her head to bless her, her father's affectionate embrace, the caring gaze of her mother, how her grandmother scolded her lovingly, the way Suraiya imitated her in every matter. It was as if the gods were trying to lift her spirit and cheer her up, to enable her to welcome the impending death in some special and mystical way. She felt a sense of gratitude overcome her.

The two masons worked fast to complete their unpleasant task. The walls had grown rapidly, reaching the level of her eyes. She realised that it was only a matter of a few minutes before the next layer of bricks was placed and she would never again see the light of the day. She tried to raise her hands in prayer but could not. She said a prayer for her mother and Suraiya. She thought of Salim.

'Taqliya,' she heard a roar that sounded like the voice of the emperor. A pair of eyes looked at her from the gap in the wall. He spoke, this time softly, in a tone that was of a father, not the emperor of Hindustan. It was a voice that held remorse. 'You have earned my respect for the second time, Anarkali. We will remember your favour and generations to come will celebrate you and your love for my son. I hope my children can make me proud like you do your father today.' He muttered a prayer. The pair of eyes disappeared.

The masons resumed their work. They placed the last layer of bricks, engulfing the enclosure in darkness. Nadira thought of Salim. He appeared before her eyes. She saw him standing at a distance looking at her. His eyes had the same passion which made her want to drown in them. He wanted to come forward and hold her but he could not move. It was as if he was held by some invisible shackles. She saw the shackles change shape, rapidly turning into faces and objects that appeared and faded. She saw Akbar, Gulbadan, and many others whom she did not recognise, holding him back. She saw the lofty image of the throne of Hindustan tied to his feet. She saw him fighting to wriggle out of the worldly manacles that held him back from taking her into his arms. He kicked and thrashed to free himself and reach her. She found his image turn hazy as her brain gasped for air. Suddenly, everything turned dark and she could no longer see him. She battled with the darkness to get another glimpse of her lover. She clutched on to each fading breath till she had no strength left. She drifted into the darkest of darkness.

# A Voice from Beyond Time

*Till the end of my life…*

*I heard the faint voice of a woman. Had Allah sent her to take me away? The voice kept getting louder. It sounded like that of my mother. I felt water on my face. I opened my eyes with some difficulty. I saw my mother holding me. For a moment I thought I was in my afterlife and my mother had come along. But why had she left Suraiya behind alone, I wondered. I could not think straight. My mother slapped my face and whispered in my ears. 'I am so happy you are fine. We were afraid it might be too late before we could retrieve you.'*

*I could not fathom what was going on. With the help of the woman accompanying my mother I jumped out of the gap the size of a window in one of the walls. I was dazed and felt giddy. I sensed we were in a tunnel. My mother held me tight, sobbing uncontrollably. I could not see the face of the woman as it was covered by a cloth wrapped around her face. My mother also had her mouth and nose covered. I realised it was because of the stench from the tunnel. The woman nodded at me and signalled us to follow her. She led the way using a lantern she held in one of her hands. In the other hand she carried a stick to ward off the bats that flew around in panic and make way through the cobwebs that stubbornly held even after the two had made their journey in.*

*We walked carefully, avoiding stepping on the rats the size of rabbits running around. None of us spoke a word except my mother who shrieked every time a rat passed over her feet. Her screams echoed and travelled far in the deafening silence of the tunnel. Every time she screamed, the woman turned to give her an angry glance. Then, we saw light appearing in the distance. It grew brighter as we approached it. We reached the exit hidden by shrubs with a camouflaged door they had left open when entering. The glare of the bright sunlight hit our eyes when we stepped out.*

*Outside, the woman took the cover off her face. Ruksana. I hugged her. Two horses stood tied to a tree nearby. My mother climbed one of them. Ruksana helped me mount behind her. We galloped away, Ruksana once again leading the way.*

*We rode the whole day. My mother and I wore a burqa so that no one could recognise us. I was snubbed by both whenever I inquired about anything. I asked about Suraiya but was told to keep quiet. I was assured that all my questions would be answered when we reach our destination. I was weak, very weak and had no strength to ask any questions. I was reminded of the time when we had fled Kabul. That time I rode behind my father.*

*When we had travelled a few miles, we found another horseman waiting for us. Suraiya sat on the horse behind him. She hugged me warmly. We continued riding, stopping only for food or relieving ourselves and sometimes to rest the horses.*

*Two days later we reached a place called Gwalior. We stopped in a guesthouse on the outskirts of the city. Here, my mother told me that Jodha had come to meet her a few days after speaking to Akbar in Fatehpur Sikri.*

*'It seems that Akbar decided to forgive you but on one condition. He did not want the two of you to meet again. Salim did not agree, he did not want to negotiate his love. Akbar decided to spare our lives nevertheless. He planned to let you escape through the secret tunnel. No one would know you were alive. Not even Salim. Only*

*Jodha, Akbar, Ruksana and I would know of this. We are to be sent far away. You are forbidden to get in touch with Salim. On that condition, Akbar also agreed to forgive his son and spare his life. But he would have to marry Meherunissa if he wanted to be made the emperor. Jodha is hopeful that in time Salim will overcome the grief of your death and agree to marry Meherunissa. Arrangements have been made for us to start a new life in Hyderabad. We have been prohibited to mention even a word about our past. The three of us have been given new identities. You are to be Sharf-un-Nisa.'*

*I felt proud that my love, Salim, refused to negotiate on our love. He did not care for his life. But I felt devastated that I was to live without him. But I was willing to make any sacrifice to see my love become the emperor of Hindustan.*

*Ruksana left us with a family in Gwalior who I learnt later were distant relatives of Raja Man Singh. They were told we were court artists on our way to Hyderabad.*

*We left for Hyderabad after resting for three days.*

*A few days later I discovered I was pregnant. I was thrilled I was carrying the child of my love. My mother agreed that I keep the child. Now, I had a reason to live and even find some happiness. Salim would always remain with me through my daughter. I named her Jodha.*

*We kept our promise and did not ever mention our past to anyone. But I will not be able to erase his memories from my heart. I miss him. I was so happy when I found out he had been anointed king. He was given the title of Jahangir. What a beautiful name. It suited him well. But I was saddened to learn that he drowned himself in wine. He married Meherunissa. She was given the title of Nur Jahan. She looked after the affairs of the empire on his behalf. She cared well for Salim. She was like Rukmani, my beloved Krishna's wife. I realised I hold no grudges against her.*

*My mother and I agreed that while we couldn't talk about our past, we should record our experiences and feelings, separately.*

*Initially, she did not think it was a good idea. But after some coaxing, she relented. We started writing our diaries. She wrote about her life and I penned my tale of love, my dance and my defiance.*

*

*Today, Jahangir visited Bhopal but I did not make any attempt to see or meet him. I kept my promise. I wanted my daughter to see her father but what was the point of that when she could not be told that her father was the emperor of Hindustan.*

*

*I pray for him and his good health every day. I even thank Nur Jahan in my prayers for taking care of my daughter's father.*

*

*Suraiya will be getting married tomorrow. His bridegroom keeps horses for the local trader. What a lovely young man he is. They are madly in love with each other. I am so happy for my sister.*

*

*Last week, my mother passed away from malaria. I feel very lonely. She stood by her daughters through thick and thin. I miss her. May Allah give her place in his kingdom!*

*

*Jodha is growing. She often asks about her father. I was scared of what will happen to her if I died suddenly. A handsome man who runs a shop across the street has proposed to me a few times. He is a fine gentleman. He is fond of Jodha. I think he will take good care of her. I have decided to marry him for the sake of my daughter.*

*

*Oh friend, I cannot tell you*
*Whether he was near or far, real or a dream.*
*Like a streak of lightning,*
*As I chained the dark one,*
*I felt a river flooding in my heart*
*Like a shining moon,*
*I devoured that liquid face.*
*I felt stars shooting around me.*
*The sky fell with my dress,*
*leaving my ravished breasts.*
*I was rocking like the earth.*
*In my storming breath*
*I could hear my ankle-bells,*
*sounding like bees.*
*Drowned in the last waters of dissolution,*
*I knew that this was not the end.*

*Says Vidyapati.*

*

*I have been married for a few months now. My husband, Dilawar Khan, is a caring father. He loves me too. I have also started liking his company. I am assured Jodha will be looked after well if I die.*

*

*Out of respect for Dilawar, I have decided to stop writing any further about my feelings for Salim with ink on these leaves. I will continue to carry him in my heart that still aches for him.*

*London, Twenty-first Century*

# Epilogue

Saima kept aside the crumbling pages of the two diaries and looked at Damini. Neither knew what to say to each other.

'You know something,' Saima spoke softly, breaking the silence, 'the prophecy of the fortune-teller that Ali's elder daughter will become famous one day did come true...'

'...not only did the prophecy come true and Anarkali became famous, she has left a lasting legacy,' Damini completed Saima's sentence.

*

Saima had been woken up by the frantic ringing of the doorbell. She found a worried Damini waiting at the door. 'What the fuck, Sam! Why aren't you answering your phone, I have been trying to call all morning,' her friend had inquired annoyingly.

'My phone was on silent. I was reading through the night. I don't know when I dozed off,' Saima had explained, climbing back on the couch.

'What was so interesting that kept you awake all night?'

She had pointed at the diaries, struggling to keep awake.

Damini's eyes had opened wide. 'Weren't you supposed to stay away from it till you turned fifty?'

'I couldn't hold back.' Saima had moaned, snuggling under the blanket.

'That's not done. Had I known you were planning to read it, I would have stayed back. Now tell me what's in those diaries,' Damini said, snatching away her blanket.

That is when Saima started recounting Anarkali's story. She narrated as many details as she recollected, holding nothing back from her friend. Damini's eyes kept opening wider as she heard the account of none other than the legendary Anarkali, co-authored with her mother. By the time Saima had finished, Damini was shaking from a surge of emotions.

'She was real ... walking on this earth in flesh and blood. I can't believe it. All this while we believed, like million others, that she was a fictional character from a Hindi film.'

'No, silly. Anarkali first featured in Imtiaz Ali Taj's seminal play *Anarkali* sometime in the early twentieth century,' Saima corrected her friend. 'Films were made on her even before *Mughal-e-Azam*. But yes, the world sees her as the imagination of a playwright. But surely, since she did exist in real time there should be some reference of her in history books. It is hard to believe that such a controversial episode remained undocumented. There must be a citation somewhere.'

Saima was already planning in her mind a visit to the library.

'How fine a writer and translator my great-grandfather was. He cleverly merged the autobiographies of two different persons and authored one of the most authoritative and moving love stories from Indian history,' Saima said.

## I

Saima landed in Delhi two months later. She and Damini had decided to cut short their trip to Vietnam and save a few days for Saima to make her first visit to India. Saima had spent the last few weeks researching on Nadira Ali. She was astounded to discover the enormity of literature available on Anarkali. So much so there was a dissertation on her in Harvard University. She also found a mention of the tomb of Anarkali in Lahore although there were differing claims about its occupant. She made up her mind to visit India and Pakistan before she joined the firm.

After dumping her bags in the hotel room, she went straight to old Delhi to pick up a copy of Imtiaz Ali Taj's play. She had searched on Google and found out that a cheap print of the publication was available in a shop in the old part of the city. That was the only text she discovered where Anarkali was discussed in some detail. She found some references to Anarkali in the seventeenth-century travel writings of two Englishmen, William Finch and Edward Terry, but they believed she was a fictional character.

Some books she read identified Anarkali as one of the early wives of Jahangir. The historian Sayed Latif was the only one who stood out as the single-most adamant supporter of the belief in the historical existence of Anarkali and the tomb of Anarkali as her last burial place. He identified Anarkali as Nadira Begum or Sharf-un-Nisa. Saima was also amused to find a poem on Anarkali penned by Pundi Seshadri, an illustrious professor of English at Benares Hindu University in India.

*The Hall of Mirrors blazed with lamps one night*
*When royal Akbar sat in crowded state*
*And held his court; with wine and song elate*
*Revelled the courtiers and it was a sight*
*To set the youthful heart aglow with light and love*
*Prince Selim cast his longing eye*
*On fair Anarkali and heaved a sigh*

She had heard that Salim kept a diary but no one knew of its contents. On the airplane, she skimmed through the translation of *The Jahangirnama* but found no reference to Anarkali in it. What baffled her the most was that no consensus existed on Anarkali's real name.

The following day she hired a cab to Fatehpur Sikri. She stopped in Agra for a day to visit the fort. She saw the quila standing majestically. She bought a ticket and went straight to the sheesh mahal and Salim's palace where Nadira would have spent those momentous moments of her life. She was transported to Anarkali's last performance. Looking at the mirrors around her in the glass palace, she thought, what a spectacle it must have been!

She visited Fatehpur Sikri the next day. A short winding road led to the royal palaces and the Jama Masjid. She marvelled at the complex comprising many historical buildings. She climbed up the steps to the Buland Darwaza and walked across to the tomb of Salim Chishti, the only structure she found made of marble. All other buildings were made of red stone. Sufi singers sat across the tomb singing melodies in praise of Allah.

She noticed a graveyard next to the dargah. A sweeper cleaned the floor, pausing at each grave to brush aside the leaves from the trees that shaded the vaults of the dead. Curious to find if Anarkali was still remembered, she inquired about her from the sweeper. With an airy flourish, he pointed past the graves to a locked gate on the right. 'The poor nartaki – Akbar wanted her dead but her lover, Jahangir, rescued her. He enabled Anarkali and her mother to flee through the length of the tunnel which goes right through to Delhi and travelled onward to Lahore, where she spent the rest of her days,' he said.

Saima was amused to hear the story. It was an enduring legend associated with Fatehpur Sikri.

## II

After spending a few days in Delhi, Saima took a connecting flight to Lahore from Dubai. Flights between India and Pakistan had been suspended owing to tensions between the two countries. In Lahore, she checked into a hotel and requested the people manning its reception to arrange a car to visit the tomb of Anarkali.

She found the whitewashed seventeenth-century octagonal tomb standing in the middle of the square garden on the southeast corner of the Punjab Civil Secretariat complex. Her research had revealed that the original structure was built in Lahori burnt brick with lime mortar. It was then situated on the bank of the Ravi which had receded years ago. The structure had been remodelled a few times. She found the following Persian couplet inscribed on the white marble cenotaph cut from a single rock in the shape of a rectangular box:

*Ta qayamat shukr goyam kard gar khwish ra*
*Aah gar man baz beenam rui yar khwish ra*
(Ah! Could I behold the face of my beloved once more
I would give thanks to my God until the day of Resurrection)

She offered a prayer for Nadira Ali and wished that the tomb would continue to represent the longstanding memory of Anarkali aka Nadira Ali, a reminder of one of the most inspiring love stories from the subcontinent.

# Acknowledgments

The idea for this book traces its roots back to a provoking conversation with my tour guide during a trip to Fatehpur Sikri a few years ago. Hurt by my probe into his account of Anarkali, the guide took a dig at me, '*Janab, agar aap ke paas apna sach nahi hai to meharbaani karke humari sach ko chotta na kareiye.*' (Sir, if you don't have your own truth, please don't belittle mine.) That affront was enough to set me on the quest for Anarkali. On the way back, this book was conceived, and in its making, I found a truth for myself and a story for Anarkali. I don't recollect the name of the guide but I do hope to find him some day to thank him for sending me on this creative and fulfilling voyage.

A historical fiction is the product of facts and fantasy. I can claim only some credit for writing it and only for the latter. The historical records of the Mughal era, particularly of the characters in this book, and the work of other writers on this period helped me set the backdrop of the story. I can't possibly start naming each book I read, or its author but Parvati Sharma's *Jahangir,* Ira Mukhoty's *Akbar,* Alex Rutherford's *Empire of the Moghul,* T.N. Murari's *Taj* deserve a mention. For the fictional portions, my imagination was generously fed by all those who have written about Anarkali, Salim and Akbar, including Syed Imtiaz Ali Taj, who wrote the Urdu play

*Anarkali*. I acknowledge them all even when I fail in mentioning each of them individually.

I am in awe of the film-makers who dared to visualise Anarkali on celluloid: K. Asif of *Mughal-e-Azam*, and before him, Nandlal Jaswantlal and Vedantam Raghavaiahwho made *Anarkali*, and even earlier than that, Charu and Prafulla Roy and R.S. Choudhury for their versions of this enigmatic character. They deserve no less than a kornish from me for providing glimpses to the Anarkali I could envision. Although hard to stay uninfluenced by the beauty of Bina Rai, Anjali Devi and Madhubala, I carved out my own visualisation of Anarkali's beauty and grace. A conversation with Anuja Chandramouli helped me discover the words to adorn my protagonist.

This book was shaped through random conversations held with travel guides and the staff of the Archaeological Survey of India during my countless trips to Fatehpur Sikri and Agra, a couple of visits to Allahabad and one even to Lahore. These exchanges inspired a creative chaos, much like the samudra manthana, the churning of the ocean, throwing up ideas which I latched on to with greed. I recognise the role of these over-a-dozen unnamed people.

The first few chapters were written in the solace of a forest guesthouse booked by my friend Basanta Rajkumar. I owe him one. That guesthouse will remain special, always.

For my protagonist, a young girl, I wanted to be sure that no injustice was caused to her in the portrayal of her feelings and perspective in the book. A colleague, Mehreen Garg, offered to read the manuscript through a young girl's lens. She made many helpful observations. I thank Mehreen for her inputs.

I am grateful to Natasha D'Cruze, a colleague fond of literature, for spending many evenings after long working hours to do the first round of copy editing. She made several valuable suggestions in the process.

Then arrived Chakrika Pandey, the talented young editor at Om Books International. She provided many remarkable insights. The book has immensely benefited from her perspectives, astute female gaze and lexis. I am confident she will go on to become a celebrity editor someday. My deepest gratitude to her.

I am thankful to Ajay Mago, the man behind Om Books International, and his team, for their support.

I am grateful to Shantanu Ray Chaudhuri, for his unwavering faith in this book, for his editorial inputs and his friendship.

The Book Bakers and Om's design team need a special mention for executing my vision of the cover of the book and for being very patient with me in the process.

This book, like all my other pursuits, happened at the cost of my family time. My wife, Asha, and children, Dev and Siya, have been unyielding in their support for all my endeavours. They never complained about my distraction, only teased me for, unexpected as it was to them coming from a no-nonsense lawyer, writing a love story. How does one even find adequate words to thank such a family? I have no words, only love for them.

Anarkali has lived alongside my family for many years. It is time to say alvida to her. I plan to visit Fatehpur Sikri after the first copy arrives, to give her a dignified departure from my mind which she has occupied for a long, long time. I can now move on.